D0389724

THE WESTERN FRONT 1914–1916

DESPATCHES FROM THE FRONT

The Commanding Officers' Reports from the Field and at Sea

THE WESTERN FRONT 1914–1916

Mons, La Cataeu, Loos, the Battle of the Somme

Introduced and compiled by
Martin Mace and John Grehan
with additional research by
Sara Mitchell

Pen & Sword
MILITARY

First published in Great Britain in 2013 by
PEN & SWORD MILITARY
An imprint of
Pen & Sword Books Ltd
47 Church Street
Barnsley
South Yorkshire
S70 2AS

Copyright © Martin Mace and John Grehan, 2013

ISBN 978-1-78159-321-9

The right of Martin Mace and John Grehan to be identified as the authors of this
work has been asserted by them in accordance with the Copyright, Designs and
Patents Act 1988.

A CIP catalogue record for this book is available from the British Library.

All rights reserved. No part of this book may be reproduced or transmitted in
any form or by any means, electronic or mechanical including photocopying,
recording or by any information storage and retrieval system, without
permission from the Publisher in writing.

Typeset by Concept, Huddersfield, West Yorkshire, HD4 5JL.
Printed and bound in England by CPI Group (UK) Ltd, Croydon CR0 4YY.

Pen & Sword Books Ltd incorporates the imprints of Pen & Sword Archaeology,
Atlas, Aviation, Battleground, Discovery, Family History, History, Maritime,
Military, Naval, Politics, Railways, Select, Social History, Transport, True Crime,
and Claymore Press, Frontline Books, Leo Cooper, Praetorian Press,
Remember When, Seaforth Publishing and Wharncliffe.

For a complete list of Pen & Sword titles please contact
PEN & SWORD BOOKS LIMITED
47 Church Street, Barnsley, South Yorkshire, S70 2AS, England
E-mail: enquiries@pen-and-sword.co.uk
Website: www.pen-and-sword.co.uk

Contents

List of Plates

A portrait of John French, 1st Earl of Ypres. He became Chief of the Imperial General Staff on 15 March 1912, and was promoted to Field Marshal on 3 June 1913.

Field Marshal Sir John French pictured with ADCs at his General Headquarters.

A portrait of Field Marshal Douglas Haig.

Field Marshal Haig reviewing troops in Canterbury, Kent.

The men of 'A' Company, 4th Battalion, Royal Fusiliers (9th Brigade, 3rd Division) pictured resting in Grand Place at Mons, Belgium.

The so-called "First Shot" Memorial near Mons.

The standard Commonwealth War Graves Commission headstone of Private John Parr of the 4th Battalion Middlesex Regiment in St Symphorien Military Cemetery near Mons, Belgium.

An artist's depiction of 24-year-old Lance Corporal Frederick William Holmes, of the 2nd Battalion, The King's Own Yorkshire Light Infantry, during the action for which he was awarded the Victoria Cross during the fighting at Le Cateau on 26 August 1914.

A photograph of the ruined battlefield of Festubert which was taken in the spring of 1919.

Men of the 7th (City of London) Battalion London Regiment ("The Shiny Seventh"), being led forward by Sergeant Hayward during the afternoon of Sunday, 16 May 1915, the second day of the Battle of Festubert.

British troops advancing across No Man's Land through a cloud of poison gas, as viewed from the trench they have just left, during the Battle of Loos, 25 September 1915.

Fighting in the Ypres Salient. The men of the Liverpool Scottish and the Honourable Artillery Company (HAC – the oldest regiment in the British Army) during the attack on Y Wood, 16 June 1915.

"Men of the New Army resting whilst en route to the front".

The calm before the storm. Troops pictured waiting, some still asleep, in a support trench shortly before Zero Hour near Beaumont Hamel on the first day of the Battle of the Somme.

The 103rd (Tyneside Irish) Brigade, part of the 34th Division, pictured advancing from the Tara-Usna Line to attack the village of La Boisselle on the morning of 1 July 1916.

One of the trenches with which the fighting on the Western Front has become synonymous.

Introduction

The clock was ticking. In light of the fact that Germany had declared war on France the previous day (following worsening events in Eastern Europe), the British Government delivered an ultimatum to the German Government on Tuesday, 4 August 1914.

Announcing the fact amid a strained silence that had fallen throughout the House of Commons, the Prime Minister, H.H. Asquith, stated: "We have repeated the request made last week to the German Government that they should give us the same assurance in regard to Belgian neutrality that was given to us and Belgium by France last week. We have asked that it should be given before midnight."

During the evening on the 4th a reply was received from Germany. As this was considered unsatisfactory, King George V held a Council which had been called for midnight. The declaration of war was then signed.

Following this momentous event, the Foreign Office issued the following official statement: "Owing to the summary rejection by the German Government of the request made by his Majesty's Government for assurances that the neutrality of Belgium will be respected, his Majesty's Ambassador to Berlin has received his passports, and his Majesty's Government declared to the German Government that a state of war exists between Great Britain and Germany as from 11 p.m. on August 4, 1914."

As patriotic fervour swept across Britain, it was generally thought that the Great European War would be over by Christmas. In fact, it dragged on for another four years, its battles and campaigns stretching around the globe to become the First World War.

The fighting that took place on the Western Front, in Flanders and France, was, by contrast so close to Britain that the guns and detonating mines could be heard in England. So close, indeed, that in the days of telephones and trains, verbal messages could be relayed back to the United Kingdom almost instantaneously and written despatches could be shipped in a matter of hours.

The British public, therefore, received a daily digest of information through the newspapers and radio but the official reports from the commanding officers were usually more considered documents, produced only at the end of a campaign or specific period. This was so that the story of the fighting, up to that particular point in time, could be covered with a degree of completeness but, unlike the battles of earlier generations which could be fought and won in a day, the battles of the First World War lasted for days, weeks and even months. Until the final shots were fired there could be no definitive conclusions to be drawn, but because of the protracted duration of First World War battles interim reports had to be submitted.

The first of these was published in The London Gazette on 8 September 1914. This account detailed the British Expeditionary Force's (BEF) initial operations in the First Word War. Published as a separate supplement, it was the first in a succession of despatches sent back to the UK by the BEF's initial commanding officer, Field Marshal Sir John French. This, along with the succeeding ones, is presented here just as it was written almost 100 years ago. It covers the movement of the BEF to France, the early battles at Mons and Le Cateau, and the first steps in the subsequent retreat. It clearly shows the confusion of those first days as the Germans attacked with surprising speed and strength.

"From information I received from French Headquarters," wrote Sir John French of events on the morning of 23 August 1914, "I understood that little more than one, or at most two, of the enemy's Army Corps, with perhaps one Cavalry Division, were in front of my position; and I was aware of no attempted outflanking movement by the enemy". The BEF was therefore in no danger. French had addressed his Corps and Cavalry Commanders at 06:00 hours with this information.

Yet just a few hours later, at 15:00 hours, fresh reports were received that the British position at Mons was about to be attacked by the Germans, not merely one or two corps but in considerable strength.

"In the meantime, about 5 p.m.," continued French, "I received a most unexpected message from General Joffre by telegraph, telling me that at least three German Corps, viz., a reserve corps, the 4th Corps and the 9th Corps, were moving on my position in front, and that the Second Corps was engaged in a turning movement from the direction of Tournay. He also informed me that the two reserve French divisions and the 5th French Army on my right were retiring."

The Allies were supposed to be on the offensive. Suddenly John French is informed that not only is the BEF about to be overwhelmed by a massive enemy force but that their Allies had retired and left the British exposed to face the brunt of the German advance.

French had to respond quickly to the rapidly changing situation as the French armies were pushed back. In his own words, the only way to save the BEF from "complete annihilation" was by a swift withdrawal. "The French were still retiring, and I had no support except such as was afforded by the

Fortress of Maubeuge; and the determined attempts of the enemy to get round my left flank assured me that it was his intention to hem me against that place and surround me. I felt that not a moment must be lost in retiring to another position."

This was successfully accomplished and French was at pains to point out that the army was saved by the skill of its generals. Amongst these men, French named Douglas Haig, the man who was to replace him as commander of the BEF.

The second of John French's despatches is remarkable for the fact that, despite the alarming reverses that the Allies had suffered, he still maintained the belief that these were only temporary setbacks and that once the situation had been stabilised the offensive could be resumed. Unlike some of the later stages of the war on the Western Front, these early encounters still involved complex manoeuvres, the despatches explaining the movements of the BEF in relation to those of the French Army.

The main feature of this second despatch, published on 18 October 1914, is the Battle of the Marne. Though less celebrated than some of the other battles of the First World War, none were of greater significance. It was at the Battle of the Marne, which was fought between 5 and 12 September 1914, that the great German drive upon Paris was halted. This Allied victory not only stopped the German advance it actually turned it back, with the Germans in turn being forced to retreat. The Germans then found positions in which they could hold their ground, and hold as much French territory as they could.

By the time of his third despatch the situation had stabilised, as French had hoped. The fighting on the Western Front now settled into the gruelling stalemate of trench warfare for which it has become synonymous. Despite all of this French still remained confident of an eventual victory.

Subsequent despatches from French, until he was superseded by Haig, take the story of the fighting on the Western Front up to the latter stages of the Battle of Loos. Included amongst these is his report on the attempt by the Royal Naval Division to help the Belgian Army in the defence of the National Redoubt of Antwerp. This despatch, published on 5 December 1914, was, unlike his other despatches which were sent to the War Office, was forwarded to and printed by the Admiralty.

Along with other factors, the controversy over French's deployment of his reserves at the Battle of Loos that eventually led to his removal from command of the BEF. In his penultimate, and tenth, despatch French was at pains to explain his use of his reserves. This, though, did him little good as his fate had already been decided by the British Cabinet. His final despatch was not written until 31 July 1916, long after he had lost his command in France.

After taking over the BEF from John French on 10 December 1915, Haig waited until 19 May 1916 before sending his first official despatch. This was the most difficult period for the French Army with the Germans having returned to the offensive at Verdun. Haig opens his despatch with reference to Verdun, explaining that no comparable effort has been made by the British forces during the duration of the fighting at Verdun.

The British would soon have to help relieve the mounting pressure that the French were under, but there were many factors to consider, as Haig explained in his third despatch: "Subject to the necessity of commencing operations before the summer was too far advanced, and with due regard to the general situation, I desired to postpone my attack as long as possible. The British Armies were growing in numbers and the supply of munitions was steadily increasing. Moreover a very large proportion of the officers and men under my command were still far from being fully trained, and the longer the attack could be deferred the more efficient they would become. On the other hand the Germans were continuing to press their attacks at Verdun, and both there and on the Italian front, where the Austrian offensive was gaining ground, it was evident that the strain might become too great to be borne unless timely action were taken to relieve it. Accordingly, while maintaining constant touch with General Joffre in regard to all these considerations, my preparations were pushed on, and I agreed, with the consent of H.M. Government, that my attack should be launched whenever the general situation required it with as great a force as I might then be able to make available."

As is well known, it was not until 1 July 1916 that Haig felt able to open the offensive on the Somme to relieve the French at Verdun. From the very first day of that terrible battle, it was clear that Haig's confidence was ill-founded. Though the Battle of the Somme ended with few appreciable gains, Haig felt able to draw some very positive conclusions: "The enemy's power has not yet been broken, nor is it yet possible to form an estimate of the time the war may last before the objects for which the Allies are fighting have been attained. But the Somme battle has placed beyond doubt the ability of the Allies to gain those objects.

"The German Army is the mainstay of the Central Powers, and a full half of that Army, despite all the advantages of the defensive, supported by the strongest fortifications, suffered defeat on the Somme this year," continued Haig. "Neither victors nor the vanquished will forget this; and, though bad weather has given the enemy a respite, there will undoubtedly be many thousands in his ranks who will begin the new campaign with little confidence in their ability to resist our assaults or to overcome our defence. Our new Armies entered the battle with the determination to win and with confidence in their power to do so. They have proved to themselves, to the enemy, and to the world that this confidence was justified, and in the fierce struggle they have been through they have learned many valuable lessons which will help them in the future."

Haig's despatches continued, though less frequently but in greater depth than those of his predecessor, until the end of the war. The last of his despatches presented in this volume deals with the fighting in the area of the River Ancre in November 1916, the final act of the Battle of the Somme, and the pursuit of the Germans as they withdrew to the Hindenburg Line.

The latter was first detected by British patrols in February 1917, whilst the main withdrawal, Operation Alberich, was completed by 15 March. A planned strategic withdrawal, as opposed to a retreat, the operation saw German troops occupy new positions on a shorter, more easily defended stretch of the front, positioned to take every tactical advantage of ground. The enemy soldiers destroyed everything on the ground that they left behind, flattening villages, poisoning wells, cutting down trees, blowing craters on roads and crossroads, and booby-trapping ruins and dugouts.

Despite the fact that Operation Alberich occurred in early 1917 – a period dealt within a second volume of Western Front despatches – its coverage in Haig's third despatch as Commander-in-Chief of the BEF, the greater part of which relates to events in 1916, means that we have opted to include it here.

*   *   *

The objective of this book is to reproduce these despatches as they were first published more than ninety years ago. Both French and Haig used abbreviations in their despatches, some of which may not be immediately obvious to the reader; consequently we have included in the book a full explanation of these. Any grammatical or spelling errors have been left uncorrected to retain the authenticity of the original documents.

These despatches have not been modified, edited or interpreted in any way. They are, therefore, the original and unique words of the British commanding officers as they saw things at the time – French's and Haig's own compelling accounts of the involvement of the British and Commonwealth armies in the fighting on the Western Front between 1914 and 1916.

Martin Mace and John Grehan
Storrington, 2013

Abbreviations

AAD – Advanced Ammunition Depot
ACI – Army Council Instruction
AD – Artillery Depot
ADC – Aide-de-Camp
ADS – Advanced Dressing Station
AF – Army Form
AG – Anti-gas
AO – Army Order
AOC – Army Ordnance Corps
AOD – Army Ordnance Depot
ARP – Ammunition Refilling Point
ARS – Advanced Regulating Station
ASC – Army Service Corps
BA – British Army
BAC – Brigade Ammunition Column
BAD – Base Ammunition Depot
Bde – Brigade
BEF – British Expeditionary Force
BGGS – Brigadier-General General Staff
BGRA – Brigadier-General Royal Artillery
BGS – Brigadier, General Staff
BM – Brigade Major
BOD – Base Ordnance Depot
Brig – Brigade
BSD – Base Supply Depot
CB – Companion of The Most Honourable Order of the Bath
CCS – Casualty Clearing Station
CDS – Corps Dressing Station
CHA – Commander Heavy Artillery
CIE – Companion of The Most Eminent Order of the Indian Empire
CMG – Companion of The Most Distinguished Order of Saint Michael and
    Saint George
CO – Commanding Officer

Co, Coy – Company
Cpl – Corporal
CQMS – Company Quartermaster Master Sergeant
CRA – Commander Royal Artillery
CSM – Company Sergeant Major
CT – Communication Trench
CVO – Commander of the Royal Victorian Order
DA – Divisional Artillery
DAC – Divisional Ammunition Column
DAP – Divisional Ammunition Park
DAQMG – Deputy Assistant Quartermaster General
DCM – Distinguished Conduct Medal
DD – Dishonourable Discharge
DDMS – Deputy Director Medical Services
Div – Division or Divisional
DO – Dug-out
DoW – Died of wounds
DRS – Divisional Rest Station
DSC – Distinguished Service Cross
DSO – Distinguished Service Order
DTMO – Divisional Trench Mortar Officer
FA – Field Ambulance
FDS – Field Dressing Station
FOO – Forward Observation Officer
FSPB – Field Service Pocket Book
GCB – Knight Grand Cross of The Most Honourable Order of the Bath
GCIE – Knight Grand Commander of The Most Eminent Order of the Indian
     Empire
GCSI – Knight Grand Commander of The Most Exalted Order of the Star of
     India
GCVO – Knight Grand Cross of The Royal Victorian Order
GHQ – General Headquarters
GOC – General Officer Commanding
GS – General Service or General Staff
GSO – General Staff Officer
GSW – Gunshot Wound
HA – Heavy Artillery
HE – High Explosive
HQ, Hqts, HdQrs – Headquarters
Hr – Hour
HT – Horse Transport

Hy – Heavy
IB – Infantry Brigade
IC – In Charge
2/IC – Second in Charge
Inf, Infy – Infantry
Inf Bde – Infantry Brigade
Infm, Info – Information
Inf Reg, Inf Regt – Infantry Regiment
Int, Intel – Intelligence
IO – Intelligence Officer
KCB – Knight Commander of The Most Honourable Order of the Bath
KCIE – Knight Commander of The Most Eminent Order of the Indian
    Empire
KCMG – Knight Commander of The Most Distinguished Order of Saint
    Michael and Saint George
KCSI – Knight Commander of The Most Exalted Order of the Star of India
KCVO – Knight Commander of the Royal Victorian Order
KHS – King's Honorary Surgeon
L.Bdr, L/Bdr – Lance Bombardier
L.Cpl, L/Cpl, L/C, Lce Cpl – Lance Corporal
L.G., L. Gun – Lewis Gun
LO – Liaison Officer
L of C, LC – Lines of Communication
L.Sgt, L/Sgt – Lance Sergeant
Lt – Lieutenant
Lt Col – Lieutenant Colonel
MC – Military Cross
MDS – Main Dressing Station
Mg, MG, M.Gun – Machine-gun
MGS – Machine-Gun Section
MM – Military Medal
MO – Medical Officer
MVO – Member of The Royal Victorian Order
NCO – Non-Commissioned Officer
OC – Officer Commanding
OIC – Officer-in-Charge
OP – Observation Post
OR, O. Rank – Other Rank(s)
Pdr – Pounder
Pl, Plt – Platoon
Pnr – Pioneer

Pt, Pte, Prvt – Private
PW, PoW – Prisoner of War
QM, Qr.Mr. – Quarter-Master
QMG – Quartermaster General
QMS – Quarter-Master Sergeant
RA – Royal Artillery
RAMC – Royal Army Medical Corps
RAP – Regimental Aid Post
Rd – Road
RE – Royal Engineers
Rec, Recce – Reconnaissance or Reconnoitre
Recd – Received
Ref – Reference
Reg, Regt – Regimental
Res – Reserve
RFA – Royal Field Artillery
RFC – Royal Flying Corps
Rfn – Rifleman
Rft – Reinforcement(s)
RHQ – Regimental Headquarters
RMA – Royal Marine Artillery
RMLI – Royal Marines Light Infantry
RMO – Regimental Medical Officer
RN – Royal Navy
RNR – Royal Naval Reserve
RNVR – Royal Naval Volunteer Reserve
RO – Routine Orders
RQMS – Regimental Quarter-Master Sergeant
RSM – Regimental Sergeant-Major
RV – Rendezvous
SAA – Small Arms Ammunition
SC – Staff Captain
Sec Lt, 2/Lt – Second Lieutenant
Sgt, Sjt – Sergeant
Sig – Signal
SL – Start line
SMO – Senior Medical Officer
SO – Staff Officer
SP – Start Point, Strong Point, or support
ST – Support Trench

TF – Territorial Force
TM – Trench Mortar
TMB – Trench Mortar Battery
TO – Transport Officer
VC – Victoria Cross
WD – War Diary
WO – Warrant Officer

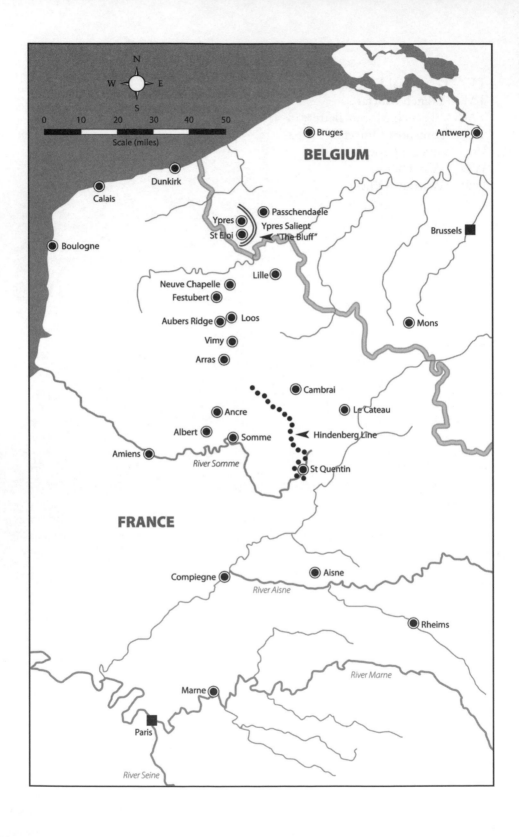

SIR JOHN FRENCH'S DESPATCH OF 7 SEPTEMBER 1914

Mons and Le Cateau

War Office, September 9, 1914.

THE following despatch has been received by the Secretary of State for War from the Field-Marshal Commanding-in-Chief, British Forces in the Field:-

7th September, 1914

MY LORD,

I have the honour to report the proceedings of the Field Force under my command up to the time of rendering this despatch.

1. The transport of the troops from England both by sea and by rail was effected in the best order and without a check. Each unit arrived at its destination in this country well within the scheduled time.

The concentration was practically complete on the evening of Friday, the 21st ultimo, and I was able to make dispositions to move the Force during Saturday, the 22nd, to positions I considered most favourable from which to commence operations which the French Commander-in-Chief, General Joffre, requested me to undertake in pursuance of his plans in prosecution of the campaign.

The line taken up extended along the line of the canal from Conde on the west, through Mons and Binche on the east. This line was taken up as follows:-

From Conde to Mons inclusive was assigned to the Second Corps, and to the right of the Second Corps from Mons the First Corps was posted. The 5th Cavalry Brigade was placed at Binche.

In the absence of my Third Army Corps I desired to keep the Cavalry Division as much as possible as a reserve to act on my outer flank, or move in support of any threatened part of the line. The forward reconnaissance was entrusted to Brigadier-General Sir Philip Chetwode with the 5th Cavalry Brigade, but I directed General Allenby to send forward a few squadrons to assist in this work.

During the 22nd and 23rd these advanced squadrons did some excellent work, some of them penetrating as far as Soignies, and several encounters took place in which our troops showed to great advantage.

2. At 6 a.m., on August 23rd, I assembled the Commanders of the First and Second Corps and Cavalry Division at a point close to the position, and explained the general situation of the Allies, and what I understood to be General Joffre's plan. I discussed with them at some length the immediate situation in front of us.

From information I received from French Headquarters I understood that little more than one, or at most two, of the enemy's Army Corps, with perhaps one Cavalry Division, were in front of my position; and I was aware of no attempted outflanking movement by the enemy. I was confirmed in this opinion by the fact that my patrols encountered no undue opposition in their reconnoitring operations. The observation of my aeroplanes seemed also to bear out this estimate. About 3 p.m. on Sunday, the 23rd, reports began coming in to the effect that the enemy was commencing an attack on the Mons line, apparently in some strength, but that the right of the position from Mons and Bray was being particularly threatened.

The Commander of the First Corps had pushed his flank back to some high ground south of Bray, and the 5th Cavalry Brigade evacuated Binche, moving slightly south: the enemy thereupon occupied Binche.

The right of the 3rd Division, under General Hamilton, was at Mons, which formed a somewhat dangerous salient; and I directed the Commander of the Second Corps to be careful not to keep the troops on this salient too long, but, if threatened seriously, to draw back the centre behind Mons. This was done before dark. In the meantime, about 5 p.m., I received a most unexpected message from General Joffre by telegraph, telling me that at least three German Corps, viz., a reserve corps, the 4th Corps and the 9th Corps, were moving on my position in front, and that the Second Corps was engaged in a turning movement from the direction of Tournay. He also informed me that the two reserve French divisions and the 5th French Army on my right were retiring, the Germans having on the previous day gained possession of the passages of the Sambre between Charleroi and Namur.

3. In view of the possibility of my being driven from the Mons position, I had previously ordered a position in rear to be reconnoitred. This position rested on the fortress of Maubeuge on the right and extended west to Jenlain, south-east of Valenciennes, on the left. The position was reported difficult to hold, because standing crops and buildings made the siting of trenches very difficult and limited the field of fire in many important localities. It nevertheless afforded a few good artillery positions.

When the news of the retirement of the French and the heavy German threatening on my front reached me, I endeavoured to confirm it by aeroplane reconnaissance; and as a result of this I determined to effect a retirement to the Maubeuge position at daybreak on the 24th. A certain amount of fighting continued along the whole line throughout the night, and at daybreak on the 24th the 2nd Division from the neighbourhood of Harmignies made a powerful demonstration as if to retake Binche. This was supported by the artillery of both the 1st and 2nd Divisions, whilst the 1st Division took up a supporting position in the neighbourhood of Peissant. Under cover of this demonstration the Second Corps retired on the line Dour – Quarouble – Frameries. The 3rd Division on the right of the Corps suffered considerable loss in this operation from the enemy, who had retaken Mons.

The Second Corps halted on this line, where they partially entrenched themselves, enabling Sir Douglas Haig with the First Corps gradually to withdraw to the new position; and he effected this without much further loss, reaching the line Bavai – Maubeuge about 7 p.m. Towards midday the enemy appeared to be directing his principal effort against our left.

I had previously ordered General Allenby with the Cavalry to act vigorously in advance of my left front and endeavour to take the pressure off.

About 7.30 a.m. General Allenby received a message from Sir Charles Fergusson, commanding 5th Division, saying that he was very hard pressed and in urgent need of support. On receipt of this message General Allenby drew in the Cavalry and endeavoured to bring direct support to the 5th Division.

During the course of this operation General De Lisle, of the 2nd Cavalry Brigade, thought he saw a good opportunity to paralyse the further advance of the enemy's infantry by making a mounted attack on his flank. He formed up and advanced for this purpose, but was held up by wire about 500 yards from his objective, and the 9th Lancers and 18th Hussars suffered severely in the retirement of the Brigade.

The 19th Infantry Brigade, which had been guarding the Line of Communications, was brought up by rail to Valenciennes on the 22nd and 23rd. On the morning of the 24th they were moved out to a position south of Quarouble to support the left flank of the Second Corps. With the assistance of the Cavalry Sir Horace Smith-Dorrien was enabled to effect his retreat to a new position; although, having two corps of the enemy on his front and one threatening his flank, he suffered great losses in doing so.

At nightfall the position was occupied by the Second Corps to the west of Bavai, the First Corps to the right. The right was protected by the Fortress of Maubeuge, the left by the 19th Brigade in position between Jenlain, and Bry, and the Cavalry on the outer flank.

4. The French were still retiring, and I had no support except such as was afforded by the Fortress of Maubeuge; and the determined attempts of the

enemy to get round my left flank assured me that it was his intention to hem me against that place and surround me. I felt that not a moment must be lost in retiring to another position.

I had every reason to believe that the enemy's forces were somewhat exhausted, and I knew that they had suffered heavy losses. I hoped, therefore, that his pursuit would not be too vigorous to prevent me effecting my object.

The operation, however, was full of danger and difficulty, not only owing to the very superior force in my front, but also to the exhaustion of the troops.

The retirement was recommenced in the early morning of the 25th to a position in the neighbourhood of Le Cateau, and rearguards were ordered to be clear of the Maubeuge – Bavai-Eth Road by 5.30 a.m.

Two Cavalry Brigades, with the Divisional Cavalry of the Second Corps, covered the movement of the Second Corps. The remainder of the Cavalry Division with the 19th Brigade, the whole under the command of General Allenby, covered the west flank.

The 4th Division commenced its detrainment at Le Cateau on Sunday, the 23rd, and by the morning of the 25th eleven battalions and a Brigade of Artillery with Divisional Staff were available for service.

I ordered General Snow to move out to take up a position with his right south of Solesmes, his left resting on the Cambrai – Le Cateau Road south of La Chaprie. In this position the Division rendered great help to the effective retirement of the Second and First Corps to the new position.

Although the troops had been ordered to occupy the Cambrai – Le Cateau – Landrecies position, and the ground had, during the 25th, been partially prepared and entrenched, I had grave doubts – owing to the information I received as to the accumulating strength of the enemy against me – as to the wisdom of standing there to fight.

Having regard to the continued retirement of the French on my right, my exposed left flank, the tendency of the enemy's western corps (II.) to envelop me, and, more than all, the exhausted condition of the troops, I determined to make a great effort to continue the retreat till I could put some substantial obstacle, such as the Somme or the Oise, between my troops and the enemy, and afford the former some opportunity of rest and reorganisation. Orders were, therefore, sent to the Corps Commanders to continue their retreat as soon as they possibly could towards the general line Vermand – St. Quentin Ribemont.

The Cavalry, under General Allenby, were ordered to cover the retirement.

Throughout the 25th and far into the evening, the First Corps continued its march on Landrecies, following the road along the eastern border of the Forêt De Mormal, and arrived at Landrecies about 10 o'clock. I had intended that the Corps should come further west so as to fill up the gap between Le Cateau and Landrecies, but the men were exhausted and could not get further in without rest.

The enemy, however, would not allow them this rest, and about 9.30 p.m. a report was received that the 4th Guards Brigade in Landrecies was heavily attacked by troops of the 9th German Army Corps who were coming through the forest on the north of the town. This brigade fought most gallantly and caused the enemy to suffer tremendous loss in issuing from the forest into the narrow streets of the town. This loss has been estimated from reliable sources at from 700 to 1,000. At the same time information reached me from Sir Douglas Haig that his 1st Division was also heavily engaged south and east of Maroilles. I sent urgent messages to the Commander of the two French Reserve Divisions on my right to come up to the assistance of the First Corps, which they eventually did. Partly owing to this assistance, but mainly to the skilful manner in which Sir Douglas Haig extricated his Corps from an exceptionally difficult position in the darkness of the night, they were able at dawn to resume their march south towards Wassigny on Guise.

By about 6 p.m. the Second Corps had got into position with their right on Le Cateau, their left in the neighbourhood of Caudry, and the line of defence was continued thence by the 4th Division towards Seranvillers, the left being thrown back.

During the fighting on the 24th and 25th the Cavalry became a good deal scattered, but by the early morning of the 26th General Allenby had succeeded in concentrating two brigades to the south of Cambrai.

The 4th Division was placed under the orders of the General Officer Commanding the Second Army Corps.

On the 24th the French Cavalry Corps, consisting of three divisions, under General Sordêt, had been in billets north of Avesnes. On my way back from Bavai, which was my "Poste de Commandement" during the fighting of the 23rd and 24th, I visited General Sordêt, and earnestly requested his co-operation and support. He promised to obtain sanction from his Army Commander to act on my left flank, but said that his horses were too tired to move before the next day. Although he rendered me valuable assistance later on in the course of the retirement, he was unable for the reasons given to afford me any support on the most critical day of all, viz., the 26th.

At daybreak it became apparent that the enemy was throwing the bulk of his strength against the left of the position occupied by the Second Corps and the 4th Division.

At this time the guns of four German Army Corps were in position against them, and Sir Horace Smith-Dorrien reported to me that he judged it impossible to continue his retirement at daybreak (as ordered) in face of such an attack.

I sent him orders to use his utmost endeavours to break off the action and retire at the earliest possible moment, as it was impossible for me to send him any support, the First Corps being at the moment incapable of movement.

The French Cavalry Corps, under General Sordêt, was coming up on our left rear early in the morning, and I sent an urgent message to him to do his utmost to come up and support the retirement of my left flank; but, owing to the fatigue of his horses he found himself unable to intervene in any way.

There had been no time to entrench the position properly, but the troops showed a magnificent front to the terrible fire which confronted them.

The Artillery, although outmatched by at least four to one, made a splendid fight, and inflicted heavy losses on their opponents.

At length it became apparent that, if complete annihilation was to be avoided, a retirement must be attempted; and the order was given to commence it about 3.30 p.m. The movement was covered with the most devoted intrepidity and determination by the Artillery, which had itself suffered heavily, and the fine work done by the Cavalry in the further retreat from the position assisted materially in the final completion of this most difficult and dangerous operation.

Fortunately the enemy had himself suffered too heavily to engage in an energetic pursuit.

I cannot close the brief account of this glorious stand of the British troops without putting on record my deep appreciation of the valuable services rendered by General Sir Horace Smith-Dorrien.

I say without hesitation that the saving of the left wing of the Army under my command on the morning of the 26th August could never have been accomplished unless a commander of rare and unusual coolness, intrepidity, and determination had been present to personally conduct the operation.

The retreat was continued far into the night of the 26th and through the 27th and 28th, on which date the troops halted on the line Noyon – Chauny – La Fere, having then thrown off the weight of the enemy's pursuit.

On the 27th and 28th I was much indebted to General Sordêt and the French Cavalry Division which he commands for materially assisting my retirement and successfully driving back some of the enemy on Cambrai.

General D'Amade also, with the 61st and 62nd French Reserve Divisions, moved down from the neighbourhood of Arras on the enemy's right flank and took much pressure off the rear of the British Forces.

This closes the period covering the heavy fighting which commenced at Mons on Sunday afternoon, 23rd August, and which really constituted a four days' battle.

At this point, therefore, I propose to close the present despatch.

I deeply deplore the very serious losses which the British Forces have suffered in this great battle; but they were inevitable in view of the fact that the British Army – only two days after a concentration by rail – was called upon to withstand a vigorous attack of five German Army Corps.

It is impossible for me to speak too highly of the skill evinced by the two General Officers commanding Army Corps; the self-sacrificing and devoted exertions of their Staffs; the direction of the troops by Divisional, Brigade and Regimental Leaders; the command of the smaller units by their officers; and the magnificent fighting spirit displayed by non-commissioned officers and men.

I wish particularly to bring to your Lordship's notice the admirable work done by the Royal Flying Corps under Sir David Henderson. Their skill, energy and perseverance have been beyond all praise. They have furnished me with the most complete and accurate information which has been of incalculable value in the conduct of the operations. Fired at constantly both by friend and foe, and not hesitating to fly in every kind of weather, they have remained undaunted throughout.

Further, by actually fighting in the air, they have succeeded in destroying five of the enemy's machines. I wish to acknowledge with deep gratitude the incalculable assistance I received from the General and Personal Staffs at Headquarters during this trying period.

Lieutenant-General Sir Archibald Murray, Chief of the General Staff; Major-General Wilson, Sub-Chief of the General Staff; and all under them have worked day and night unceasingly with the utmost skill, self-sacrifice, and devotion; and the same acknowledgment is due by me to Brigadier-General Hon. W. Lambton, my Military Secretary, and the Personal Staff.

In such operations as I have described the work of the Quartermaster-General is of an extremely onerous nature. Major-General Sir William Robertson has met what appeared to be almost insuperable difficulties with his characteristic energy, skill and determination; and it is largely owing to his exertions that the hardships and sufferings of the troops – inseparable from such operations – were not much greater.

Major-General Sir Nevil Macready, the Adjutant-General, has also been confronted with most onerous and difficult tasks in connection with disciplinary arrangements and the preparation of casualty lists. He has been indefatigable in his exertions to meet the difficult situations which arose.

I have not yet been able to complete the list of officers whose names I desire to bring to your Lordship's notice for services rendered during the period under review; and, as I understand it is of importance that this despatch should no longer be delayed, I propose to forward this list, separately, as soon as I can.

I have the honour to be,
Your Lordship's most obedient Servant,
(Signed) J.D.P. FRENCH, Field-Marshal,
Commander-in-Chief,
British Forces in the Field.

SIR JOHN FRENCH'S DESPATCHES OF 17 SEPTEMBER 1914 AND 8 OCTOBER 1914

The Retreat from Le Cateau, the Battle of the Marne and the Battle of the Aisne

War Office, October 18*th*, 1914.

THE following despatches have been received by the Secretary of State for War from the Field-Marshal Commanding-in-Chief, British Forces in the Field:-

I.

17th September, 1914.

MY LORD,

In continuation of my despatch of September 7th, I have the honour to report the further progress of the operations of the Forces under my command from August 28th. On that evening the retirement of the Force was followed closely by two of the enemy's cavalry columns, moving south-east from St. Quentin.

The retreat in this part of the field was being covered by the 3rd and 5th Cavalry Brigades. South of the Somme General Gough, with the 3rd Cavalry Brigade, threw back the Uhlans of the Guard with considerable loss.

General Chetwode, with the 5th Cavalry Brigade, encountered the eastern column near Cérizy, moving south. The Brigade attacked and routed the column, the leading German regiment suffering very severe casualties and being almost broken up.

The 7th French Army Corps was now in course of being railed up from the south to the east of Amiens. On the 29th it nearly completed its detrainment, and the French 6th Army got into position on my left, its right resting on Roye.

The 5th French Army was behind the line of the Oise between La Fère and Guise.

The pursuit of the enemy was very vigorous; some five or six German corps were on the Somme, facing the 5th Army on the Oise. At least two corps were advancing towards my front, and were crossing the Somme east and west of Ham. Three or four more German corps were opposing the 6th French Army on my left.

This was the situation at 1 o'clock on the 29th, when I received a visit from General Joffre at my headquarters.

I strongly represented my position to the French Commander-in-Chief, who was most kind, cordial, and sympathetic, as he has always been. He told me that he had directed the 5th French Army on the Oise to move forward and attack the Germans on the Somme, with a view to checking pursuit. He also told me of the formation of the Sixth French Army on my left flank, composed of the 7th Army Corps, four Reserve Divisions, and Sordêt's Corps of Cavalry.

I finally arranged with General Joffre to effect a further short retirement towards the line Compiègne-Soissons, promising him, however, to do my utmost to keep always within a day's march of him.

In pursuance of this arrangement the British Forces retired to a position a few miles north of the line Compiegne-Soissons on the 29th.

The right flank of the German Army was now reaching a point which appeared seriously to endanger my line of communications with Havre. I had already evacuated Amiens, into which place a German reserve division was reported to have moved.

Orders were given to change the base to St. Nazaire, and establish an advance base at Le Mans. This operation was well carried out by the Inspector General of Communications.

In spite of a severe defeat inflicted upon the Guard 10th and Guard Reserve Corps of the German Army by the 1st and 3rd French Corps on the right of the 5th Army, it was not part of General Joffre's plan to pursue this advantage; and a general retirement on to the line of the Marne was ordered, to which the French Forces in the more eastern theatre were directed to conform.

A new Army (the 9th) had been formed from three corps in the south by General Joffre, and moved into the space between the right of the 5th and left of the 4th Armies.

Whilst closely adhering to his strategic conception to draw the enemy on at all points until a favourable situation was created from which to assume the offensive, General Joffre found it necessary to modify from day to day the methods by which he sought to attain this object, owing to the development of the enemy's plans and changes in the general situation.

In conformity with the movements of the French Forces, my retirement continued practically from day to day. Although we were not severely pressed by the enemy, rearguard actions took place continually.

On the 1st September, when retiring from the thickly wooded country to the south of Compiègne, the 1st Cavalry Brigade was overtaken by some German cavalry. They momentarily lost a Horse Artillery battery, and several officers and men were killed and wounded. With the help, however, of some detachments from the 3rd Corps operating on their left, they not only recovered their own guns but succeeded in capturing twelve of the enemy's.

Similarly, to the eastward, the 1st Corps, retiring south, also got into some very difficult forest country, and a somewhat severe rearguard action ensued at Villers-Cotterets, in which the 4th Guards Brigade suffered considerably.

On September 3rd the British Forces were in position south of the Marne between Lagny and Signy-Signets. Up to this time I had been requested by General Joffre to defend the passages of the river as long as possible, and to blow up the bridges in my front. After I had made the necessary dispositions, and the destruction of the bridges had been effected, I was asked by the French Commander-in-Chief to continue my retirement to a point some 12 miles in rear of the position I then occupied, with a view to taking up a second position behind the Seine. This retirement was duly carried out. In the meantime the enemy had thrown bridges and crossed the Marne in considerable force, and was threatening the Allies all along the line of the British Forces and the 5th and 9th French Armies. Consequently several small outpost actions took place.

On Saturday, September 5th, I met the French Commander-in-Chief at his request, and he informed me of his intention to take the offensive forthwith, as he considered conditions were very favourable to success.

General Joffre announced to me his intention of wheeling up the left flank of the 6th Army, pivoting on the Marne and directing it to move on the Ourcq; cross and attack the flank of the 1st German Army, which was then moving in a south-easterly direction east of that river.

He requested me to effect a change of front to my right – my left resting on the Marne and my right on the 5th Army – to fill the gap between that army and the 6th. I was then to advance against the enemy in my front and join in the general offensive movement.

These combined movements practically commenced on Sunday, September 6th, at sunrise; and on that day it may be said that a great battle opened on a front extending from Ermenonville, which was just in front of the left flank of the 6th French Army, through Lizy on the Marne, Mauperthuis, which was about the British centre, Courtecon, which was the left of the 5th French Army, to Esternay and Charleville, the left of the 9th Army under General Foch, and so along the front of the 9th, 4th, and 3rd French Armies to a point north of the fortress of Verdun.

This battle, in so far as the 6th French Army, the British Army, the 5th French Army and the 9th French Army were concerned, may be said to have concluded on the evening of September 10th, by which time the Germans had been driven back to the line Soissons – Reims, with a loss of thousands of prisoners, many guns, and enormous masses of transport. About the 3rd September the enemy appears to have changed his plans and to have determined to stop his advance South direct upon Paris; for on the

4th September air reconnaissances showed that his main columns were moving in a south-easterly direction generally east of a line drawn through Nanteuil and Lizy on the Ourcq.

On the 5th September several of these columns were observed to have crossed the Marne; whilst German troops, which were observed moving south-east up the left bank of the Ourcq on the 4th, were now reported to be halted and facing that river. Heads of the enemy's columns were seen crossing at Changis, La Ferté, Nogent, Château Thierry and Mezy. Considerable German columns of all arms were seen to be converging on Montmirail, whilst before sunset large bivouacs of the enemy were located in the neighbourhood of Coulommiers, south of Rebais, La Ferté-Gaucher and Dagny.

I should conceive it to have been about noon on the 6th September, after the British Forces had changed their front to the right and occupied the line Jouy – Le Chatel – Faremoutiers – Villeneuve Le Comte, and the advance of the 6th French Army north of the Marne towards the Ourcq became apparent, that the enemy realised the powerful threat that was being made against the flank of his columns moving south-east, and began the great retreat which opened the battle above referred to.

On the evening of the 6th September, therefore, the fronts and positions of the opposing armies were roughly as follows:-

ALLIES.

6th French Army. – Right on the Marne at Meaux, left towards Betz.

British Forces. – On the line Dagny – Coulommiers – Maison.

5th French Army. – At Courtagon, right on Esternay.

Conneau's Cavalry Corps. – Between the right of the British and the left of the French 5th Army

GERMANS.

4th Reserve and 2nd Corps. – East of the Ourcq and facing that river.

9th Cavalry Division. – West of Crecy.

2nd Cavalry Division. – North of Coulommiers.

4th Corps. – Rebais.

3rd and 7th Corps. – South-west of Montmirail.

All these troops constituted the 1st German Army, which was directed against the French 6th Army on the Ourcq, and the British Forces, and the left of the 5th French Army south of the Marne.

The 2nd German Army (IX., X., X.R. and Guard) was moving against the centre and right of the 5th French Army and the 9th French Army.

On the 7th September both the 5th and 6th French Armies were heavily engaged on our flank. The 2nd and 4th Reserve German Corps on the Ourcq vigorously opposed the advance of the French towards that river, but did not prevent the 6th Army from gaining some headway, the Germans themselves suffering serious losses. The French 5th Army threw the enemy back to the line of the Petit Morin river after inflicting severe losses upon them, especially about Montceaux, which was carried at the point of the bayonet.

The enemy retreated before our advance, covered by his 2nd and 9th and Guard Cavalry Divisions, which suffered severely.

Our Cavalry acted with great vigour, especially General De Lisle's Brigade with the 9th Lancers and 18th Hussars.

On the 8th September the enemy continued his retreat northward, and our Army was successfully engaged during the day with strong rearguards of all arms on the Petit Morin River, thereby materially assisting the progress of the French Armies on our right and left, against whom the enemy was making his greatest efforts. On both sides the enemy was thrown back with very heavy loss. The First Army Corps encountered stubborn resistance at La Trétoire (north of Rebais). The enemy occupied a strong position with infantry and guns on the northern bank of the Petit Morin River; they were dislodged with considerable loss. Several machine guns and many prisoners were captured, and upwards of two hundred German dead were left on the ground.

The forcing of the Petit Morin at this point was much assisted by the Cavalry and the 1st Division, which crossed higher up the stream.

Later in the day a counter attack by the enemy was well repulsed by the First Army Corps, a great many prisoners and some guns again falling into our hands.

On this day (8th September) the Second Army Corps encountered considerable opposition, but drove back the enemy at all points with great loss, making considerable captures.

The Third Army Corps also drove back considerable bodies of the enemy's infantry and made some captures.

On the 9th September the First and Second Army Corps forced the passage of the Marne and advanced some miles to the north of it. The Third Corps encountered considerable opposition, as the bridge at La Ferté was destroyed and the enemy held the town on the opposite bank in some strength, and thence persistently obstructed the construction of a bridge; so the passage was not effected until after nightfall.

During the day's pursuit the enemy suffered heavy loss in killed and wounded, some hundreds of prisoners fell into our hands and a battery of eight machine guns was captured by the 2nd Division.

On this day the 6th French Army was heavily engaged west of the River Ourcq. The enemy had largely increased his force opposing them; and very heavy fighting ensued, in which the French were successful throughout.

The left of the 5th French Army reached the neighbourhood of Château Thierry after the most severe fighting, having driven the enemy completely north of the river with great loss.

The fighting of this Army in the neighbourhood of Montmirail was very severe. The advance was resumed at daybreak on the 10th up to the line of the Ourcq, opposed by strong rearguards of all arms. The 1st and 2nd Corps, assisted by the Cavalry Division on the right, the 3rd and 5th Cavalry Brigades on the left, drove the enemy northwards. Thirteen guns, seven machine guns, about 2,000 prisoners, and quantities of transport fell into our hands. The enemy left many dead on the field. On this day the French 5th and 6th Armies had little opposition.

As the 1st and 2nd German Armies were now in full retreat, this evening marks the end of the battle which practically commenced on the morning of the 6th instant; and it is at this point in the operations that I am concluding the present despatch.

Although I deeply regret to have had to report heavy losses in killed and wounded throughout these operations, I do not think they have been excessive in view of the magnitude of the great fight, the outlines of which I have only been able very briefly to describe, and the demoralisation and loss in killed and wounded which are known to have been caused to the enemy by the vigour and severity of the pursuit.

In concluding this despatch I must call your Lordship's special attention to the fact that from Sunday, August 23rd, up to the present date (September 17th), from Mons back almost to the Seine, and from the Seine to the Aisne, the Army under my command has been ceaselessly engaged without one single day's halt or rest of any kind.

Since the date to which in this despatch I have limited my report of the operations, a great battle on the Aisne has been proceeding. A full report of this battle will be made in an early further despatch.

It will, however, be of interest to say here that, in spite of a very determined resistance on the part of the enemy, who is holding in strength and great tenacity a position peculiarly favourable to defence, the battle which commenced on the evening of the 12th instant has, so far, forced the enemy back from his first position, secured the passage of the river, and inflicted great loss upon him, including the capture of over 2,000 prisoners and several guns.

I have the honour to be,
Your Lordship's most obedient Servant,
(Signed) J.D.P. FRENCH, Field-Marshal,
Commanding-in-Chief,
The British Forces in the Field.

II.

8th October, 1914.

My LORD,

I have the honour to report the operations in which the British Forces in France have been engaged since the evening of the 10th September.

1. In the early morning of the 11th the further pursuit of the enemy was commenced; and the three Corps crossed the Ourcq practically unopposed, the Cavalry reaching the line of the Aisne River; the 3rd and 5th Brigades south of Soissons, the 1st, 2nd and 4th on the high ground at Couvrelles and Cerseuil.

On the afternoon of the 12th from the opposition encountered by the 6th French Army to the west of Soissons, by the 3rd Corps south-east of that place, by the 2nd Corps south of Missy and Vailly, and certain indications all along the line, I formed the opinion that the enemy had, for the moment at any rate, arrested his retreat and was preparing to dispute the passage of the Aisne with some vigour.

South of Soissons the Germans were holding Mont de Paris against the attack of the right of the French 6th Army when the 3rd Corps reached the neighbourhood of Buzancy, southeast of that place. With the assistance of the Artillery of the 3rd Corps the French drove them back across the river at Soissons, where they destroyed the bridges.

The heavy artillery fire which was visible for several miles in a westerly direction in the valley of the Aisne showed that the 6th French Army was meeting with strong opposition all along the line.

On this day the Cavalry under General Allenby reached the neighbourhood of Braine and did good work in clearing the town and the high ground beyond it of strong hostile detachments. The Queen's Bays are particularly mentioned by the General as having assisted greatly in the success of this operation. They were well supported by the 3rd Division, which on this night bivouacked at Brenelle, south of the river.

The 5th Division approached Missy, but were unable to make headway.

The 1st Army Corps reached the neighbourhood of Vauxcéré without much opposition.

In this manner the Battle of the Aisne commenced.

2. The Aisne Valley runs generally East and West, and consists of a flat-bottomed depression of width varying from half a mile to two miles, down which the river follows a winding course to the West at some points near the southern slopes of the valley and at others near the northern. The high ground both on the north and south of the river is approximately 400 feet

above the bottom of the valley and is very similar in character, as are both slopes of the valley itself, which are broken into numerous rounded spurs and re-entrants. The most prominent of the former are the Chivre spur on the right bank and Sermoise spur on the left. Near the latter place the general plateau on the south is divided by a subsidiary valley of much the same character, down which the small River Vesle flows to the main stream near Sermoise. The slopes of the plateau overlooking the Aisne on the north and south are of varying steepness, and are covered with numerous patches of wood, which also stretch upwards and backwards over the edge on to the top of the high ground. There are several villages and small towns dotted about in the valley itself and along its sides, the chief of which is the town of Soissons.

The Aisne is a sluggish stream of some 170 feet in breadth, but, being 15 feet deep in the centre, it is unfordable. Between Soissons on the west and Villers on the east (the part of the river attacked and secured by the British Forces) there are eleven road bridges across it. On the north bank a narrow-gauge railway runs from Soissons to Vailly, where it crosses the river and continues eastward along the south bank. From Soissons to Sermoise a double line of railway runs along the south bank, turning at the latter place up the Vesle Valley towards Bazoches.

The position held by the enemy is a very strong one, either for a delaying action or for a defensive battle. One of its chief military characteristics is that from the high ground on neither side can the top of the plateau on the other side be seen except for small stretches. This is chiefly due to the woods on the edges of the slopes. Another important point is that all the bridges are under either direct or high angle artillery fire.

The tract of country above described, which lies north of the Aisne, is well adapted to concealment, and was so skilfully turned to account by the enemy as to render it impossible to judge the real nature of his opposition to our passage of the river, or to accurately gauge his strength; but I have every reason to conclude that strong rearguards of at least three army corps were holding the passages on the early morning of the 13th.

3. On that morning I ordered the British Forces to advance and make good the Aisne.

The 1st Corps and the Cavalry advanced on the river. The 1st Division was directed on Chanouille viâ the canal bridge at Bourg, and the 2nd Division on Courtecon and Presles viâ Pont-Arcy and on the canal to the north of Braye viâ Chavonne. On the right the Cavalry and 1st Division met with slight opposition, and found a passage by means of the canal which crosses the river by an aqueduct. The Division was therefore able to press on, supported by the Cavalry Division on its outer flank, driving back the enemy in front of it.

On the left the leading troops of the 2nd Division reached the river by 9 o'clock. The 5th Infantry Brigade were only enabled to cross, in single file and under considerable shell fire, by means of the broken girder of the bridge which was not entirely submerged in the river. The construction of a pontoon bridge was at once undertaken, and was completed by 5 o'clock in the afternoon.

On the extreme left the 4th Guards Brigade met with severe opposition at Chavonne, and it was only late in the afternoon that it was able to establish a foothold on the northern bank of the river by ferrying one battalion across in boats.

By nightfall the 1st Division occupied the area Moulins – Paissy – Geny, with posts in the village of Vendresse.

The 2nd Division bivouacked as a whole on the southern bank of the river, leaving only the 5th Brigade on the north bank to establish a bridge head.

The Second Corps found all the bridges in front of them destroyed, except that of Condé, which was in possession of the enemy, and remained so until the end of the battle.

In the approach to Missy, where the 5th Division eventually crossed, there is some open ground which was swept by heavy fire from the opposite bank. The 13th Brigade was, therefore, unable to advance; but the 14th, which was directed to the east of Venizel at a less exposed point, was rafted across, and by night established itself with its left at St. Marguérite. They were followed by the 15th Brigade; and later on both the 14th and 15th supported the 4th Division on their left in repelling a heavy counter-attack on the Third Corps. On the morning of the 13th the Third Corps found the enemy had established himself in strength on the Vregny Plateau. The road bridge at Venizel was repaired during the morning, and a reconnaissance was made with a view to throwing a pontoon bridge at Soissons.

The 12th Infantry Brigade crossed at Venizel, and was assembled at Bucy Le Long by 1 p.m., but the bridge was so far damaged that artillery could only be man-handled across it. Meanwhile the construction of a bridge was commenced close to the road bridge at Venizel. At 2 p.m. the 12th Infantry Brigade attacked in the direction of Chivres and Vregny with the object of securing the high ground east of Chivres, as a necessary preliminary to a further advance northwards. This attack made good progress, but at 5.30 p.m. the enemy's artillery and machine-gun fire from the direction of Vregny became so severe that no further advance could be made. The positions reached were held till dark.

The pontoon bridge at Venizel was completed at 5.30 p.m., when the 10th Infantry Brigade crossed the river and moved to Bucy Le Long.

The 19th Infantry Brigade moved to Billy Sur Aisne, and before dark all the artillery of the Division had crossed the river, with the exception of the Heavy Battery and one Brigade of Field Artillery.

During the night the positions gained by the 12th Infantry Brigade to the east of the stream running through Chivres were handed over to the 5th Division.

The section of the Bridging Train allotted to the Third Corps began to arrive in the neighbourhood of Soissons late in the afternoon, when an attempt to throw a heavy pontoon bridge at Soissons had to be abandoned, owing to the fire of the enemy's heavy howitzers.

In the evening the enemy retired at all points and entrenched himself on the high ground about two miles north of the river along which runs the Chemin-des-Dames. Detachments of Infantry, however, strongly entrenched in commanding points down slopes of the various spurs, were left in front of all three corps with powerful artillery in support of them. During the night of the 13th and on the 14th and following days the Field Companies were incessantly at work night and day. Eight pontoon bridges and one foot bridge were thrown across the river under generally very heavy artillery fire, which was incessantly kept up on to most of the crossings after completion. Three of the road bridges, i.e., Venizel, Missy and Vailly, and the railway bridge east of Vailly were temporarily repaired so as to take foot traffic and the Villers Bridge made fit to carry weights up to six tons.

Preparations were also made for the repair of the Missy, Vailly and Bourg Bridges so as to take mechanical transport.

The weather was very wet and added to the difficulties by cutting up the already indifferent approaches, entailing a large amount of work to repair and improve.

The operations of the Field Companies during this most trying time are worthy of the best traditions of the Royal Engineers.

4. On the evening of the 14th it was still impossible to decide whether the enemy was only making a temporary halt, covered by rearguards, or whether he intended to stand and defend the position.

With a view to clearing up the situation, I ordered a general advance.

The action of the First Corps on this day under the direction and command of Sir Douglas Haig was of so skilful, bold and decisive a character that he gained positions which alone have enabled me to maintain my position for more than three weeks of very severe fighting on the north bank of the river.

The Corps was directed to cross the line Moulins – Moussy by 7 a.m.

On the right the General Officer Commanding the 1st Division directed the 2nd Infantry Brigade (which was in billets and bivouacked about

Moulins), and the 25th Artillery Brigade (less one battery), under General Bulfin, to move forward before daybreak, in order to protect the advance of the Division sent up the valley to Vendresse. An officers' patrol sent out by this Brigade reported a considerable force of the enemy near the factory north of Troyon, and the Brigadier accordingly directed two regiments (the King's Royal Rifles and the Royal Sussex Regiment) to move at 3 a.m. The Northamptonshire Regiment was ordered to move at 4 a.m. to occupy the spur east of Troyon. The remaining regiment of the Brigade (the Loyal North Lancashire Regiment) moved at 5.30 a.m. to the village of Vendresse. The factory was found to be held in considerable strength by the enemy, and the Brigadier ordered the Loyal North Lancashire Regiment to support the King's Royal Rifles and the Sussex Regiment. Even with this support the force was unable to make headway, and on the arrival of the 1st Brigade the Coldstream Guards were moved up to support the right of the leading Brigade (the 2nd), while the remainder of the 1st Brigade supported its left.

About noon the situation was, roughly, that the whole of these two brigades were extended along a line running east and west, north of the line Troyon and south of the Chemin-des-Dames. A party of the Loyal North Lancashire Regiment had seized and were holding the factory. The enemy held a line of entrenchments north and east of the factory in considerable strength, and every effort to advance against this line was driven back by heavy shell and machine-gun fire. The morning was wet and a heavy mist hung over the hills, so that the 25th Artillery Brigade and the Divisional Artillery were unable to render effective support to the advanced troops until about 9 o'clock.

By 10 o'clock the 3rd Infantry Brigade had reached a point one mile south of Vendresse, and from there it was ordered to continue the line of the 1st Brigade and to connect with and help the right of the 2nd Division. A strong hostile column was found to be advancing, and by a vigorous counter stroke with two of his battalions the Brigadier checked the advance of this column and relieved the pressure on the 2nd Division. From this period until late in the afternoon the fighting consisted of a series of attacks and counter attacks. The counter strokes by the enemy were delivered at first with great vigour, but later on they decreased in strength, and all were driven off with heavy loss.

On the left the 6th Infantry Brigade had been ordered to cross the river and to pass through the line held during the preceding night by the 5th Infantry Brigade and occupy the Courtecon Ridge, whilst a detached force, consisting of the 4th Guards Brigade and the 36th Brigade, Royal Field Artillery, under Brigadier-General Perceval, were ordered to proceed to a point east of the village of Ostel.

The 6th Infantry Brigade crossed the river at Pont-Arcy, moved up the valley towards Braye, and at 9 a.m. had reached the line Tilleul – La Buvelle.

On this line they came under heavy artillery and rifle fire, and were unable to advance until supported by the 34th Brigade, Royal Field Artillery, und the 44th Howitzer Brigade and the Heavy Artillery.

The 4th Guards Brigade crossed the river at 10 a.m. and met with very heavy opposition. It had to pass through dense woods; field artillery support was difficult to obtain; but one section of a field battery pushed up to and within the firing line. At 1 p.m. the left of the Brigade was south of the Ostel Ridge.

At this period of the action the enemy obtained a footing between the First and Second Corps, and threatened to cut the communications of the latter.

Sir Douglas Haig was very hardly pressed and had no reserve in hand. I placed the Cavalry Division at his disposal, part of which he skilfully used to prolong and secure the left flank of the Guards Brigade. Some heavy fighting ensued, which resulted in the enemy being driven back with heavy loss.

About 4 o'clock the weakening of the counter attacks by the enemy and other indications tended to show that his resistance was decreasing, and a general advance was ordered by the Army Corps Commander. Although meeting with considerable opposition and coming under very heavy artillery and rifle fire, the position of the corps at the end of the day's operations extended from the Chemin-des-Dames on the right, through Chivy, to Le Cour de Soupir, with the 1st Cavalry Brigade extending to the Chavonne – Soissons road.

On the right the corps was in close touch with the French Moroccan troops of the 18th Corps, which were entrenched in echelon to its right rear. During the night they entrenched this position. Throughout the Battle of the Aisne this advanced and commanding position was maintained, and I cannot speak too highly of the valuable services rendered by Sir Douglas Haig and the Army Corps' under his command. Day after day and night after night the enemy's infantry has been hurled against him in violent counter attack which has never on any one occasion succeeded, whilst the trenches all over his position have been under continuous heavy artillery fire.

The operations of the First Corps on this day resulted in the capture of several hundred prisoners, some field pieces, and machine guns.

The casualties were very severe, one brigade alone losing three of its four Colonels.

The 3rd Division commenced a further advance and had nearly reached the plateau of Aizy when they were driven back by a powerful counter attack supported by heavy artillery. The division, however, fell back in the best order, and finally entrenched itself about a mile north of Vailly Bridge, effectively covering the passage.

The 4th and 5th Divisions were unable to do more than maintain their ground.

5. On the morning of the 15th, after close examination of the position, it became clear to me that the enemy was making a determined stand; and this view was confirmed by reports which reached me from the French Armies fighting on my right and left, which clearly showed that a strongly entrenched line of defence was being taken up from the north of Compiègne, eastward and south-eastward, along the whole valley of the Aisne up to and beyond Reims.

A few days previously the Fortress of Maubeuge fell, and a considerable quantity of siege artillery was brought down from that place to strengthen the enemy's position in front of us. During the 15th shells fell in our position which have been judged by experts to be thrown by eight-inch siege guns with a range of 10,000 yards. Throughout the whole course of the battle our troops have suffered very heavily from this fire, although its effect latterly was largely mitigated by more efficient and thorough entrenching, the necessity for which I impressed strongly upon Army Corps Commanders. In order to assist them in this work all villages within the area of our occupation were searched for heavy entrenching tools, a large number of which were collected.

In view of the peculiar formation of the ground on the north side of the river between Missy and Soissons, and its extraordinary adaptability to a force on the defensive, the 5th Division found it impossible to maintain its position on the southern edge of the Chivres Plateau, as the enemy in possession of the village of Vregny to the west was able to bring a flank fire to bear upon it. The Division had, therefore, to retire to a line the left of which was at the village of Marguérite, and thence ran by the north edge of Missy back to the river to the east of that place.

With great skill and tenacity Sir Charles Fergusson maintained this position throughout the whole battle, although his trenches were necessarily on lower ground than that occupied by the enemy on the southern edge of the plateau, which was only 400 yards away.

General Hamilton with the 3rd Division vigorously attacked to the north, and regained all the ground he had lost on the 15th, which throughout the battle has formed a most powerful and effective bridge head.

6. On the 16th the 6th Division came up into line.

It had been my intention to direct the First Corps to attack and seize the enemy's position on the Chemin-des-Dames, supporting it with this new reinforcement. I hoped from the position thus gained to bring effective fire to bear across the front of the 3rd Division which, by securing the advance of the latter, would also take the pressure off the 5th Division and the Third Corps.

But any further advance of the First Corps would have dangerously exposed my right flank. And, further, I learned from the French Commander-in-Chief that he was strongly reinforcing the 6th French Army on my left, with the intention of bringing up the Allied left to attack the enemy's flank and thus compel his retirement. I therefore sent the 6th Division to join the Third Corps with orders to keep it on the south side of the river, as it might be available in general reserve.

On the 17th, 18th and 19th the whole of our line was heavily bombarded, and the First Corps was constantly and heavily engaged. On the afternoon of the 17th the right flank of the 1st Division was seriously threatened. A counter attack was made by the Northamptonshire Regiment in combination with the Queen's, and one battalion of the Divisional Reserve was moved up in support. The Northamptonshire Regiment, under cover of mist, crept up to within a hundred yards of the enemy's trenches and charged with the bayonet, driving them out of the trenches and up the hill. A very strong force of hostile infantry was then disclosed on the crest line. This new line was enfiladed by part of the Queen's and the King's Royal Rifles, which wheeled to their left on the extreme right of our infantry line, and were supported by a squadron of cavalry on their outer flank. The enemy's attack was ultimately driven back with heavy loss.

On the 18th, during the night, the Gloucestershire Regiment advanced from their position near Chivy, filled in the enemy's trenches and captured two maxim guns.

On the extreme right the Queen's were heavily attacked, but the enemy was repulsed with great loss. About midnight the attack was renewed on the First Division, supported by artillery fire, but was again repulsed.

Shortly after midnight an attack was made on the left of the 2nd Division with considerable force, which was also thrown back.

At about 1 p.m. on the 19th the 2nd Division drove back a heavy infantry attack strongly supported by artillery fire. At dusk the attack was renewed and again repulsed. On the 18th I discussed with the General Officer Commanding the Second Army Corps and his Divisional Commanders the possibility of driving the enemy out of Condé, which lay between his two Divisions, and seizing the bridge which has remained throughout in his possession.

As, however, I found that the bridge was closely commanded from all points on the south side and that satisfactory arrangements were made to prevent any issue from it by the enemy by day or night, I decided that it was not necessary to incur the losses which an attack would entail, as, in view of the position of the Second and Third Corps, the enemy could make no use of Condé, and would be automatically forced out of it by any advance which might become possible for us.

7. On this day information reached me from General Joffre that he had found it necessary to make a new plan, and to attack and envelop the German right flank.

It was now evident to me that the battle in which we had been engaged since the 12th instant must last some days longer until the effect of this new flank movement could be felt and a way opened to drive the enemy from his positions.

It thus became essential to establish some system of regular relief in the trenches, and I have used the infantry of the 6th Division for this purpose with good results. The relieved brigades were brought back alternately south of the river, and, with the artillery of the 6th Division, formed a general reserve on which I could rely in case of necessity.

The Cavalry has rendered most efficient and ready help in the trenches, and have done all they possibly could to lighten the arduous and trying task which has of necessity fallen to the lot of the Infantry.

On the evening of the 19th and throughout the 20th the enemy again commenced to show considerable activity. On the former night a severe counter-attack on the 3rd Division was repulsed with considerable loss, and from early on Sunday morning various hostile attempts were made on the trenches of the 1st Division. During the day the enemy suffered another severe repulse in front of the 2nd Division, losing heavily in the attempt. In the course of the afternoon the enemy made desperate attempts against the trenches all along the front of the First Corps, but with similar results.

After dark the enemy again attacked the 2nd Division, only to be again driven back. Our losses on these two days were considerable, but the number, as obtained, of the enemy's killed and wounded vastly exceeded them.

As the troops of the First Army Corps were much exhausted by this continual fighting, I reinforced Sir Douglas Haig with a brigade from the reserve, and called upon the 1st Cavalry Division to assist them.

On the night of the 21st another violent counter-attack was repulsed by the 3rd Division, the enemy losing heavily.

On the 23rd the four six-inch howitzer batteries, which I had asked to be sent from home, arrived. Two batteries were handed over to the Second Corps and two to the First Corps. They were brought into action on the 24th with very good results.

Our experiences in this campaign seem to point to the employment of more heavy guns of a larger calibre in great battles which last for several days, during which time powerful entrenching work on both sides can be carried out.

These batteries were used with considerable effect on the 24th and the following days.

8. On the 23rd the action of General de Castelnau's Army on the Allied left developed considerably, and apparently withdrew considerable forces of the enemy away from the centre and east. I am not aware whether it was due to this cause or not, but until the 26th it appeared as though the enemy's opposition in our front was weakening. On that day, however, a very marked renewal of activity commenced. A constant and vigorous artillery bombardment was maintained all day, and the Germans in front of the 1st Division were observed to be "sapping" up to our lines and trying to establish new trenches. Renewed counter-attacks were delivered and beaten off during the course of the day, and in the afternoon a well-timed attack by the 1st Division stopped the enemy's entrenching work. During the night of 27th-28th the enemy again made the most determined attempts to capture the trenches of the 1st Division, but without the slightest success.

Similar attacks were reported during these three days all along the line of the Allied front, and it is certain that the enemy then made one last great effort to establish ascendancy. He was, however, unsuccessful everywhere, and is reported to have suffered heavy losses. The same futile attempts were made all along our front up to the evening of the 28th, when they died away, and have not since been renewed.

On former occasions I have brought to your Lordship's notice the valuable services performed during this campaign by the Royal Artillery.

Throughout the Battle of the Aisne they have displayed the same skill, endurance and tenacity, and I deeply appreciate the work they have done.

Sir David Henderson and the Royal Flying Corps under his command have again proved their incalculable value. Great strides have been made in the development of the use of aircraft in the tactical sphere by establishing effective communication between aircraft and units in action.

It is difficult to describe adequately and accurately the great strain to which officers and men were subjected almost every hour of the day and night throughout this battle. I have described above, the severe character of the artillery fire which was directed from morning till night, not only upon the trenches, but over the whole surface of the ground occupied by our Forces. It was not until a few days before the position was evacuated that the heavy guns were removed and the fire slackened. Attack and counter-attack occurred at all hours of the night and day throughout the whole position, demanding extreme vigilance, and permitting only a minimum of rest.

The fact that between the 12th September to the date of this despatch the total numbers of killed, wounded and missing reached the figures amounting to 561 officers, 12,980 men, proves the severity of the struggle.

The tax on the endurance of the troops was further increased by the heavy rain and cold which prevailed for some ten or twelve days of this trying time.

The Battle of the Aisne has once more demonstrated the splendid spirit, gallantry and devotion which animates the officers and men of His Majesty's Forces.

With reference to the last paragraph of my despatch of 7th September, I append the names of officers, non-commissioned officers and men brought forward for special mention by Army Corps commanders and heads of departments for services rendered from the commencement of the campaign up to the present date.

I entirely agree with these recommendations and beg to submit them for your Lordship's consideration.

I further wish to bring forward the names of the following officers who have rendered valuable service:- General Sir Horace Smith-Dorrien and Lieutenant-General Sir Douglas Haig (commanding First and Second Corps respectively) I have already mentioned in the present and former despatches for particularly marked and distinguished service in critical situations.

Since the commencement of the campaign they have carried out all my orders and instructions with the utmost ability.

Lieutenant-General W.P. Pulteney took over the command of the Third Corps just before the commencement of the Battle of the Marne. Throughout the subsequent operations he showed himself to be a most capable commander in the field and has rendered very valuable service.

Major-General E.H.H. Allenby and Major-General H. de la P. Gough have proved themselves to be Cavalry leaders of a high order, and I am deeply indebted to them. The undoubted moral superiority which our Cavalry has obtained over that of the enemy has been due to the skill with which they have turned to the best account the qualities inherent in the splendid troops they command.

In my despatch of 7th September I mentioned the name of Brigadier-General Sir David Henderson and his valuable work in command of the Royal Flying Corps; and I have once more to express my deep appreciation of the help he has since rendered me.

Lieutenant-General Sir Archibald Murray has continued to render me invaluable help as Chief of the Staff; and in his arduous and responsible duties he has been ably assisted by Major-General Henry Wilson, Sub-Chief.

Lieutenant-General Sir Nevil Macready and Lieutenant-General Sir William Robertson have continued to perform excellent service as Adjutant-General and Quartermaster-General respectively.

The Director of Army Signals, Lieutenant-Colonel J.S. Fowler, has materially assisted the operations by the skill and energy which he has displayed in the working of the important department over which he presides.

My Military Secretary, Brigadier-General the Hon. W. Lambton, has performed his arduous and difficult duties with much zeal and great efficiency.

I am anxious also to bring to your Lordship's notice the following names of officers of my Personal Staff, who throughout these arduous operations have shown untiring zeal and energy in the performance of their duties:-

Aides-de-Camp.
Lieutenant-Colonel Stanley Barry.
Lieutenant-Colonel Lord Brooke.
Major Fitzgerald Watt.

Extra Aide-de-Camp.
Captain the Hon. F.E. Guest.

Private Secretary.
Lieutenant-Colonel Brindsley Fitzgerald.

Major His Royal Highness Prince Arthur of Connaught, K.G., joined my Staff as Aide-de-Camp on the 14th September.

His Royal Highness's intimate knowledge of languages enabled me to employ him with great advantage on confidential missions of some importance, and his services have proved of considerable value.

I cannot close this despatch without informing your Lordship of the valuable services rendered by the Chief of the French Military Mission at my Headquarters, Colonel Victor Huguet, of the French Artillery. He has displayed tact and judgment of a high order in many difficult situations, and has rendered conspicuous service to the Allied cause.

I have the honour to be,
Your Lordship's most obedient Servant,
(Signed) J.D.P. FRENCH, Field-Marshal,
Commanding-in-Chief,
The British Army in the Field.

SIR JOHN FRENCH'S DESPATCH OF 20 NOVEMBER 1914

The BEF's move to Flanders, and the First Battle of Ypres

War Office, November 29th, 1914.

THE following despatch has been received by the Secretary of State for War from the Field-Marshal Commanding-in-Chief, British Forces in the Field:-

General Headquarters,
20th November, 1914.

MY LORD,

1. I have the honour to submit a further despatch recounting the operations of the Field Force under my command throughout the battle of Ypres – Armentières.

Early in October a study of the general situation strongly impressed me with the necessity of bringing the greatest possible force to bear in support of the northern flank of the Allies, in order to effectively outflank the enemy and compel him to evacuate his positions.

At the same time the position on the Aisne, as described in the concluding paragraphs of my last despatch, appeared to me to warrant a withdrawal of the British Forces from the positions they then held.

The enemy had been weakened by continual abortive and futile attacks, whilst the fortification of the position had been much improved.

I represented these views to General Joffre, who fully agreed.

Arrangements for withdrawal and relief having been made by the French General Staff, the operation commenced on the 3rd October; and the 2nd Cavalry Division, under General Gough, marched for Compiègne *en route* for the new theatre.

The Army Corps followed in succession at intervals of a few days, and the move was completed on the 19th October, when the First Corps, under Sir Douglas Haig, completed its detrainment at St. Omer.

That this delicate operation was carried out so successfully is in great measure due to the excellent feeling which exists between the French and British Armies; and I am deeply indebted to the Commander-in-Chief and the French General Staff for their cordial and most effective co-operation.

As General Foch was appointed by the Commander-in-Chief to supervise the operations of all the French troops north of Noyon, I visited his headquarters at Doullens on 8th October and arranged joint plans of operations as follows:-

The Second Corps to arrive on the line Aire – Bethune on the 11th October, to connect with the right of the French 10th Army and, pivoting on its left, to attack in flank the enemy who were opposing the 10th French Corps in front.

The Cavalry to move on the northern flank of the Second Corps and support its attack until the Third Corps, which was to detrain at St. Omer on the 12th, should come up. They were then to clear the front and act on the northern flank of the Third Corps in a similar manner, pending the arrival of the First Corps from the Aisne.

The 3rd Cavalry Division and 7th Division, under Sir Henry Rawlinson, which were then operating in support of the Belgian Army and assisting its withdrawal from Antwerp, to be ordered to co-operate as soon as circumstances would allow.

In the event of these movements so far overcoming the resistance of the enemy as to enable a forward movement to be made, all the Allied Forces to march in an easterly direction. The road running from Bethune to Lille was to be the dividing line between the British and French Forces, the right of the British Army being directed on Lille.

2. The great battle, which is mainly the subject of this despatch, may be said to have commenced on October 11th, on which date the 2nd Cavalry Division, under General Gough, first came into contact with the enemy's cavalry who were holding some woods to the north of the Bethune – Aire Canal. These were cleared of the enemy by our cavalry, which then joined hands with the Divisional Cavalry of the 6th Division in the neighbourhood of Hazebrouck. On the same day the right of the 2nd Cavalry Division connected with the left of the Second Corps which was moving in a north-easterly direction after crossing the above mentioned canal.

By the 11th October Sir Horace Smith-Dorrien had reached the line of the canal between Aire and Bethune. I directed him to continue his march on the 12th, bringing up his left in the direction of Merville. Then he was to move East to the line Laventie – Lorgies, which would bring him on the immediate left of the French Army and threaten the German flank.

On the 12th this movement was commenced. The 5th Division connected up with the left of the French Army north of Annequin. They moved to the attack of the Germans who were engaged at this point with the French; but the enemy once more extended his right in some strength to meet the threat against his flank. The 3rd Division, having crossed the canal, deployed on the left of the 5th; and the whole Second Corps again advanced to the attack, but were unable to make much headway owing to the difficult character of the ground upon which they were operating, which was similar to that usually found in manufacturing districts and was covered with mining works, factories, buildings, etc. The ground throughout this country is remarkably flat, rendering effective artillery support very difficult.

Before nightfall, however, they had made some advance and had successfully driven back hostile counter attacks with great loss to the enemy and destruction of some of his machine guns. On and after the 13th October the object of the General Officer Commanding the Second Corps was to wheel to his right, pivoting on Givenchy to get astride the La Bassée – Lille Road in the neighbourhood of Fournes, so as to threaten the right flank and rear of the enemy's position on the high ground south of La Bassée.

This position of La Bassée has throughout the battle defied all attempts at capture, either by the French or the British.

On this day Sir Horace Smith-Dorrien could make but little progress. He particularly mentions the fine fighting of the Dorsets, whose Commanding Officer, Major Roper, was killed. They suffered no less than 400 casualties, 130 of them being killed, but maintained all day their hold on Pont Fixe. He also refers to the gallantry of the Artillery.

The fighting of the Second Corps continued throughout the 14th in the same direction. On this day the Army suffered a great loss, in that the Commander of the 3rd Division, General Hubert Hamilton, was killed.

On the 15th the 3rd Division fought splendidly, crossing the dykes, with which this country is intersected, with planks; and driving the enemy from one entrenched position to another in loop-holed villages, till at night they pushed the Germans off the Estaires – La Bassée Road, and establishing themselves on the line Pont de Ham – Croix Barbée.

On the 16th the move was continued until the left flank of the Corps was in front of the village of Aubers, which was strongly held. This village was captured on the 17th by the 9th Infantry Brigade; and at dark on the same day the Lincolns and Royal Fusiliers carried the village of Herlies at the point of the bayonet after a fine attack, the Brigade being handled with great dash by Brigadier-General Shaw.

At this time, to the best of our information, the Second Corps were believed to be opposed by the 2nd, 4th, 7th and 9th German Cavalry Divisions, supported by several battalions of Jaegers and a part of the 14th German Corps.

On the 18th powerful counter attacks were made by the enemy all along the front of the Second Corps, and were most gallantly repulsed; but only slight progress could be made. From the 19th to the 31st October the Second Corps carried on a most gallant fight in defence of their position against very superior numbers, the enemy having been reinforced during that time by at least one Division of the 7th Corps, a brigade of the 3rd Corps and the whole of the 14th Corps, which had moved north from in front of the French 21st Corps.

On the 19th the Royal Irish Regiment, under Major Daniell, stormed and carried the village of Le Pilly, which they held and entrenched. On the 20th, however, they were cut off and surrounded, suffering heavy losses.

On the morning of the 22nd the enemy made a very determined attack on the 5th Division, who were driven out of the village of Violaines, but they were sharply counter-attacked by the Worcesters and Manchesters, and prevented from coming on.

The left of the Second Corps being now somewhat exposed, Sir Horace Smith-Dorrien withdrew the line during the night to a position he had previously prepared, running generally from the eastern side of Givenchy, east of Neuve Chapelle to Fauquissart.

On the 24th October the Lahore Division of the Indian Army Corps, under Major General Watkis, having arrived, I sent them to the neighbourhood of Lacon to support the Second Corps.

Very early on this morning the enemy commenced a heavy attack, but, owing to the skilful manner in which the artillery was handled and the targets presented by the enemy's infantry as it approached, they were unable to come to close quarters. Towards the evening a heavy attack developed against the 7th Brigade, which was repulsed, with very heavy loss to the enemy, by the Wiltshires and the Royal West Kents. Later, a determined attack on the 18th Infantry Brigade drove the Gordon Highlanders out of their trenches, which were retaken by the Middlesex Regiment, gallantly led by Lieutenant-Colonel Hull.

The 8th Infantry Brigade (which had come into line on the left of the Second Corps) was also heavily attacked, but the enemy was driven off.

In both these cases the Germans lost very heavily, and left large numbers of dead and prisoners behind them.

The Second Corps was now becoming exhausted, owing to the constant reinforcements of the enemy, the length of line which it had to defend and the enormous losses which it had suffered.

3. By the evening of the 11th October the Third Corps had practically completed its detrainment at St. Omer, and was moved east to Hazebrouck, where the Corps remained throughout the 12th.

On the morning of the 13th the advanced guard of the Corps, consisting of the 19th Infantry Brigade and a Brigade of Field Artillery, occupied the position of the line Strazeele Station – Caestre – St. Sylvestre.

On this day I directed General Pulteney to move towards the line Armentières – Wytschaete; warning him, however, that should the Second Corps require his aid he must be prepared to move South-East to support it.

A French Cavalry Corps under General Conneau was operating between the Second and Third Corps.

The Fourth German Cavalry Corps, supported by some Jaeger Battalions, was known to be occupying the position in the neighbourhood of Meteren; and they were believed to be further supported by the advanced guard of another German Army Corps.

In pursuance of his orders, General Pulteney proceeded to attack the enemy in his front.

The rain and fog which prevailed prevented full advantage being derived from our much superior artillery. The country was very much enclosed and rendered difficult by heavy rain. The enemy were, however, routed; and the position taken at dark, several prisoners being captured. During the night the Third Corps made good the attacked position and entrenched it.

As Bailleul was known to be occupied by the enemy, arrangements were made during the night to attack it; but reconnaissances sent out on the morning of the 14th showed that they had withdrawn, and the town was taken by our troops at 10 a.m. on that day, many wounded Germans being found and taken in it.

The Corps then occupied the line St. Jans Cappel – Bailleul.

On the morning of the 15th the Third Corps were ordered to make good the line of the Lys from Armentières to Sailly, which, in the face of considerable opposition and very foggy weather, they succeeded in doing, the 6th Division at Sailly – Bac St. Maur and the 4th Division at Nieppe.

The enemy in its front having retired, the Third Corps on the night of the 17th occupied the line Bois Grenier – Le Gheir.

On the 18th the enemy were holding a line from Radinghem on the south, through Perenchies and Frelinghien on the north, whence the German troops which were opposing the Cavalry Corps occupied the east bank of the river as far as Wervick.

On this day I directed the Third Corps to move down the valley of the Lys and endeavour to assist the Cavalry Corps in making good its position on the right bank. To do this it was necessary first to drive the enemy eastward towards Lille. A vigorous offensive in the direction of Lille was assumed, but the enemy was found to have been considerably reinforced, and but little progress was made.

The situation of the Third Corps on the night of the 18th was as follows:-

The 6th Division was holding the line Radingham – La Vallée – Emnetières – Capinghem – Premesques – Railway Line 300 yards east of

Halte. The 4th Divison were holding the line from L'Epinette to the river at a point 400 yards south of Frelinghein, and thence to a point half a mile south-east of Le Gheir. The Corps Reserve was at Armentières Station, with right and left flanks of Corps in close touch with French Cavalry and the Cavalry Corps. Since the advance from Bailleul the enemy's forces in front of the Cavalry and Third Corps had been strongly reinforced, and on the night of the 17th they were opposed by three or four divisions of the enemy's cavalry, the 19th Saxon Corps and at least one division of the 7th Corps. Reinforcements for the enemy were known to be coming up from the direction of Lille.

4. Following the movements completed on the 11th October, the 2nd Cavalry Division pushed the enemy back through Flêtre and Le Coq de Paille, and took Mont des Cats, just before dark, after stiff fighting.

On the 14th the 1st Cavalry Division joined up, and the whole Cavalry Corps under General Allenby, moving north, secured the high ground above Berthen, overcoming considerable opposition.

With a view to a further advance east, I ordered General Allenby, on the 15th, to reconnoitre the line of the River Lys, and endeavour to secure the passages on the opposite bank, pending the arrival of the Third and Fourth Corps.

During the 15th and 16th this reconnaissance was most skilfully and energetically carried out in the face of great opposition, especially along the lower line of the river.

These operations were continued throughout the 17th, 18th and 19th; but, although valuable information was gained, and strong forces of the enemy held in check, the Cavalry Corps was unable to secure passages or to establish a permanent footing on the eastern bank of the river.

5. At this point in the history of the operations under report it is necessary that I should return to the co-operation of the forces operating in the neighbourhood of Ghent and Antwerp under Lieutenant-General Sir Henry Rawlinson, as the action of his force about this period exercised, in my opinion, a great influence on the course of the subsequent operations.

This force, consisting of the 3rd Cavalry Division, under Major-General the Hon. Julian Byng, and the 7th Division, under Major-General Capper, was placed under my orders by telegraphic instructions from your Lordship.

On receipt of these instructions I directed Sir Henry Rawlinson to continue his operations in covering and protecting the withdrawal of the Belgian Army, and subsequently to form the left column in the eastward advance of the British Forces. These withdrawal operations were concluded about the 16th October, on which date the 7th Division was posted to the east of Ypres on a line extending from Zandvoorde through Gheluvelt to Zonnebeke. The 3rd Cavalry Division was on its left towards Langemarck and Poelcappelle.

In this position Sir Henry Rawlinson was supported by the 87th French Territorial Division in Ypres and Vlamertinghe, and by the 89th French Territorial Division at Poperinghe. On the night of the 16th I informed Sir Henry Rawlinson of the operations which were in progress by the Cavalry Corps and the Third Corps, and ordered him to conform to those movements in an easterly direction, keeping an eye always to any threat which might be made against him from the north-east.

A very difficult task was allotted to Sir Henry Rawlinson and his command. Owing to the importance of keeping possession of all the ground towards the north which we already held, it was necessary for him to operate on a very wide front, and, until the arrival of the First Corps in the northern theatre – which I expected about the 20th – I had no troops available with which to support or reinforce him.

Although on this extended front he had eventually to encounter very superior forces, his troops, both Cavalry and Infantry, fought with the utmost gallantry, and rendered very signal service. On the 17th four French Cavalry Divisions deployed on the left of the 3rd Cavalry Division, and drove back advanced parties of the enemy beyond the Forêt d'Houthulst.

As described above, instructions for a vigorous attempt to establish the British Forces east of the Lys were given on the night of the 17th to the Second, Third and Cavalry Corps.

I considered, however, that the possession of Menin constituted a very important point of passage, and would much facilitate the advance of the rest of the Army. So I directed the General Officer Commanding the Fourth Corps to advance the 7th Division upon Menin, and endeavour to seize that crossing on the morning of the 18th.

The left of the 7th Division was to be supported by the 3rd Cavalry Brigade, and further north by the French Cavalry in the neighbourhood of Roulers.

Sir Henry Rawlinson represented to me that large hostile forces were advancing upon him from the east and north-east, and that his left flank was severely threatened.

I was aware of the threats from that direction, but hoped that at this particular time there was no greater force coming from the north-east than could be held off by the combined efforts of the French and British Cavalry, and the Territorial troops supporting them until the passage at Menin could be seized and the First Corps brought up in support.

Sir Henry Rawlinson probably exercised a wise judgment in not committing his troops to this attack in their somewhat weakened condition; but the result was that the enemy's continued possession of the passage at Menin certainly facilitated his rapid reinforcement of his troops and thus rendered any further advance impracticable.

On the morning of the 20th October the 7th Division and 3rd Cavalry Division had retired to their old position extending from Zandvoorde through Kruiseik and Gheluvelt to Zonnebeke.

6. On the 19th October the First Corps, coming from the Aisne, had completed its detrainment and was concentrated between St. Omer and Hazebrouck.

A question of vital importance now arose for decision.

I knew that the enemy were by this time in greatly superior strength on the Lys, and that the Second, Third, Cavalry and Fourth Corps were holding a much wider front than their numbers and strength warranted.

Taking these facts alone into consideration it would, have appeared wise to throw the First Corps in to strengthen the line; but this would have left the country north and east of Ypres and the Ypres Canal open to a wide turning movement by the 3rd Reserve Corps and at least one Landwehr Division which I knew to be operating in that region. I was also aware that the enemy was bringing large reinforcements up from the East which could only be opposed for several days by two or three French Cavalry Divisions, some French Territorial troops, and the Belgian Army.

After the hard fighting it had undergone the Belgian Army was in no condition to withstand, unsupported, such an attack; and unless some substantial resistance could be offered to this threatened turning movement, the Allied flank must be turned and the Channel Ports laid bare to the enemy.

I judged that a successful movement of this kind would be fraught with such disastrous consequences that the risk of operating on so extended a front must be undertaken; and I directed Sir Douglas Haig to move with the First Corps to the north of Ypres.

From the best information at my disposal I judged at this time that the considerable reinforcements which the enemy had undoubtedly brought up during the 16th, 17th and 18th had been directed principally on the line of the Lys and against the Second Corps at La Bassée; and that Sir Douglas Haig would probably not be opposed north of Ypres by much more than the 3rd Reserve Corps, which I knew to have suffered considerably in its previous operations, and perhaps one or two Landwehr Divisions.

At a personal interview with Sir Douglas Haig on the evening of the 19th October I communicated the above information to him, and instructed him to advance with the First Corps through Ypres to Thourout. The object he was to have in view was to be the capture of Bruges and subsequently, if possible, to drive the enemy towards Ghent. In case of an unforeseen situation arising, or the enemy proving to be stronger than anticipated, he was to decide, after passing Ypres, according to the situation, whether to attack the enemy lying to the North or the hostile forces advancing from the East: I had arranged for the French Cavalry to operate on the left of the First Corps and the 3rd Cavalry Division, under General Byng, on its right.

The Belgian Army were rendering what assistance they could by entrenching themselves on the Ypres Canal and the Yser River; and the troops, although in the last stage of exhaustion, gallantly maintained their positions, buoyed up with the hope of substantial British and French support.

I fully realised the difficult task which lay before us, and the onerous rôle which the British Army was called upon to fulfil.

That success has been attained, and all the enemy's desperate attempts to break through our line frustrated, is due entirely to the marvellous fighting power and the indomitable courage and tenacity of officers, non-commissioned officers and men.

No more arduous task has ever been assigned to British soldiers; and in all their splendid history there is no instance of their having answered so magnificently to the desperate calls which of necessity were made upon them.

Having given these orders to Sir Douglas Haig, I enjoined a defensive rôle upon the Second and Third and Cavalry Corps, in view of the superiority of force which had accumulated in their front. As regards the Fourth Corps, I directed Sir Henry Rawlinson to endeavour to conform generally to the movements of the First Corps.

On the 20th October they reached the line from Elverdinghe to the cross roads one and a half miles north-west of Zonnebeke.

On the 21st the Corps was ordered to attack and take the line Poelcappelle – Passchendaele.

Sir Henry Rawlinson's Command was moving on the right of the First Corps, and French troops, consisting of Cavalry and Territorials, moved on their left under the orders of General Bidon.

The advance was somewhat delayed owing to the roads being blocked; but the attack progressed favourably in face of severe opposition, often necessitating the use of the bayonet. Hearing of heavy attacks being made upon the 7th Division and the 2nd Cavalry Division on his right, Sir Douglas Haig ordered his reserve to be halted on the north-eastern outskirts of Ypres.

Although threatened by a hostile movement from the Forêt d'Houthulst, our advance was successful until about 2 o'clock in the afternoon, when the French Cavalry Corps received orders to retire west of the canal.

Owing to this and the demands made on him by the Fourth Corps, Sir Douglas Haig was unable to advance beyond the line Zonnebeke – St. Julien – Langemarck – Bixschoote.

As there was reported to be congestion with French troops at Ypres, I went there on the evening of the 21st and met Sir Douglas Haig and Sir Henry Rawlinson. With them I interviewed General De Mitry, Commanding the French Cavalry, and General Bidon, Commanding the French Territorial Divisions.

They promised me that the town would at once be cleared of the troops, and that the French Territorials would immediately move out and cover the left of the flank of the First Corps.

I discussed the situation with the General Officers Commanding the First and Fourth Army Corps, and told them that, in view of the unexpected reinforcements coming up of the enemy, it would probably be impossible to carry out the original rôle assigned to them. But I informed them that I had that day interviewed the French Commander-in-Chief, General Joffre, who told me that he was bringing up the 9th French Army Corps to Ypres, that more French troops would follow later, and that he intended – in conjunction with the Belgian troops – to drive the Germans East. General Joffre said that he would be unable to commence this movement before the 24th; and I directed the General Officers Commanding the First and Fourth Corps to strengthen their positions as much as possible and be prepared to hold their ground for two or three days, until the French offensive movement on the North could develop.

It now became clear to me that the utmost we could do to ward off any attempts of the enemy to turn our flank to the North, or to break in from the eastward was to maintain our present very extended front, and to hold fast our positions until French reinforcements could arrive from the South.

During the 22nd the necessity of sending support to the Fourth Corps on his right somewhat hampered the General Officer Commanding the First Corps; but a series of attacks all along his front had been driven back during the day with heavy loss to the enemy. Late in the evening the enemy succeeded in penetrating a portion of the line held by the Cameron Highlanders north of Pilkem.

At 6 a.m. on the morning of the 23rd a counter attack to recover the lost trenches was made by the Queen's Regiment, the Northamptons, and the King's Royal Rifles, under Major-General Bulfin. The attack was very strongly opposed and the bayonet had to be used. After severe fighting during most of the day the attack was brilliantly successful, and over six hundred prisoners were taken.

On the same day an attack was made on the 3rd Infantry Brigade. The enemy advanced with great determination, but with little skill, and consequently the loss inflicted on him was exceedingly heavy; some fifteen hundred dead were seen in the neighbourhood of Langemarck. Correspondence found subsequently on a captured German Officer stated that the effectives of this attacking Corps were reduced to 25 per cent, in the course of the day's fighting.

In the evening of this day a division of the French 9th Army Corps came up into line and took over the portion of the line held by the 2nd Division, which, on the 24th, took up the ground occupied by the 7th Division from Poelzelhoek to the Becelaere – Passchendaele Road. On the 24th and 25th October repeated attacks by the enemy were brilliantly repulsed.

On the night of the 24th-25th the 1st Division was relieved by French Territorial troops and concentrated about Zillebeke.

During the 25th the 2nd Division, with the 7th on its right and the French 9th Corps on its left, made good progress towards the North-East, capturing some guns and prisoners. On the 27th October I went to the headquarters of the First Corps at Hooge to personally investigate the condition of the 7th Division.

Owing to constant marching and fighting, ever since its hasty disembarkation, in aid of the Antwerp Garrison, this division had suffered great losses, and were becoming very weak. I therefore decided temporarily to break up the Fourth Corps and place the 7th Division with the First Corps under the command of Sir Douglas Haig.

The 3rd Cavalry Division was similarly detailed for service with the First Corps.

I directed the Fourth Corps Commander to proceed, with his Staff, to England, to watch and supervise the mobilization of his 8th Division, which was then proceeding.

On receipt of orders, in accordance with the above arrangement, Sir Douglas Haig redistributed the line held by the First Corps as follows:-

(a) 7th Division from the Chateau east of Zandvoorde to the Menin Road.
(b) 1st Division from the Menin Road to a point immediately west of Reytel Village.
(c) 2nd Division to near Moorslede – Zonnebeke Road.

On the early morning of the 29th October a heavy attack developed against the centre of the line held by the First Corps, the principal point of attack being the cross roads one mile east of Gheluvelt. After severe fighting – nearly the whole of the Corps being employed in counter attack – the enemy began to give way at about 2 p.m.; and by dark the Kruiseik Hill had been recaptured and the 1st Brigade had re-established most of the line north of the Menin Road.

Shortly after daylight on the 30th another attack began to develop in the direction of Zandvoorde, supported by heavy artillery fire. In face of this attack the 3rd Cavalry Division had to withdraw to the Klein Zillebeke ridge. This withdrawal involved the right of the 7th Division.

Sir Douglas Haig describes the position at this period as serious, the Germans being in possession of Zandvoorde Ridge.

Subsequent investigation showed that the enemy had been reinforced at this point by the whole German Active Fifteenth Corps.

The General Officer Commanding First Corps ordered the line Gheluvelt to the corner of the canal to be held at all costs. When this line was taken up the 2nd Brigade was ordered to concentrate in rear of the 1st Division and the 4th Brigade line. One battalion was placed in reserve in the woods one mile south of Hooge.

Further precautions were taken at night to protect this flank, and the Ninth French Corps sent three battalions and one Cavalry Brigade to assist.

The First Corps' communications through Ypres were threatened by the advance of the Germans towards the canal; so orders were issued for every effort to be made to secure the line then held and, when this had been thoroughly done, to resume the offensive.

An order taken from a prisoner who had been captured on this day purported to emanate from the German General, Von Beimling, and said that the Fifteenth German Corps, together with the 2nd Bavarian and Thirteenth Corps, were entrusted with the task of breaking through the line to Ypres; and that the Emperor himself considered the success of this attack to be one of vital importance to the successful issue of the war.

Perhaps the most important and decisive attack (except that of the Prussian Guard on 15th November) made against the First Corps during the whole of its arduous experiences in the neighbourhood of Ypres took place on the 31st October.

General Moussy, who commanded the detachment which had been sent by the French Ninth Corps on the previous day to assist Sir Douglas Haig on the right of the First Corps, moved to the attack early in the morning, but was brought to a complete standstill, and could make no further progress.

After several attacks and counter attacks during the course of the morning along the Menin – Ypres – road, south-east of Gheluvelt, an attack against that place developed in great force, and the line of the 1st Division was broken. On the south the 7th Division and General Bulfin's detachment were being heavily shelled. The retirement of the 1st Division exposed the left of the 7th Division, and owing to this the Royal Scots Fusiliers, who remained in their trenches, were cut off and surrounded. A strong infantry attack was developed against the right of the 7th Division at 1.30 p.m.

Shortly after this the Headquarters of the 1st and 2nd Divisions were shelled. The General Officer Commanding 1st Division was wounded, three Staff Officers of the 1st Division and three of the 2nd Division were killed. The General Officer Commanding the 2nd Division also received a severe shaking, and was unconscious for a short time. General Landon assumed command of the 1st Division.

On receiving a report about 2.30 p.m. from General Lomax that the 1st Division had moved back and that the enemy was coming on in strength, the General Officer Commanding the First Corps issued orders that the line, Frezenberg – Westhoek – bend of the main road – Klein Zillebeke – bend of canal, was to be held at all costs.

The 1st Division rallied on the line of the woods east of the bend of the road, the German advance by the road being checked by enfilade fire from the north.

The attack against the right of the 7th Division forced the 22nd Brigade to retire, thus exposing the left of the 2nd Brigade. The General Officer Commanding the 7th Division used his reserve, already posted on his flank, to restore the line; but, in the meantime, the 2nd Brigade, finding their left flank exposed, had been forced to withdraw. The right of the 7th Division thus advanced as the left of the 2nd Brigade went back, with the result that the right of the 7th Division was exposed, but managed to hold on to its old trenches till nightfall. Meantime, on the Menin road, a counter-attack delivered by the left of the 1st Division and the right of the 2nd Division against the right flank of the German line was completely successful, and by 2.30 p.m. Gheluvelt had been retaken with the bayonet, the 2nd Worcestershire Regiment being to the fore in this, admirably supported by the 42nd Brigade, Royal Field Artillery. The left of the 7th Division, profiting by their capture of Gheluvelt, advanced almost to its original line; and connection between the 1st and 7th Divisions was re-established. The recapture of Gheluvelt released the 6th Cavalry Brigade, till then held in support of the 1st Division. Two regiments of this brigade were sent at once to clear the woods to the south-east, and close the gap in the line between the 7th Division and 2nd Brigade. They advanced with much dash, partly mounted and partly dismounted; and, surprising the enemy in the woods, succeeded in killing large numbers and materially helped to restore the line. About 5 p.m. the French Cavalry Brigade also came up to the cross-roads just east of Hooge, and at once sent forward a dismounted detachment to support our 7th Cavalry Brigade.

Throughout the day the extreme right and left of the First Corps' line held fast, the left being only slightly engaged, while the right was heavily shelled and subjected to slight infantry attacks. In the evening the enemy were steadily driven back from the woods on the front of the 7th Division and 2nd Brigade; and by 10 p.m. the line as held in the morning had practically been reoccupied.

During the night touch was restored between the right of the 7th Division and left of the 2nd Brigade, and the Cavalry were withdrawn into reserve, the services of the French Cavalry being dispensed with.

As a result of the day's fighting eight hundred and seventy wounded were evacuated.

I was present with Sir Douglas Haig at Hooge between 2 and 3 o'clock on this day, when the 1st Division were retiring. I regard it as the most critical moment in the whole of this great battle. The rally of the 1st Division and the recapture of the village of Gheluvelt at such a time was fraught with momentous consequences. If any one unit can be singled out for especial praise it is the Worcesters.

7. In the meantime the centre of my line, occupied by the Third and Cavalry Corps, was being heavily pressed by the enemy in ever increasing force.

On the 20th October advanced posts of the 12th Brigade of the 4th Division, Third Corps, were forced to retire, and at dusk it was evident that the Germans were likely to make a determined attack. This ended in the occupation of Le Gheir by the enemy.

As the position of the Cavalry at St. Yves was thus endangered, a counter-attack was decided upon and planned by General Hunter-Weston and Lieutenant-Colonel Anley. This proved entirely successful, the Germans being driven back with great loss and the abandoned trenches reoccupied. Two hundred prisoners were taken and about forty of our prisoners released.

In these operations the staunchness of the King's Own Regiment and the Lancashire Fusiliers was most commendable. These two battalions were very well handled by Lieutenant-Colonel Butler of the Lancashire Fusiliers.

I am anxious to bring to special notice the excellent work done throughout this battle by the Third Corps under General Pulteney's command. Their position in the right central part of my line was of the utmost importance to the general success of the operations. Besides the very undue length of front which the Corps was called upon to cover (some 12 or 13 miles), the position presented many weak spots, and was also astride of the River Lys, the right bank of which from Frelinghein downwards was strongly held by the enemy. It was impossible to provide adequate reserves, and the constant work in the trenches tried the endurance of officers and men to the utmost. That the

Corps was invariably successful in repulsing the constant attacks, sometimes in great strength, made against them by day and by night is due entirely to the skilful manner in which the Corps was disposed by its Commander, who has told me of the able assistance he has received throughout from his Staff, and the ability and resource displayed by Divisional, Brigade and Regimental leaders in using the ground and the means of defence at their disposal to the very best advantage.

The courage, tenacity, endurance and cheerfulness of the men in such unparalleled circumstances are beyond all praise.

During the 22nd and 23rd and 24th October frequent attacks were made along the whole line of the Third Corps, and especially against the 16th Infantry Brigade; but on all occasions the enemy was thrown back with loss.

During the night of the 25th October the Leicestershire Regiment were forced from their trenches by shells blowing in the pits they were in; and after investigation by the General Officers Commanding the 16th and 18th Infantry Brigades it was decided to throw back the line temporarily in this neighbourhood.

On the evening of the 29th October the enemy made a sharp attack on Le Gheir, and on the line to the north of it, but were repulsed.

About midnight a very heavy attack developed against the 19th Infantry Brigade south of Croix Maréchal. A portion of the trenches of the Middlesex Regiment was gained by the enemy and held by him for some hours till recaptured with the assistance of the detachment from the Argyll and Sutherland Highlanders from Brigade Reserve. The enemy in the trenches were all bayoneted or captured. Later information from prisoners showed that there were twelve battalions opposite the 19th Brigade. Over two hundred dead Germans were left lying in front of the Brigade's trenches, and forty prisoners were taken.

On the evening of the 30th the line of the 11th Infantry Brigade in the neighbourhood of St. Yves was broken. A counter-attack carried out by Major Prowse with the Somerset Light Infantry restored the situation. For his services on this occasion this officer was recommended for special reward.

On the 31st October it became necessary for the 4th Division to take over the extreme right of the 1st Cavalry Division's trenches, although this measure necessitated a still further extension of the line held by the Third Corps.

8. On October 20th, while engaged in the attempt to force the line of the River Lys, the Cavalry Corps was attacked from the South and East. In the evening the 1st Cavalry Division held the line St. Yves – Messines: the 2nd Cavalry Division from Messines through Garde Dieu along the Wambeck to Houthem and Kortewilde.

At 4 p.m. on the 21st October a heavy attack was made on the 2nd Cavalry Division, which was compelled to fall back to the line Messines – 9th kilo stone on the Warneton-Oostaverne Road – Hollebeke.

On the 22nd I directed the 7th Indian Infantry Brigade, less one battalion, to proceed to Wulverghem in support of the Cavalry Corps. General Allenby sent two battalions to Wytschaete and Voormezeele to be placed under the orders of General Gough, Commanding the 2nd Cavalry Division.

On the 23rd, 24th and 25th several attacks were directed against the Cavalry Corps and repulsed with loss to the enemy.

On the 26th October I directed General Allenby to endeavour to regain a more forward line, moving in conjunction with the 7th Division. But the latter being apparently quite unable to take the offensive, the attempt had to be abandoned.

On October 30th heavy infantry attacks, supported by powerful artillery fire, developed against the 2nd and 3rd Cavalry Divisions, especially against the trenches about Hollebeke held by the 3rd Cavalry Brigade. At 1.30 p.m. this Brigade was forced to retire, and the 2nd Cavalry Brigade, less one regiment, was moved across from the 1st Cavalry Division to a point between Oostaverne and St. Eloi in support of the 2nd Cavalry Division.

The 1st Cavalry Division in the neighbourhood of Messines was also threatened by a heavy infantry column.

General Allenby still retained the two Indian Battalions of the 7th Indian Brigade, although they were in a somewhat exhausted condition.

After a close survey of the positions and consultations with the General Officer Commanding the Cavalry Corps, I directed four battalions of the Second Corps, which had lately been relieved from the trenches by the Indian Corps, to move to Neuve Eglise under General Shaw, in support of General Allenby.

The London Scottish Territorial Battalion was also sent to Neuve Eglise.

It now fell to the lot of the Cavalry Corps, which had been much weakened by constant fighting, to oppose the advance of two nearly fresh German Army Corps for a period of over forty-eight hours, pending the arrival of a French reinforcement. Their action was completely successful. I propose to send shortly a more detailed account of the operation.

After the critical situation in front of the Cavalry Corps, which was ended by the arrival of the head of the French 16th Army Corps, the 2nd Cavalry Division was relieved by General Conneau's French Cavalry Corps and concentrated in the neighbourhood of Bailleul.

The 1st Cavalry Division continued to hold the line of trenches east of Wulverghem.

From that time to the date of this despatch the Cavalry Divisions have relieved one another at intervals, and have supported by their artillery the attacks made by the French throughout that period on Hollebeke, Wytschaete and Messines.

The Third Corps in its position on the right of the Cavalry Corps continued throughout the same period to repel constant attacks against its front, and suffered severely from the enemy's heavy artillery fire.

The artillery of the 4th Division constantly assisted the French in their attacks.

The General Officer Commanding Third Corps brings specially to my notice the excellent behaviour of the East Lancashire Regiment, the Hampshire Regiment and the Somersetshire Light Infantry in these latter operations; and the skilful manner in which they were handled by General Hunter-Weston, Lieutenant-Colonel Butler and the Battalion Commanders.

9. The Lahore Division arrived in its concentration area in rear of the Second Corps on the 19th and 20th October.

I have already referred to the excellent work performed by the battalions of this Division which were supporting the Cavalry. The remainder of the Division from the 25th October onwards were heavily engaged in assisting the 7th Brigade of the Second Corps in fighting round Neuve Chappelle. Another Brigade took over some ground previously held by the French 1st Cavalry Corps, and did excellent service.

On the 28th October especially the 47th Sikhs and the 20th and 21st Companies of the 3rd Sappers and Miners distinguished themselves by their gallant conduct in the attack on Neuve Chappelle, losing heavily in officers and men.

After the arrival of the Meerut Division at Corps Headquarters the Indian Army Corps took over the line previously held by the Second Corps, which was then partially drawn back into reserve. Two and a half brigades of British Infantry and a large part of the Artillery of the Second Corps still remained to assist the Indian Corps in defence of this line. Two and a half battalions of these brigades were returned to the Second Corps when the Ferozepore Brigade joined the Indian Corps after its support of the Cavalry further North.

The Secunderbad Cavalry Brigade arrived in the area during the 1st and 2nd November, and the Jodhpur Lancers came about the same time. These were all temporarily attached to the Indian Corps.

Up to the date of the present despatch the line held by the Indian Corps has been subjected to constant bombardment by the enemy's heavy artillery, followed up by infantry attacks.

On two occasions these attacks were severe.

On the 13th October the 8th Gurkha Rifles of the Bareilly Brigade were driven from their trenches, and on the 2nd November a serious attack was developed against a portion of the line west of Neuve Chapelle. On this occasion the line was to some extent pierced, and was consequently slightly bent back.

The situation was prevented from becoming serious by the excellent leadership displayed by Colonel Norie, of the 2nd Gurkha Rifles.

Since their arrival in this country, and their occupation of the line allotted to them, I have been much impressed by the initiative and resource displayed by the Indian troops. Some of the ruses they have employed to deceive the enemy have been attended with the best results, and have doubtless kept superior forces in front of them at bay.

The Corps of Indian Sappers and Miners have long enjoyed a high reputation for skill and resource. Without going into detail, I can confidently assert that throughout their work in this campaign they have fully justified that reputation.

The General Officer Commanding the Indian Army Corps describes the conduct and bearing of these troops in strange and new surroundings to have been highly satisfactory, and I am enabled, from my own observation, to fully corroborate his statement.

Honorary Major-General H.H. Sir Pratap Singh Bahadur, G.C.S.I., G.C.V.O., K.C.B., A.D.C., Maharaja-Regent of Jodhpur; Honorary Lieutenant H.H. The Maharaja of Jodhpur; Honorary Colonel H.H. Sir Ganga Singh Bahadur, G.C.S.I., G.C.I.E., A.D.C., Maharaja of Bikanir; Honorary Major H.H. Sir Madan Singh Bahadur, K.C.S.I., K.C.I.E., Maharaja-Dhiraj of Kishengarh; Honorary Captain The Honourable Malik Umar Hayat Khan, C.I.E., M.V.O., Tiwana; Honorary Lieutenant Raj-Kumar Hira Singh of Panna; Honorary Lieutenant Maharaj-Kumar Hitendra Narayan of Cooch Behar; Lieutenant Malik Mumtaz Mahomed Khan, Native Indian Land Forces; Resaldar Khwaja Mahomed Khan Bahadur, Queen Victoria's Own Corps of Guides; Honorary Captain Shah Mirza Beg, are serving with the Indian contingents.

10. Whilst the whole of the line has continued to be heavily pressed, the enemy's principal efforts since the 1st November have been concentrated upon breaking through the line held by the First British and 9th French Corps, and thus gaining possession of the town of Ypres. From the 2nd November onwards the 27th, the 15th and parts of the Bavarian 13th and 2nd German Corps, besides other troops, were all directed against this northern line.

About the 10th instant, after several units of these Corps had been completely shattered in futile attacks, a division of the Prussian Guard, which had been operating in the neighbourhood of Arras, was moved up to this area with great speed and secrecy. Documents found on dead officers prove that the Guard had received the Emperor's special commands to break through and succeed where their comrades of the line had failed.

They took a leading part in the vigorous attacks made against the centre on the 11th and 12th; but, like their comrades, were repulsed with enormous loss.

Throughout this trying period Sir Douglas Haig, ably assisted by his Divisional and Brigade Commanders, held the line with marvellous tenacity and undaunted courage.

Words fail me to express the admiration I feel for their conduct, or my sense of the incalculable services they rendered. I venture to predict that their deeds during these days of stress and trial will furnish some of the most brilliant chapters which will be found in the military history of our time.

The First Corps was brilliantly supported by the 3rd Cavalry Division under General Byng. Sir Douglas Haig has constantly brought this officer's eminent services to my notice. His troops were repeatedly called upon to restore the situation at critical points, and to fill gaps in the line caused by the tremendous losses which occurred.

Both Corps and Cavalry Division Commanders particularly bring to my notice the name of Brigadier-General Kavanagh, Commanding the 7th Cavalry Brigade, not only for his skill but his personal bravery and dash. This was particularly noticeable when the 7th Cavalry Brigade was brought up to support the French troops when the latter were driven back near the village of Klein Zillebeke on the night of the 7th November. On this occasion I regret to say Colonel Gordon Wilson, Commanding the Royal Horse Guards, and Major the Hon. Hugh Dawnay, Commanding the 2nd Life Guards, were killed.

In these two officers the Army has lost valuable cavalry leaders.

Another officer whose name was particularly mentioned to me was that of Brigadier-General FitzClarence, V.C., Commanding the 1st Guards Brigade. He was, unfortunately, killed in the night attack of the 11th November. His loss will be severely felt.

The First Corps Commander informs me that on many occasions Brigadier-General the Earl of Cavan, Commanding the 4th Guards Brigade, was conspicuous for the skill, coolness and courage with which he led his troops, and for the successful manner in which he dealt with many critical situations.

I have more than once during this campaign brought forward the name of Major-General Bulfin to Your Lordship's notice. Up to the evening of the 2nd November, when he was somewhat severely wounded, his continued to be of great value.

On the 5th November I despatched eleven battalions of the Second Corps, all considerably reduced in strength, to relieve the infantry of the 7th Division, which was then brought back into general reserve.

Three more battalions of the same Corps, the London Scottish and Hertfordshire Battalions of Territorials, and the Somersetshire and Leicestershire Regiments of Yeomanry, were subsequently sent to reinforce the troops fighting to the east of Ypres.

General Byng in the case of the Yeomanry Cavalry Regiments and Sir Douglas in that of the Territorial Battalions speak in high terms of their conduct in the field and of the value of their support.

The battalions of the Second Corps took a conspicuous part in repulsing the heavy attacks delivered against this part of the line. I was obliged to despatch them immediately after their trying experiences in the southern part of the line and when they had had a very insufficient period of rest; and, although they gallantly maintained these northern positions until relieved by the French, they were reduced to a condition of extreme exhaustion.

The work performed by the Royal Flying Corps has continued to prove of the utmost value to the success of the operations.

I do not consider it advisable in this despatch to go into any detail as regards the duties assigned to the Corps and the nature of their work, but almost every day new methods for employing them, both strategically and tactically, are discovered and put into practice.

The development of their use and employment has indeed been quite extraordinary, and I feel sure that no effort should be spared to increase their numbers and perfect their equipment and efficiency. In the period covered by this despatch Territorial Troops have been used for the first time in the Army under my command.

The units actually engaged have been the Northumberland, Northamptonshire, North Somerset, Leicestershire and Oxfordshire Regiments of Yeomanry Cavalry; and the London Scottish, Hertfordshire, Honourable Artillery Company and the Queen's Westminster Battalions of Territorial Infantry.

The conduct and bearing of these units under fire, and the efficient manner in which they carried out the various duties assigned to them, have imbued me with the highest hope as to the value and help of Territorial Troops generally.

Units which I have mentioned above, other than these, as having been also engaged, have by their conduct fully justified these hopes.

Regiments and battalions as they arrive come into a temporay camp of instruction, which is formed at Headquarters, where they are closely inspected, their equipment examined, so far as possible perfected, and such instruction as can be given to them in the brief time available in the use of machine guns, etc., is imparted.

Several units have now been sent up to the front besides those I have already named, but have not yet been engaged.

I am anxious in this despatch to bring to Your Lordship's special notice the splendid work which has been done throughout the campaign by the Cyclists of the Signal Corps.

Carrying despatches and messages at all hours of the day and night in every kind of weather, and often traversing bad roads blocked with transport, they have been conspicuously successful in maintaining an extraordinary degree of efficiency in the service of communications.

Many casualties have occurred in their ranks, but no amount of difficulty or danger has ever checked the energy and ardour which has distinguished their Corps throughout the operations.

11. As I close this despatch there are signs in evidence that we are possibly in the last stages of the battle of Ypres – Armentières.

For several days past the enemy's artillery fire has considerably slackened, and infantry attack has practically ceased.

In remarking upon the general military situation of the Allies as it appears to me at the present moment, it does not seem to be clearly understood that the operations in which we have been engaged embrace nearly all the Continent of Central Europe from East to West. The combined French, Belgian and British Armies in the West and the Russian Army in the East are opposed to the united forces of Germany and Austria acting as a combined army between us.

Our enemies elected at the commencement of the war to throw the weight of their forces against the armies in the West, and to detach only a comparatively weak force, composed of very few first-line troops and several corps of the second and third lines, to stem the Russian advance till the Western Forces could be completely defeated and overwhelmed.

Their strength enabled them from the outset to throw greatly superior forces against us in the West. This precluded the possibility of our taking a vigorous offensive, except when the miscalculations and mistakes made by their commanders opened up special opportunities for a successful attack and pursuit.

The battle of the Marne was an example of this, as was also our advance from St. Omer and Hazebrouck to the line of the Lys at the commencement of this battle. The rôle which our armies in the West have consequently been called upon to fulfil has been to occupy strong defensive positions, holding the ground gained and inviting the enemy's attack; to throw these attacks back, causing the enemy heavy losses in his retreat and following him up with powerful and successful counter-attacks to complete his discomfiture.

The value and significance of the rôle fulfilled since the commencement of hostilities by the Allied Forces in the West lies in the fact that at the moment when the Eastern Provinces of Germany are in imminent danger of being overrun by the numerous and powerful armies of Russia, nearly the whole of the active army of Germany is tied down to a line of trenches extending from the Fortress of Verdun on the Alsatian Frontier round to the sea at Nieuport, east of Dunkirk (a distance of 260 miles), where they are held, much reduced in numbers and morale by the successful action of our troops in the West.

I cannot speak too highly of the valuable services rendered by the Royal Artillery throughout the battle.

In spite of the fact that the enemy has brought up guns in support of his attacks of great range and shell power ours have succeeded throughout in preventing the enemy from establishing anything in the nature of an artillery superiority. The skill, courage and energy displayed by their commanders have been very marked.

The General Officer Commanding Third Corps, who had special means of judging, makes mention of the splendid work performed by a number of young Artillery officers, who in the most gallant manner pressed forward in the vicinity of the firing line in order that their guns may be able to shoot at the right targets at the right moment.

The Royal Engineers have, as usual, been indefatigable in their efforts to assist the infantry in field fortification and trench work.

I deeply regret the heavy casualities which we have suffered; but the nature of the fighting has been very desperate, and we have been assailed by vastly superior numbers. I have every reason to know that throughout the course of the battle we have placed at least three times as many of the enemy hors de combat in dead, wounded and prisoners.

Throughout these operations General Foch has strained his resources to the utmost to afford me all the support he could; and an expression of my warm gratitude is also due to General D'Urbal, Commanding the 8th French Army on my left, and General Maud'huy, Commanding the 10th French Army on my right.

I have many recommendations to bring to Your Lordship's notice for gallant and distinguished service performed by officers and men in the period

under report. These will be submitted shortly, as soon as they can be collected.

I have the honour to be,
Your Lordship's most obedient Servant,
J.D.P. FRENCH,
Field-Marshal, Commanding-in-Chief,
The British Forces in the Field

SIR JOHN FRENCH'S DESPATCH OF NOVEMBER 1914

Antwerp

Admiralty, 5th December, 1914.

The following despatch has been received from Field-Marshal Sir J.D.P. French, G.C.B., G.C.V.O., K.C.M.G., covering a despatch from Major-General A. Paris, C.B., R.M.A., relating to the operations round Antwerp from the 3rd to the 9th October.

From Sir J.D.P. French, Field-Marshal, Commander-in-Chief,
to the Secretary of the Admiralty.

In forwarding this report to the Army Council at the request of the Lords Commissioners of the Admiralty, I have to state that, from a comprehensive review of all the circumstances, the force of Marines and Naval Brigades which assisted in the defence of Antwerp was handled by General Paris with great skill and boldness.

Although the results did not include the actual saving of the fortress, the action of the force under General Paris certainly delayed the enemy for a considerable time, and assisted the Belgian Army to be withdrawn in a condition to enable it to reorganize and refit, and regain its value as a fighting force. The destruction of war material and ammunition – which, but for the intervention of this force, would have proved of great value to the enemy – was thus able to be carried out.

The assistance which the Belgian Army has rendered throughout the subsequent course of the operations on the canal and the Yeser river has been a valuable asset to the allied cause, and such help must be regarded as an outcome of the intervention of General Paris's force. I am further of opinion that the moral effect produced on the minds of the Belgian Army by this necessarily desperate attempt to bring them succour, before it was too late, has been of great value to their use and efficiency as a fighting force.

J.D.P. FRENCH,
Field-Marshal,
Commanding-in-Chief.

From the Secretary of the Admiralty to Field Marshal Sir J.D.P. French, Commanding-in-Chief. (Enclosure in No. 1.)

Admiralty,
2nd November, 1914.

Sir,

I am commanded by My Lords Commissioners of the Admiralty to transmit herewith a despatch from Major-General Paris, reporting the proceedings of the Division round Antwerp from the 3rd to 9th October, with a view to its being considered by you and forwarded to the Army Council with your survey of the operations as a whole.

I am, etc.,
W. GRAHAM GREENE

From Major-General A. Paris, C.B., commanding Royal Naval Division, to the Secretary of the Admiralty. (Sub-enclosure in No. 1.)

31st October, 1914.

Regarding the operations round Antwerp from 3rd to 9th October, I have the honour to report as follows:-

The Brigade (2,200 all ranks) reached Antwerp during the night 3rd-4th October, and early on the 4th occupied, with the 7th Belgian Regiment, the trenches facing Lierre, with advanced post on the River Nethe, relieving some exhausted Belgian troops.

The outer forts on this front had already fallen and bombardment of the trenches was in progress. This increased in violence during the night and early morning of 5th October, when the advanced posts were driven in and the enemy effected a crossing of the river, which was not under fire from the trenches.

About midday the 7th Belgian Regiment was forced to retire, thus exposing my right flank. A vigorous counter-attack, gallantly led by Colonel Tierchon, 2nd Chasseurs, assisted by our aeroplanes, restored the position, late in the afternoon.

Unfortunately, an attempt made by the Belgian troops during the night (5th-6th October) to drive the enemy across the river failed, and resulted in the evacuation of practically the whole of the Belgian trenches.

The few troops now capable of another counter-attack were unable to make any impression, and the position of the Marine Brigade became untenable.

The bombardment, too, was very violent, but the retirement of the Brigade was well carried out, and soon after midday (6th October) an intermediate position, which had been hastily prepared, was occupied.

The two Naval Brigades reached Antwerp during the night, 5th-6th October. The 1st Brigade moved out in the afternoon of 5th to assist the withdrawal to the main 2nd Line of Defence. The retirement was carried out during the night, 6th-7th October, without opposition, and the Naval Division occupied the intervals between the forts on the 2nd Line of Defence.

The bombardment of the town, forts and trenches began at midnight, 7th-8th October, and continued with increasing intensity until the evacuation of the fortress.

As the water supply had been cut, no attempt could be made to subdue the flames, and soon 100 houses were burning. Fortunately, there was no wind, or the whole town and bridges must have been destroyed.

During the day (8th October) it appeared evident that the Belgian Army could not hold the forts any longer. About 5.30 p.m. I considered that if the Naval Division was to avoid disaster an immediate retirement under cover of darkness was necessary. General De Guise, the Belgian Commander, was in complete agreement. He was most chivalrous and gallant, insisting on giving orders that the roads and bridges were to be cleared for the passage of the British troops.

The retirement began about 7.30 p.m., and was carried out under very difficult conditions. The enemy were reported in force (a Division plus a Reserve Brigade) on our immediate line of retreat, rendering necessary a detour of 15 miles to the north.

All the roads were crowded with Belgian troops, refugees, herds of cattle, and all kinds of vehicles, making inter-communication a practical impossibility. Partly for these reasons, partly on account of fatigue, and partly from at present unexplained causes large numbers of the 1st Naval Brigade became detached, and I regret to say are either prisoners or interned in Holland. Marching all night (8th to 9th October), one battalion of 1st Brigade, the 2nd Brigade and Royal Marine Brigade, less one battalion, entrained at St. Gillies Waes and effected their retreat without further incident.

The Battalion (Royal Marine Brigade) Rear Guard of the whole force, also entrained late in the afternoon together with many hundreds of refugees, but at Morbeke the line was cut, the engine derailed, and the enemy opened fire.

There was considerable confusion. It was dark and the agitation of the refugees made it difficult to pass any orders. However, the battalion behaved admirably, and succeeded in fighting its way through, but with a loss in missing of more than half its number. They then marched another 10 miles to Selzaate and entrained there.

Colonel Seely and Colonel Bridges were not part of my command, but they rendered most skilful and helpful services during the evacuation.

The casualties are approximately-

1st Naval Brigade and 2nd Naval Brigade, 5 killed, 64 wounded, 2,040 missing.
Royal Marine Brigade, 23 killed, 103 wounded, 388 missing.

In conclusion, I would call your attention to the good services rendered by the following officers and men during the operations-

OFFICERS.

Staff-
  Lieut.-Colonel A.H. Ollivant, R.A.
  Major Richardson, N.Z. Staff Corps.
  Fleet Surgeon E.J. Finch, R.N.
1st Brigade-
  Lieutenant G.G. Grant, R.N.V.R.
  Sub-Lieutenant C.O.F. Modin, R.N.V.R.
2nd Brigade-
  Commodore O. Backhouse, R.N., Commanding Brigade.
  Captain W.L. Maxwell, Brigade Major.
  Sub-Lieutenant H.C. Hedderwick, R.N.V.R.
Royal Marine Brigade-
  Lieut-Colonel C. Mc.N. Parsons, R.M.L.I., in command most of the
    time.
  Major A.H. French, R.M.L.I., 10th Battalion.
  Lieutenant D.J. Gowney, R.M.L.I., 10th Battalion.

MEN.

Naval Brigade-
  Chief Petty Officer B.H. Ellis, No. 748, B Co., R.N.V.R., London.
  Chief Petty Officer Payne, D Co.
  Petty Officer (Acting) W. Wallace, O.N., Dev., 211,130.
  Stoker Petty Officer W.S. Cole, O.N., Ch. 100,113.
  Leading Seaman (Acting) H.D. Lowe, R.N.R., Dev., No. B.2542.
  Ordinary Seaman G. Ripley, new Army recruit, C Co. (now R.N.V.R.).
  Ordinary Seaman T. Machen, new Army recruit, C Co. (now R.N.V.R.).
Royal Marine Brigade-
  Serjeant-Major (Acting) Galliford.
  Quartermaster-Serjeant Kenny, R.F.R., Ch. A. 426.
  Serjeant G.H. Bruce, R.F.R., Ch. A. 631.
  Lance-Corporal T.C. Frank, Ch. 17817.
  Lance-Corporal W.J. Cook, Ply. 7685.
  Private G.H. Hall, R.F.R., Ch. B. 194.

Private C.J. Fleet, R.F.R., Ch. B. 1585.
Private S. Lang, Ch. 18446.
Serjeant E. Walch (R. Naval Auxiliary Sick Berth Reserve), S.B. 508.

I have the honour to be, Sir,
Your obedient Servant,
A. PARIS, Major-General,
General Officer Commanding-in-Chief.

SIR JOHN FRENCH'S DESPATCH OF 2 FEBRUARY 1915

Visit of King George, Operations During the First Winter of the War

TUESDAY, 16 FEBRUARY, 1915.

The following Despatch was received on the 12th February, 1915:-

From the Field-Marshal Commanding-in-Chief, The British Army in the Field.

To the Secretary of State for War, War Office, London, S.W.

General Headquarters,
2nd February, 1915.

MY LORD,

I have the honour to forward a further report on the operations of the Army under my command.

1. In the period under review the salient feature was the presence of His Majesty the King in the Field. His Majesty arrived at Headquarters on the 30th November, and left on the 5th December.

At a time when the strength and endurance of the troops had been tried to the utmost throughout the long and arduous Battle of Ypres – Armentiéres the presence of His Majesty in their midst was of the greatest possible help and encouragement.

His Majesty visited all parts of the extensive area of operations and held numerous inspections of the troops behind the line of trenches.

On the 16th November Lieutenant His Royal Highness the Prince of Wales, K.G., Grenadier Guards, joined my Staff as Aide-de-Camp.

2. Since the date of my last report the operations of the Army under my command have been subject almost entirely to the limitations of weather.

History teaches us that the course of campaigns in Europe, which have been actively prosecuted during the months of December and January, have been largely influenced by weather conditions. It should, however, be thoroughly understood throughout the country that the most recent development of armaments and the latest methods of conducting warfare have added greatly to the difficulties and drawbacks of a vigorous winter campaign.

To cause anything more than a waste of ammunition long-range artillery fire requires constant and accurate observation; but this most necessary condition is rendered impossible of attainment in the midst of continual fog and mist.

Again, armies have now grown accustomed to rely largely on aircraft reconnaissance for accurate information of the enemy; but the effective performance of this service is materially influenced by wind and weather.

The deadly accuracy, range and quick-firing capabilities of the modern rifle and machine gun require that a fire-swept zone be crossed in the shortest possible space of time by attacking troops. But if men are detained under the enemy's fire by the difficulty of emerging from a water-logged trench, and by the necessity of passing over ground knee-deep in holding mud and slush, such attacks become practically prohibitive owing to the losses they entail.

During the exigencies of the heavy fighting which ended in the last week of November the French and British Forces had become somewhat mixed up, entailing a certain amount of difficulty in matters of supply and in securing unity of command.

By the end of November I was able to concentrate the Army under my command in one area, and, by holding a shorter line, to establish effective reserves.

By the beginning of December there was a considerable falling off in the volume of artillery fire directed against our front by the enemy. Reconnaissance and reports showed that a certain amount of artillery had been withdrawn. We judged that the cavalry in our front, with the exception of one Division of the Guard, had disappeared.

There did not, however, appear to have been any great diminution in the numbers of infantry holding the trenches.

3. Although both artillery and rifle fire were exchanged with the enemy every day, and sniping went on more or less continuously during the hours of daylight, the operations which call for special record or comment are comparatively few.

During the last week in November some successful minor night operations were carried out in the 4th Corps.

On the night of the 23rd-24th November a small party of the 2nd Lincolnshire Regiment, under Lieutenant E.H. Impey, cleared three of the enemy's advanced trenches opposite the 25th Brigade and withdrew without loss.

On the night of the 24th-25th Captain J.R. Minshull Ford, Royal Welsh Fusiliers, and Lieutenant E.L. Morris, Royal Engineers, with 15 men of the Royal Engineers and Royal Welsh Fusiliers, successfully mined and blew up a group of farms immediately in front of the German trenches on the Touquet

– Bridoux Road which had been used by German snipers. On the night of the 26th-27th November a small party of the 2nd Scots Guards, under Lieutenant Sir E.H.W. Hulse, Bt., rushed the trenches opposite the 20th Brigade; and after pouring a heavy fire into them returned with useful information as to the strength of the Germans and the position of machine guns.

The trenches opposite the 25th Brigade were rushed the same night by a patrol of the 2nd Rifle Brigade, under Lieutenant E. Durham.

On the 23rd November the 112th Regiment of the 14th German Army Corps succeeded in capturing some 800 yards of the trenches held by the Indian Corps, but the General Officer Commanding the Meerut Division organized a powerful counter-attack, which lasted throughout the night. At daybreak on the 24th November the line was entirely re-established. The operation was a costly one, involving many casualties, but the enemy suffered far more heavily.

We captured over 100 prisoners, including 3 officers, as well as 3 machine guns and 2 trench mortars.

On December 7th the concentration of the Indian Corps was completed by the arrival of the Sirhind Brigade from Egypt.

On December 9th the enemy attempted to commence a strong attack against the 3rd Corps, particularly in front of the trenches held by the Argyll and Sutherland Highlanders and the Middlesex Regiment.

They were driven back with heavy loss, and did not renew the attempt. Our casualties were very slight.

During the early days of December certain indications along the whole front of the Allied Line induced the French Commanders and myself to believe that the enemy had withdrawn considerable forces from the Western Theatre.

Arrangements were made with the Commander of the 8th French Army for an attack to be commenced on the morning of December 14th.

Operations began at 7 a.m. by a combined heavy artillery bombardment, by the two French and the 2nd British Corps.

The British objectives were the Petit Bois and the Maedelsteed Spur, lying respectively to the west and south-west of the village of Wytschaete.

At 7.45 a.m. the Royal Scots, with great dash, rushed forward and attacked the former, while the Gordon Highlanders attacked the latter place.

The Royal Scots, commanded by Major F.J. Duncan, D.S.O., in face of a terrible machine gun and rifle fire, carried the German trench on the west edge of the Petit Bois, capturing two machine guns and 53 prisoners, including one officer.

The Gordon Highlanders, with great gallantry, advanced up the Maedelsteed Spur, forcing the enemy to evacuate their front trench. They were, however, losing heavily, and found themselves unable to get any further. At nightfall they were obliged to fall back to their original position.

Captain C. Boddam-Whetham and Lieutenant W.F.R. Dobie showed splendid dash, and with a few men entered the enemy's leading trenches; but they were all either killed or captured. Lieutenant G.R.V. Hume-Gore and Lieutenant W.H. Paterson also distinguished themselves by their gallant leading.

Although not successful, the operation was most creditable to the fighting spirit of the Gordon Highlanders, most ably commanded by Major A.W.F. Baird, D.S.O.

As the 32nd French Division on the left had been unable to make any progress, the further advance of our infantry into the Wytschaete Wood was not practicable.

Possession of the western edge of the Petit Bois was, however, retained.

The ground was devoid of cover and so water-logged that a rapid advance was impossible, the men sinking deep in the mud at every step they took.

The artillery throughout the day was very skilfully handled by the C.R.A.'s of the 3rd, 4th and 5th Divisions: Major-General F.D.V. Wing, C.B., Brigadier-General G.F. Milne, C.B., D.S.O., and Brigadier-General J.E.W. Headlam, C.B., D.S.O.

The casualties during the day were about 17 officers and 407 other ranks. The losses of the enemy were very considerable, large numbers of dead being found in the Petit Bois and also in the communicating trenches in front of the Gordon Highlanders, in one of which a hundred were counted by a night patrol.

On this day the artillery of the 4th Division, 3rd Corps, was used in support of the attack, under orders of the General Officer Commanding 2nd Corps.

The remainder of the 3rd Corps made demonstrations against the enemy with a view to preventing him from detaching troops to the area of operations of the 2nd Corps.

From the 15th to the 17th December the offensive operations which were commenced on the 14th were continued, but were confined chiefly to artillery bombardment.

The infantry advance against Wytschaete Wood was not practicable until the French on our left could make some progress to afford protection to that flank.

On the 17th it was agreed that the plan of attack as arranged should be modified; but I was requested to continue demonstrations along my line in order to assist and support certain French operations which were being conducted elsewhere.

4. In his desire to act with energy up to his instructions to demonstrate and occupy the enemy, the General Officer Commanding the Indian Corps decided to take the advantage of what appeared to him a favourable opportunity to launch attacks against the advanced trenches in his front on the 18th and 19th December.

The attack of the Meerut Division on the left was made on the morning of the 19th with energy and determination, and was at first attended with considerable success, the enemy's advanced trenches being captured. Later on, however, a counter attack drove them back to their original position with considerable loss.

The attack of the Lahore Division commenced at 4.30 a.m. It was carried out by two companies each of the 1st Highland Light Infantry and the 1st Battalion, 4th Gurkha Rifles, of the Sirhind Brigade, under Lieutenant-Colonel E.W.H. Ronaldson. This attack was completely successful, two lines of the enemy's trenches being captured with little loss. Before daylight the captured trenches were filled with as many men as they would hold. The front was very restricted, communication to the rear impossible.

At daybreak it was found that the position was practically untenable. Both flanks were in the air, and a supporting attack, which was late in starting, and, therefore, conducted during daylight, failed; although attempted with the greatest gallantry and resolution.

Lieutenant-Colonel Ronaldson held on till dusk, when the whole of the captured trenches had to be evacuated, and the detachment fell back to its original line.

By the night of the 19th December nearly all the ground gained during the day had been lost. From daylight on the 20th December the enemy commenced a heavy fire from artillery and trench mortars on the whole front of the Indian Corps. This was followed by infantry attacks, which were in especial force against Givenchy, and between that place and La Quinque Rue. At about 10 a.m. the enemy succeeded in driving back the Sirhind Brigade, and capturing a considerable part of Givenchy, but the 57th Rifles and 9th Bhopals, north of the canal, and the Connaught Rangers, south of it, stood firm.

The 15th Sikhs of the Divisional Reserve were already supporting the Sirhind Brigade. On the news of the retirement of the latter being received, the 47th Sikhs were also sent up to reinforce General Brunker. The 1st Manchester Regiment, 4th Suffolk Regiment, and two battalions of French Territorials under General Carnegy were ordered to launch a vigorous counter attack from Pont Fixe through Givenchy to retake by a flank attack the trenches lost by the Sirhind Brigade.

Orders were sent to General Carnegy to divert his attack on Givenchy Village, and to re-establish the situation there.

A battalion of the 58th French Division was sent to Annequin in support.

About 5 p.m. a gallant attack by the 1st Manchester Regiment and one company of the 4th Suffolk Regiment had captured Givenchy, and had cleared the enemy out of the two lines of trenches to the North-East. To the east of the village the 9th Bhopal Infantry and 57th Rifles had maintained their positions, but the enemy were still in possession of our trenches to the north of the village.

General Macbean, with the Secunderabad Cavalry Brigade, 2nd Battalion, 8th Gurkha Rifles, and the 47th Sikhs, was sent up to support General Brunker, who at 2 p.m. directed General Macbean to move to a position of readiness in the second line trenches from Maris northward, and to counter-attack vigorously if opportunity offered.

Some considerable delay appears to have occurred and it was not until 1 a.m. on the 21st that the 47th Sikhs and the 7th Dragoon Guards under the command of Lieutenant-Colonel H.A. Lempriere, D.S.O., of the latter regiment, were launched in counter-attack.

They reached the enemy's trenches, but were driven out by enfilade fire, their gallant Commander being killed.

The main attack by the remainder of General Macbean's force, with the remnants of Lieutenant-Colonel Lempriere's detachment (which had again been rallied), was finally pushed in at about 4.30 a.m., and also failed.

In the northern section of the defensive line the retirement of the 2nd Battalion, 2nd Gurkha Rifles, at about 10 a.m. on the 20th, had left the flank of the 1st Seaforth Highlanders, on the extreme right of the Meerut Division line, much exposed. This battalion was left shortly afterwards completely in the air by the retirement of the Sirhind Brigade.

The 58th Rifles, therefore, were ordered to support the left of the Seaforth Highlanders, to fill the gap created by the retirement of the Gurkhas.

During the whole of the afternoon strenuous efforts were made by the Seaforth Highlanders to clear the trenches to their right and left. The 1st Battalion, 9th Gurkha Rifles, reinforced the 2nd Gurkhas near the orchard where the Germans were in occupation of the trenches abandoned by the latter regiment. The Garhwal Brigade was being very heavily attacked, and their trenches and loopholes were much damaged; but the brigade continued to hold its front and attack, connecting with the 6th Jats on the left of the Dehra Dun Brigade.

No advance in force was made by the enemy, but the troops were pinned to their ground by heavy artillery fire, the Seaforth Highlanders especially suffering heavily.

Shortly before nightfall the 2nd Royal Highlanders on the right of the Seaforth Highlanders had succeeded in establishing touch with the Sirhind

Brigade; and the continuous line (though dented near the orchard) existed throughout the Meerut Division.

Early in the afternoon of December 20th orders were sent to the 1st Corps, which was then in general army reserve, to send an infantry brigade to support the Indian Corps.

The 1st Brigade was ordered to Bethune, and reached that place at midnight on 20th-21st December. Later in the day Sir Douglas Haig was ordered to move the whole of the 1st Division in support of the Indian Corps.

The 3rd Brigade reached Bethune between 8 a.m. and 9 a.m. on the 21st, and on the same date the 2nd Brigade arrived at Lacon at 1 p.m.

The 1st Brigade was directed on Givenchy, via Pont Fixe, and the 3rd Brigade, through Gorre, on the trenches evacuated by the Sirhind Brigade.

The 2nd Brigade was directed to support; the Dehra Dun Brigade being placed at the disposal of the General Officer Commanding Meerut Division.

At 1 p.m. the General Officer Commanding 1st Division directed the 1st Brigade in attack from the west of Givenchy in a north-easterly direction, and the 3rd Brigade from Festubert in an east-north-easterly direction, the object being to pass the position originally held by us and to capture the German trenches 400 yards to the east of it.

By 5 p.m. the 1st Brigade had obtained a hold in Givenchy, and the ground south as far as the canal; and the 3rd Brigade had progressed to a point half a mile west of Festubert.

By nightfall the 1st South Wales Borderers and the 2nd Welsh Regiment of the 3rd Brigade had made a lodgment in the original trenches to the northeast of Festubert, the 1st Gloucestershire Regiment continuing the line southward along the track east of Festubert. The 1st Brigade had established itself on the east side of Givenchy.

By 3.p.m. the 3rd Brigade was concentrated at Le Touret, and was ordered to retake the trenches which had been lost by the Dehra Dun Brigade.

By 10 p.m. the support trenches west of the orchard had been carried, but the original fire trenches had been so completely destroyed that they could not be occupied.

This operation was performed by the 1st Loyal North Lancashire Regiment and the 1st Northamptonshire Regiment, supported by the 2nd King's Royal Rifle Corps, in reserve. Throughout this day the units of the Indian Corps rendered all the assistance and support they could in view of their exhausted condition.

At 1 p.m. on the 22nd Sir Douglas Haig took over command from Sir James Willcocks. The situation in the front line was then approximately as follows:-

South of the La Bassée Canal the Connaught Rangers of the Ferozepore Brigade had not been attacked. North of the canal a short length of our original line was still held by the 9th Bhopals and the 57th Rifles of the same brigade. Connecting with the latter was the 1st Brigade holding the village of Givenchy and its eastern and northern approaches. On the left of the 1st Brigade was the 3rd Brigade. Touch had been lost between the left of the former and the right of the latter. The 3rd Brigade held a line along, and in places advanced to, the east of the Festubert Road. Its left was in communication with the right of the Meerut Division line, where troops of the 2nd Brigade had just relieved the 1st Seaforth Highlanders. To the north, units of the 2nd Brigade held an indented line west of the orchard, connecting with half of the 2nd Royal Highlanders, half of the 41st Dogras and the 1st Battalion, 9th Gurkha Rifles. From this point to the north the 6th Jats and the whole of the Garhwal Brigade occupied the original line which they had held from the commencement of the operations. The relief of most units of the southern sector was effected on the night of 22nd December. The Meerut Division remained under the orders of the 1st Corps, and was not completely withdrawn until the 27th December.

In the evening the position at Givenchy was practically re-established, and the 3rd Brigade had re-occupied the old line of trenches.

During the 23rd the enemy's activities ceased, and the whole position was restored to very much its original condition.

In my last despatch I had occasion to mention the prompt and ready help I received from the Lahore Division, under the command of Major-General H.B.B. Watkis, C.B., which was thrown into action immediately on arrival, when the British Forces were very hard pressed during the battle of Ypres – Armentiéres.

The Indian troops have fought with the utmost steadfastness and gallantry whenever they have been called upon.

Weather conditions were abnormally bad, the snow and floods precluding any active operations during the first three weeks of January.

5. At 7.30 a.m. on the 25th January the enemy began to shell Bethune, and at 8 a.m. a strong hostile infantry attack developed south of the canal, preceded by a heavy bombardment of artillery, minenwerfers and, possibly, the explosion of mines, though the latter is doubtful. The British line south of the canal formed a pronounced salient from the canal on the left, thence running forward toward the railway triangle and back to the main La Bassée – Bethune Road, where it joined the French. This line was occupied by half a battalion of the Scots Guards, and half a battalion of the Coldstream Guards, of the

1st Infantry Brigade. The trenches in the salient were blown in almost at once; and the enemy's attack penetrated this line. Our troops retired to a partially prepared second line, running approximately due north and south from the canal to the road, some 500 yards west of the railway triangle. This second line had been strengthened by the construction of a keep half way between the canal and the road. Here the other two half battalions of the above-mentioned regiments were in support.

These supports held up the enemy who, however, managed to establish himself in the brick stacks and some communication trenches between the keep, the road and the canal – and even beyond and west of the keep on either side of it.

The London Scottish had in the meantime been sent up in support, and a counter-attack was organised with the 1st Royal Highlanders, part of the 1st Cameron Highlanders, and the 2nd King's Royal Rifle Corps, the latter regiment having been sent forward from the Divisional Reserve.

The counter-attack was delayed in order to synchronise with a counter-attack north of the canal which was arranged for 1 p.m.

At 1 p.m. these troops moved forward, their flanks making good progress near the road and the canal, but their centre being held up. The 2nd Royal Sussex Regiment was then sent forward, late in the afternoon, to reinforce. The result was that the Germans were driven back far enough to enable a somewhat broken line to be taken up, running from the culvert on the railway, almost due south to the keep, and thence south-east to the main road.

The French left near the road had also been attacked and driven back a little, but not to so great an extent as the British right. Consequently, the French left was in advance of the British right and exposed to a possible flank attack from the north.

The Germans did not, however, persevere further in their attack.

The above-mentioned line was strengthened during the night; and the 1st Guards Brigade, which had suffered severely, was withdrawn into reserve and replaced by the 2nd Infantry Brigade. While this was taking place another, and equally severe attack was delivered north of the canal against the village of Givenchy.

At 8.15 a.m., after a heavy artillery bombardment with high explosive shells, the enemy's infantry advanced under the effective fire of our artillery, which, however, was hampered by the constant interruption of telephonic communication between the observers and batteries. Nevertheless, our artillery fire, combined with that of the infantry in the fire trenches, had the effect of driving the enemy from his original direction of advance, with the result that his troops crowded together on the north-east corner of the village and broke through into the centre of the village as far as the keep, which had been previously put in a state of defence. The Germans had lost heavily, and a well-timed local counter-attack, delivered by the reserves of the 2nd Welsh Regiment and 1st South Wales Borderers, and by a company of the 1st Royal Highlanders (lent by the 1st Brigade as a working party – this company was at work on the keep at the time), was completely successful, with the result that, after about an hour's street fighting, all who had broken into the village were either captured or killed; and the original line round the village was re-established by noon.

South of the village, however, and close to the canal, the right of the 2nd Royal Munster Fusiliers fell back in conformity with the troops south of the canal; but after dark that regiment moved forward and occupied the old line.

During the course of the attack on Givenchy the enemy made five assaults on the salient at the north-east of the village about French Farm, but was repulsed every time with heavy loss.

6. On the morning of the 29th January attacks were made on the right of the 1st Corps, south of the canal in the neighbourhood of La Bassée.

The enemy (part of the 14th German Corps), after a severe shelling, made a violent attack with scaling ladders on the keep, also to the north and south of it. In the keep and on the north side the Sussex Regiment held the enemy off, inflicting on him serious losses. On the south side the hostile infantry succeeded in reaching the Northamptonshire Regiment's trenches; but were immediately counterattacked and all killed. Our artillery co-operated well with the infantry in repelling the attack.

In this action our casualties were inconsiderable, but the enemy lost severely, more than 200 of his killed alone being left in front of our position.

7. On the 1st February a fine piece of work was carried out by the 4th Brigade in the neighbourhood of Cuinchy.

Some of the 2nd Coldstream Guards were driven from their trenches at 2.30 a.m., but made a stand some twenty yards east of them in a position which they held till morning.

A counter-attack, launched at 3.15 a.m. by one company of the Irish Guards and half a company of the 2nd Coldstream Guards, proved unsuccessful, owing to heavy rifle fire from the east and south.

At 10.5 a.m., acting under orders of the 1st Division, a heavy bombardment was opened on the lost ground for ten minutes; and this was followed immediately by an assault by about 50 men of the 2nd Coldstream Guards with bayonets, led by Captain A. Leigh Bennett, followed by 30 men of the Irish Guards, led by Second Lieutenant F.F. Graham, also with bayonets. These were followed by a party of Royal Engineers with sand bags and wire.

All the ground which had been lost was brilliantly retaken; the 2nd Coldstream Guards also taking another German trench and capturing two machine guns.

Thirty-two prisoners fell into our hands.

The General Officer Commanding 1st Division describes the preparation by the artillery as "splendid, the high explosive shells dropping in the exact spot with absolute precision." In forwarding his report on this engagement, the General Officer Commanding First Army writes as follows:-

> "Special credit is due-
>
> "(i) To Major-General Haking, Commanding 1st Division, for the prompt manner in which he arranged this counterattack and for the general plan, of action, which was crowned with success.
>
> "(ii) To the General Officer Commanding the 4th Brigade (Lord Cavan) for the thorough manner in which he carried out the orders of the General Officer Commanding the Division.
>
> "(iii) To the regimental officers, non-commissioned officers and men of the 2nd Coldstream Guards and Irish Guards, who, with indomitable pluck, stormed two sets of barricades, captured three German trenches, two machine guns, and killed or made prisoners many of the enemy."

8. During the period under report the Royal Flying Corps has again performed splendid service.

Although the weather was almost uniformly bad and the machines suffered from constant exposure, there have been only thirteen days on which no actual reconnaissance has been effected. Approximately, one hundred thousand miles have been flown.

In addition to the daily and constant work of reconnaissance and co-operation with the artillery, a number of aerial combats have been fought, raids carried out, detrainments harassed, parks and petrol depôts bombed, etc.

Various successful bomb-dropping raids have been carried out, usually against the enemy's aircraft material. The principle of attacking hostile aircraft whenever and wherever seen (unless highly important information is being delivered) has been adhered to, and has resulted in the moral fact that enemy machines invariably beat immediate retreat when chased.

Five German aeroplanes are known to have been brought to the ground, and it would appear probable that others, though they have managed to reach their own lines, have done so in a considerably damaged condition.

9. In my despatch of 20th November, 1914, I referred to the reinforcement of Territorial Troops which I had received, and I mentioned several units which had already been employed in the fighting line.

In the positions which I held for some years before the outbreak of this war I was brought into close contact with the Territorial Force, and I found every reason to hope and believe that, when the hour of trial arrived, they would justify every hope and trust which was placed in them.

The Lords Lieutenant of Counties and the Associations which worked under them bestowed a vast amount of labour and energy on the organization of the Territorial Force; and I trust it may be some recompense to them to know that I, and the principal Commanders serving under me, consider that the Territorial Force has far more than justified the most sanguine hopes that any of us ventured to entertain of their value and use in the field. Commanders of Cavalry Divisions are unstinted in their praise of the manner in which the Yeomanry regiments attached to their brigades have done their duty, both in and out of action. The service of Divisional Cavalry is now almost entirely performed by Yeomanry, and Divisional Commanders report that they are very efficient.

Army Corps Commanders are loud in their praise of the Territorial Battalions which form part of nearly all the brigades at the front in the first line, and more than one of them have told me that these battalions are fast approaching – if they have not already reached – the standard of efficiency of Regular Infantry.

I wish to add a word about the Officers Training Corps. The presence of the Artists' Rifles (28th Battalion, The London Regiment) with the Army in France enabled me also to test the value of this organization.

Having had some experience in peace of the working of the Officers Training Corps, I determined to turn the Artists' Rifles (which formed part of the Officers Training Corps in peace time) to its legitimate use. I therefore established the battalion as a Training Corps for Officers in the field.

The cadets pass through a course, which includes some thoroughly practical training as all cadets do a tour of 48 hours in the trenches, and afterwards write a report on what they see and notice. They also visit an observation post of a battery or group of batteries, and spend some hours there.

A Commandant has been appointed, and he arranges and supervises the work, sets schemes for practice, administers the school, delivers lectures, and reports on the candidates.

The cadets are instructed in all branches of military training suitable for platoon commanders. Machine gun tactics, a knowledge of which is so necessary for all junior officers, is a special feature of the course of instruction.

When first started the school was able to turn out officers at the rate of 75 a month. This has since been increased to 100.

Reports received from Divisional and Army Corps Commanders on officers who have been trained at the school are most satisfactory.

10. Since the date of my last report I have been able to make a close personal inspection of all the units in the command. I was most favourably impressed by all I saw.

The troops composing the Army in France have been subjected to as severe a trial as it is possible to impose upon any body of men. The desperate fighting described in my last despatch had hardly been brought to a conclusion when they were called upon to face the rigours and hardships of a winter campaign. Frost and snow have alternated with periods of continuous rain.

The men have been called upon to stand for many hours together almost up to their waists in bitterly cold water, only separated by one or two hundred yards from a most vigilant enemy. Although every measure which science and medical knowledge could suggest to mitigate these hardships was employed, the sufferings of the men have been very great.

In spite of all this they presented, at the inspections to which I have referred, a most soldier-like, splendid, though somewhat war-worn appearance. Their spirit remains high and confident; their general health is excellent, and their condition most satisfactory.

I regard it as most unfortunate that circumstances have prevented any account of many splendid instances of courage and endurance, in the face of almost unparalleled hardship and fatigue in war, coming regularly to the knowledge of the public.

Reinforcements have arrived from England with remarkable promptitude and rapidity. They have been speedily drafted into the ranks, and most of the units I inspected were nearly complete when I saw them. In appearance and quality the drafts sent out have exceeded my most sanguine expectations, and I consider the Army in France is much indebted to the Adjutant-General's Department at the War Office for the efficient manner in which its requirements have been met in this most essential respect.

With regard to these inspections, I may mention in particular the fine appearance presented by the 27th and 28th Divisions, composed principally of battalions which had come from India. Included in the former division was the Princess Patricia's Royal Canadian Regiment. They are a magnificent set of men, and have since done excellent work in the trenches.

It was some three weeks after the events recorded in paragraph 4 that I made my inspection of the Indian Corps, under Sir James Willcocks. The appearance they presented was most satisfactory, and fully confirmed my first opinion that the Indian troops only required rest, and a little acclimatizing, to bring out all their fine inherent fighting qualities.

I saw the whole of the Indian Cavalry Corps, under Lieutenant-General Rimington, on a mounted parade soon after their arrival. They are a magnificent body of Cavalry, and will, I feel sure, give the best possible account of themselves when called upon.

In the meantime, at their own particular request, they have taken their turn in the trenches and performed most useful and valuable service.

11. The Rt. Rev. Bishop Taylor Smith, C.V.O., D.D., Chaplain-General to the Forces, arrived at my Headquarters on 6th January, on a tour of inspection throughout the command.

The Cardinal Archbishop of Westminster has also visited most of the Irish Regiments at the front and the principal centres on the Line of Communications.

In a quiet and unostentatious manner the chaplains of all denominations have worked with devotion and energy in their respective spheres.

The number with the forces in the field at the commencement of the war was comparatively small, but towards the end of last year the Rev. J.M. Simms, D.D., K.H.C., Principal Chaplain, assisted by his Secretary, the Rev. W. Drury, reorganised the branch, and placed the spiritual welfare of the soldier on a more satisfactory footing. It is hoped that the further increase of personnel may be found possible.

I cannot speak too highly of the devoted manner in which all chaplains, whether with the troops in the trenches, or in attendance on the sick and wounded in casualty clearing stations and hospitals on the line of communications, have worked throughout the campaign. Since the commencement of hostilities the work of the Royal Army Medical Corps has been carried out with untiring zeal, skill and devotion. Whether at the front under conditions such as obtained during the fighting on the Aisne, when casualties were heavy and accommodation for their reception had to be improvised, or on the line of communications, where an average of some 11,000 patients have been daily under treatment, the organisation of the Medical Services has always been equal to the demands made upon it.

The careful system of sanitation introduced into the Army has, with the assistance of other measures, kept the troops free from any epidemic, in support of which it is to be noticed that since the commencement of the war some 500 cases only of enteric have occurred.

The organisation for the first time in war of Motor Ambulance Convoys is due to the initiative and organising powers of Surgeon-General T.J. O'Donnell, D.S.O., ably assisted by Major P. Evans, Royal Army Medical Corps.

Two of these convoys, composed entirely of Red Cross Society personnel, have done excellent work under the superintendence of Regular Medical Officers.

Twelve Hospital Trains ply between the front and the various bases. I have visited several of the trains when halted in stations, and have found them conducted with great comfort and efficiency. During the more recent phase of the campaign the creation of Rest Depôts at the front has materially reduced the wastage of men to the Line of Communications.

Since the latter part of October, 1914, the whole of the medical arrangements have been in the hands of Surgeon-General Sir A.T. Sloggett, C.M.G., K.H.S., under whom Surgeon-General T.P. Woodhouse and Surgeon-General T.J. O'Donnell have been responsible for the organisation on the Line of Communications and at the front respectively.

12. The exceptional and peculiar conditions brought about by the weather have caused large demands to be made upon the resources and skill of the Royal Engineers.

Every kind of expedient has had to be thought out and adopted to keep the lines of trenches and defence work effective.

The Royal Engineers have shown themselves as capable of overcoming the ravages caused by violent rain and floods as they have been throughout in neutralising the effect of the enemy's artillery.

In this connection I wish particularly to mention the excellent services performed by my Chief Engineer, Brigadier-General G.H. Fowke, who has been indefatigable in supervising all such work. His ingenuity and skill have been most valuable in the local construction of the various expedients which experience has shown to be necessary in prolonged trench warfare.

13. I have no reason to modify in any material degree my views of the general military situation, as expressed in my despatch of November 20th, 1914.

14. I have once more gratefully to acknowledge the valuable help and support I have received throughout this period from General Foch, General D'Urbal and General Maud'huy of the French Army.

I have the honour to be,
Your Lordship's most obedient Servant,
J.D.P. FRENCH,
Field-Marshal,
Commanding-in-Chief,
The British Army in the Field.

SIR JOHN FRENCH'S DESPATCH OF 5 APRIL 1915

Battle of Neuve Chapelle

WEDNESDAY, 14 APRIL, 1915.

From the Field-Marshal Commanding-in-Chief, The British Army in the Field.

To the Secretary of State for War, War Office, London, S.W.

> *General Headquarters,*
> *5th April*, 1915.

MY LORD,

I have the honour to report the operations of the Forces, under my command since the date of my last despatch, 2nd February, 1915.

1. The event of chief interest and importance which has taken place is the victory achieved over the enemy at the Battle of Neuve Chapelle, which was fought on the 10th, 11th and 12th of March. The main attack was delivered by troops of the First Army under the command of General Sir Douglas Haig, supported by a large force of Heavy Artillery, a Division of Cavalry and some Infantry of the general reserve.

Secondary and holding attacks and demonstrations were made along the front of the Second Army under the direction of its Commander, General Sir Horace Smith-Dorrien.

Whilst the success attained was due to the magnificent bearing and indomitable courage displayed by the troops of the 4th and Indian Corps, I consider that the able and skilful dispositions which were made by the General Officer Commanding First Army contributed largely to the defeat of the enemy and to the capture of his position. The energy and vigour with which General Sir Douglas Haig handled his command show him to be a leader of great ability and power.

Another action of considerable importance was brought about by a surprise attack of the Germans made on the 14th March against the 27th Division holding the trenches east of St. Eloi. A large force of artillery was concentrated in this area under cover of mist, and a heavy volume of fire was suddenly brought to bear on the trenches at 5 p.m. This artillery attack was accompanied by two mine explosions; and, in the confusion caused by these and the suddenness of the attack, the position of St. Eloi was captured and held for some hours by the enemy.

Well directed and vigorous counter attacks, in which the troops of the 5th Army Corps showed great bravery and determination, restored the situation by the evening of the 15th.

A more detailed account of these operations will appear in subsequent pages of this despatch.

2. On the 6th February a brilliant action by troops of the 1st Corps materially improved our position in the area south, of the La Bassée Canal. During the previous night parties of Irish Guards and of the 3rd Battalion Coldstream Guards had succeeded in gaining ground whence converging fire could be directed on the flanks and rear of certain "brickstacks" occupied by the Germans, which had been for some time a source of considerable annoyance.

At 2 p.m. the affair commenced with a severe bombardment of the "brickstacks" and the enemy's trenches. A brisk attack by the 3rd Coldstream Guards and Irish Guards from our trenches west of the "brickstacks" followed, and was supported by fire from the flanking positions which had been seized the previous night by the same regiments. The attack succeeded, the "brickstacks" were occupied without difficulty, and a line established north and south through a point about forty yards east of the "brickstacks."

The casualties suffered by the 5th Corps throughout the period under review, and particularly during the month of February, have been heavier than those in other parts of the line. I regret this; but I do not think, taking all the circumstances into consideration, that they were unduly numerous. The position then occupied by the 5th Corps has always been a very vulnerable part of our line; the ground is marshy, and trenches are most difficult to construct and maintain. The 27th and 28th Divisions of the 5th Corps have had no previous experience of European warfare, and a number of the units composing it had only recently returned from service in tropical climates. In consequence, the hardships of a rigorous winter campaign fell with greater weight upon these Divisions than upon any other in the command.

Chiefly owing to these causes, the 5th Corps, up to the beginning of March, was constantly engaged in counter-attack to retake trenches and ground which had been lost.

In their difficult and arduous task, however, the troops displayed the utmost gallantry and devotion; and it is most creditable to the skill and energy of their leaders that I am able to report how well they have surmounted all their difficulties, that the ground first taken over by them is still intact, and held with little greater loss than is incurred by troops in all other parts of the line.

On the 14th February the 82nd Brigade of the 27th Division was driven from its trenches east of St. Eloi; but by 7 a.m. on the 15th all these trenches had been recaptured, fifteen prisoners taken, and sixty German dead counted in front of the trenches. Similarly in the 28th Division trenches were lost by the 85th Brigade and retaken the following night.

During the month of February the enemy made several attempts to get through all along the line, but he was invariably repulsed with loss. A particularly vigorous attempt was made on the 17th February against the trenches held by the Indian Corps, but it was brilliantly repulsed. On February 28th a successful minor attack was made on the enemy's trenches near St. Eloi by small parties of the Princess Patricia's Canadian Light Infantry. The attack was divided into three small groups, the whole under the command of Lieutenant Crabbe: No. 1 Group under Lieutenant Papineau, No. 2 Group under Serjeant Patterson, and No. 3 Group under Company Serjeant-Major Lloyd.

The head of the party got within fifteen or twenty yards of the German trench and charged; it was dark at the time (about 5.15 a.m.).

Lieutenant Crabbe, who showed the greatest dash and *élan*, took his party over everything in the trench until they had gone down it about eighty yards, when they were stopped by a barricade of sandbags and timber. This party, as well as the others, then pulled down the front face of the German parapet. A number of Germans were killed and wounded, and a few prisoners were taken.

The services performed by this distinguished corps have continued to be very valuable since I had occasion to refer to them in my last despatch. They have been most ably organised, trained and commanded by Lieutenant-Colonel F.D. Farquhar, D.S.O., who, I deeply regret to say, was killed while superintending some trench work on the 20th March. His loss will be deeply felt.

A very gallant attack was made by the 4th Battalion of the King's Royal Rifle Corps of the 80th Brigade on the enemy's trenches in the early hours of March 2nd. The Battalion was led by Major Widdrington, who launched it at 12.30 a.m. (he himself being wounded during its progress), covered by an extremely accurate and effective artillery fire. About sixty yards of the enemy's trench were cleared, but the attack was brought to a standstill by a very strong barricade, in attempting to storm which several casualties were incurred.

3. During the month of February I arranged with General Foch to render the 9th French Corps, holding the trenches on my left, some much-needed rest by sending the three Divisions of the British Cavalry Corps to hold a portion of the French trenches, each division for a period of ten days alternately.

It was very gratifying to me to note once again in this campaign the eager readiness which the Cavalry displayed to undertake a rôle which does not properly belong to them in order to support and assist their French comrades.

In carrying out this work leaders, officers and men displayed the same skill and energy which I have had reason to comment upon in former despatches.

The time passed by the Cavalry in the French trenches was, on the whole, quiet and uneventful, but there are one or two incidents calling for remark.

At about 1.45 a.m. on 16th February a half hearted attack was made against the right of the line held by the 2nd Cavalry Division, but it was easily repulsed by rifle fire, and the enemy left several dead in front of the trenches. The attack was delivered against the second and third trenches from the right of the line of this Division.

At 6 a.m. on the 21st the enemy blew up one of the 2nd Cavalry Division trenches, held by the 16th Lancers, and some adjoining French trenches. The enemy occupied forty yards of our trench and tried to advance, but were stopped. An immediate counter-attack by the supporting squadron was stopped by machine-gun fire. The line was established opposite the gap, and a counter-attack by two squadrons and one company of French reserve was ordered. At 5.30 p.m., 2nd Cavalry Division reported that the counter-attack did not succeed in retaking the trench blown in, but that a new line had been established forty yards in rear of it, and that there was no further activity on the part of the enemy. At 10 p.m. the situation was unchanged.

The Commander of the Indian Cavalry Corps expressed a strong desire that the troops under his command should gain some experience in trench warfare. Arrangements were made, therefore, with the General Officer Commanding the Indian Corps, in pursuance of which the various units of the Indian Cavalry Corps have from time to time taken a turn in the trenches, and have thereby gained some valuable experience.

4. About the end of February many vital considerations induced me to believe that a vigorous offensive movement by the Forces under my command should be planned and carried out at the earliest possible moment.

Amongst the more important reasons which convinced me of this necessity were:- The general aspect of the Allied situation through-out Europe, and particularly the marked success of the Russian Army in repelling the violent onslaughts of Marshal Von Hindenburg; the apparent weakening of the enemy in my front, and the necessity for assisting our Russian Allies to the utmost by holding as many hostile troops as possible in the Western Theatre; the efforts to this end which were being made by the French Forces at Arras and Champagne; and, perhaps the most weighty consideration of all, the need of fostering the offensive spirit in the troops under my command after the trying and possibly enervating experiences which they had gone through of a severe winter in the trenches.

In a former despatch I commented upon the difficulties and drawbacks which the winter weather in this climate imposes upon a vigorous offensive. Early in March these difficulties became greatly lessened by the drying up of the country and by spells of brighter weather.

I do not propose in this despatch to enter at length into the considerations which actuated me in deciding upon the plan, time and place of my attack, but Your Lordship is fully aware of these.

As mentioned above, the main attack was carried out by units of the First Army, supported by troops of the Second Army and the general reserve.

The object of the main attack was to be the capture of the village of Neuve Chapelle and the enemy's position at that point, and the establishment of our line as far forward as possible to the east of that place.

The object, nature and scope of the attack, and instructions for the conduct of the operation were communicated by me to Sir Douglas Haig in a secret memorandum dated 19th February.

The main topographical feature of this part of the theatre is a marked ridge which runs south-west from a point two miles south-west of Lille to the village of Fournes, whence two spurs run out, one due west to a height known as Haut Pommereau, the other following the line of the main road to Illies.

The buildings of the village of Neuve Chapelle run along the Rue du Bois-Fauquisart Road. There is a triangle of roads just north of the village. This area consists of a few big houses, with walls, gardens, orchards, etc., and here, with the aid of numerous machine guns, the enemy had established a strong post which flanked the approaches to the village.

The Bois du Biez, which lies roughly south-east of the village of Neuve Chapelle, influenced the course of this operation.

Full instructions as to assisting and supporting the attack were issued to the Second Army. The battle opened at 7.30 a.m. on the 10th March by a powerful artillery bombardment of the enemy's position at Neuve Chapelle. The artillery bombardment had been well prepared and was most effective, except on the extreme northern portion of the front of attack.

At 8.5 a.m. the 23rd (left) and 25th (right) Brigades of the 8th Division assaulted the German trenches on the north-west of the village.

At the same hour the Garhwal Brigade of the Meerut Division, which occupied the position to the south of Neuve Chapelle, assaulted the German trenches in its front.

The Garhwal Brigade and the 25th Brigade carried the enemy's lines of entrenchments where the wire entanglements had been almost entirely swept away by our shrapnel fire. The 23rd Brigade, however, on the north-east, was held up by the wire entanglements, which were not sufficiently cut.

At 8.5 a.m. the artillery turned on to Neuve Chapelle, and at 8.35 a.m. the advance of the infantry was continued.

The 25th and Garhwal Brigades pushed on eastward and north-eastward respectively, and succeeded in getting a footing in the village. The 23rd Brigade was still held up in front of the enemy's wire entanglements, and could not progress. Heavy losses were suffered, especially in the Middlesex Regiment and the Scottish Rifles. The progress, however, of the 25th Brigade into Neuve Chapelle immediately to the south of the 23rd Brigade had the effect of turning the southern flank of the enemy's defences in front of the 23rd Brigade.

This fact, combined with powerful artillery support, enabled the 23rd Brigade to get forward between 10 and 11 a.m., and by 11 a.m. the whole of the village of Neuve Chapelle and the roads leading northward and south-westward from the eastern end of that village were in our hands.

During this time our artillery completely cut off the village and the surrounding country from any German reinforcements which could be thrown into the fight to restore the situation by means of a curtain of shrapnel fire. Prisoners subsequently reported that all attempts at reinforcing the front line were checked.

Steps were at once taken to consolidate the position won.

Considerable delay occurred after the capture of the Neuve Chapelle position. The infantry was greatly disorganised by the violent nature of the attack and by its passage through the enemy's trenches and the buildings of the village. It was necessary to get units to some extent together before pushing on. The telephonic communication being cut by the enemy's fire rendered communication between front and rear most difficult. The fact of the left of the 23rd Brigade having been held up had kept back the 8th Division, and had involved a portion of the 25th Brigade in fighting to the north out of its proper direction of advance. All this required adjustment. An orchard held by the enemy north of Neuve Chapelle also threatened the flank of an advance towards the Aubers Ridge.

I am of opinion that this delay would not have occurred had the clearly expressed order of the General Officer Commanding First Army been more carefully observed.

The difficulties above enumerated might have been overcome at an earlier period of the day if the General Officer Commanding 4th Corps had been able to bring his reserve brigades more speedily into action.

As it was, the further advance did not commence before 3.30 p.m.

The 21st Brigade was able to form up in the open on the left without a shot being fired at it, thus showing that at the time the enemy's resistance had been paralysed. The Brigade pushed forward in the direction of Moulin Du Pietre.

At first it made good progress, but was subsequently held up by the machine gun fire from the houses and from a defended work in the line of the German entrenchments opposite the right of the 22nd Brigade.

Further to the south the 24th Brigade, which had been directed on Pietre, was similarly held up by machine-guns in the houses and trenches at the road junction six hundred yards northwest of Pietre.

The 25th Brigade, on the right of the 24th, was also held up by machine-guns from a bridge held by the Germans, over the River Des Layes, which is situated to the north-west of the Bois Du Biez.

Whilst two Brigades of the Meerut Division were establishing themselves on the new line, the Dehra Dun Brigade, supported by the Jullundur Brigade of the Lahore Division, moved to the attack of the Bois Du Biez, but were held up on the line of the River Des Layes by the German post at the bridge which enfiladed them and brought them to a standstill.

The defended bridge over the River Des Layes and its neighbourhood immediately assumed considerable importance. Whilst artillery fire was brought to bear, as far as circumstances would permit, on this point, Sir Douglas Haig directed the 1st Corps to despatch one or more battalions of the 1st Brigade in support of the troops attacking the bridge. Three battalions were thus sent to Richebourg St. Vaast. Darkness coming on, and the enemy having brought up reinforcements, no further progress could be made, and the Indian Corps and 4th Corps proceeded to consolidate the position they had gained.

Whilst the operations which I have thus briefly recorded were going on, the 1st Corps, in accordance with orders, delivered an attack in the morning from Givenchy, simultaneously with that against Neuve Chapelle; but, as the enemy's wire was insufficiently cut, very little progress could be made, and the troops at this point did little more than hold fast the Germans in front of them.

On the following day, March 11th, the attack was renewed by the 4th and Indian Corps, but it was soon seen that a further advance would be impossible until the artillery had dealt effectively with the various houses and defended localities which held up the troops along the entire front. Efforts were made to direct the artillery fire accordingly; but owing to the weather conditions, which did not permit of aerial observation, and the fact that nearly all the telephonic communications between the artillery observers and their batteries had been cut, it was impossible to do so with sufficient accuracy. Even when our troops which were pressing forward occupied a house here and there, it was not possible to stop our artillery fire, and the infantry had to be withdrawn.

The two principal points which barred the advance were the same as on the preceding day – namely, the enemy's position about Moulin de Pietre and at the bridge over the River des Layes. On the 12th March the same unfavourable conditions as regards weather prevailed, and hampered artillery action.

Although the 4th and Indian Corps most gallantly attempted to capture the strongly fortified positions in their front, they were unable to maintain themselves, although they succeeded in holding them for some hours.

Operations on this day were chiefly remarkable for the violent counterattacks, supported by artillery, which were delivered by the Germans, and the ease with which they were repulsed. As most of the objects for which the operations had been undertaken had been attained, and as there were reasons why I considered it inadvisable to continue the attack at that time, I directed Sir Douglas Haig on the night of the 12th to hold and consolidate the ground which had been gained by the 4th and Indian Corps, and to suspend further offensive operations for the present.

On the morning of the 12th I informed the General Officer Commanding 1st Army that he could call on the 2nd Cavalry Division, under General Gough, for immediate support in the event of the successes of the First Army opening up opportunities for its favourable employment. This Division and a Brigade of the North Midland Division, which was temporarily attached to it was moved forward for this purpose.

The 5th Cavalry Brigade, under Sir Philip Chetwode, reached the Rue Bacquerot at 4 p.m., with a view to rendering immediate support; but he was informed by the General Officer Commanding 4th Corps that the situation was not so favourable as he had hoped it would be, and that no further action by the cavalry was advisable.

General Gough's command, therefore, retired to Estaires.

The artillery of all kinds was handled with the utmost energy and skill and rendered invaluable support in the prosecution of the attack.

The losses during these three days' fighting were, I regret to say, very severe, numbering-

190 officers and 2,337 other ranks, killed.
359 officers and 8,174 other ranks, wounded.
23 officers and 1,728 other ranks, missing.

But the results attained were, in my opinion, wide and far reaching.

The enemy left several thousand dead on the battlefield which were seen and counted; and we have positive information that upwards of 12,000 wounded were removed to the northeast and east by train.

Thirty officers and 1,657 other ranks of the enemy were captured.

I can best express my estimate of this battle by quoting an extract from a Special Order of the Day which I addressed to Sir Douglas Haig and the First Army at its conclusion:-

"I am anxious to express to you personally my warmest appreciation of the skilful manner in which you have carried out your orders, and my fervent and most heartfelt appreciation of the magnificent gallantry and devoted, tenacious courage displayed by all ranks whom you have ably led to success and victory."

5. Some operations in the nature of holding attacks, carried out by troops of the Second Army, were instrumental in keeping the enemy in front of them occupied, and preventing reinforcements being sent from those portions of the front to the main point of attack.

At 12.30 a.m. on the 12th March the 17th Infantry Brigade of the 4th Division, 3rd Corps, engaged in an attack on the enemy which resulted in the capture of the village of L'Epinette and adjacent farms.

Supported by a brisk fire from the 18th Infantry Brigade, the 17th Infantry Brigade, detailed for the attack, assaulted in two columns converging, and obtained the first houses of the village without much loss. The remainder of the village was very heavily wired, and the enemy got away by means of communication trenches while our men were cutting through the wire.

The enemy suffered considerable loss; our casualties being 5 officers and 30 other ranks, killed and wounded.

The result of this operation was that an advance of 300 yards was made on a front of half a mile.

All attempts to retake this position have been repulsed with heavy loss to the enemy.

The General Officer Commanding the Second Corps arranged for an attack on a part of the enemy's position to the south-west of the village of Wytschaete which he had timed to commence at 10 a.m. on the 12th March. Owing to dense fog, the assault could not be made until 4 o'clock in the afternoon.

It was then commenced by the Wiltshire and Worcestershire Regiments, but was so hampered by the mist and the approach of darkness that nothing more was effected than holding the enemy to his ground.

The action of St. Eloi referred to in the first paragraph of this despatch commenced at 5 p.m. on the 14th March by a very heavy cannonade which was directed against our trenches in front of St. Eloi, the village itself and the approaches to it. There is a large mound lying to the south-east of the village.

When the artillery attack was at its height a mine was exploded under this mound, and a strong hostile infantry attack was immediately launched against the trenches and the mound.

Our artillery opened fire at once, as well as our infantry, and inflicted considerable losses on the enemy during their advance; but, chiefly owing to the explosion of the mine and the surprise of the overwhelming artillery attack, the enemy's infantry had penetrated the first line of trenches at some points. As a consequence the garrisons of other works which had successfully resisted the assault were enfiladed and forced to retire just before it turned dark.

A counter attack was at once organised by the General Officer Commanding 82nd Brigade, under the orders of the General Officer Commanding 27th Division, who brought up a reserve brigade to support it.

The attack was launched at 2 a.m., and the 82nd Brigade succeeded in recapturing the portion of the village of St. Eloi which was in the hands of the enemy and a portion of the trenches east of it. At 3 a.m. the 80th Brigade in support took more trenches to the east and west of the village.

The counter attack, which was well carried out under difficult conditions, resulted in the recapture of all lost ground of material importance.

It is satisfactory to be able to record that, though the troops occupying the first line of trenches were at first overwhelmed, they afterwards behaved very gallantly in the counter-attack for the recovery of the lost ground; and the following units earned and received the special commendation, of the Army Commander:- The 2nd Royal Irish Fusiliers, the 2nd Duke of Cornwall's Light Infantry, the 1st Leinster Regiment, the 4th Rifle Brigade and the Princess Patricia's Canadian Light Infantry.

A vigorous attack made by the enemy on the 17th to recapture these trenches was repulsed with great loss.

Throughout the period under review night enterprises by smaller or larger patrols, which were led with consummate skill and daring, have been very active along the whole line.

A moral superiority has thus been established, and valuable information has been collected.

I cannot speak too highly of the invincible courage and the remarkable resource displayed by these patrols.

The troops of the 3rd Corps have particularly impressed me by their conduct of these operations.

6. The work of the Royal Flying Corps throughout this period, and especially during the operations of the 10th, 11th, and 12th March, was of the greatest value. Though the weather on March 10th and on the subsequent days was very unfavourable for aerial work, on account of low-lying clouds and mist, a

remarkable number of hours flying of a most valuable character were effected, and continuous and close reconnaissance was maintained over the enemy's front.

In addition to the work of reconnaissance and observation of artillery fire, the Royal Flying Corps was charged with the special duty of hampering the enemy's movements by destroying various points on his communications. The railways at Menin, Courtrai, Don and Douai were attacked, and it is known that very extensive damage was effected at certain of these places. Part of a troop train was hit by a bomb, a wireless installation near Lille is believed to have been effectively destroyed, and a house in which the enemy had installed one of his Headquarters was set on fire. These afford other instances of successful operations of this character. Most of the objectives mentioned were attacked at a height of only 100 to 150 feet. In one case the pilot descended to about 50 feet above the point he was attacking.

Certain new and important forms of activity, which it is undesirable to specify, have been initiated and pushed forward with much vigour and success.

There have been only eight days during the period under review on which reconnaissances have not been made. A total of approximately 130,000 miles have been flown – almost entirely over the enemy's lines.

No great activity has been shown over our troops on the part of the enemy's aircraft, but they have been attacked whenever and wherever met with, and usually forced down or made to seek refuge in their own lines.

7. In my last despatch I referred to the remarkable promptitude and rapidity with which reinforcements arrived in this country from England. In connection with this it is of interest to call attention to the fact that, in spite of the heavy casualties incurred in the fighting between the 10th and 15th March, all deficiencies, both in officers and rank and file, were made good within a few days of the conclusion of the battle.

The drafts for the Indian Contingents have much improved of late, and are now quite satisfactory. Since the date of my last report the general health of the Army has been excellent; enteric has decreased, and there has been no recurrence on any appreciable scale of the "foot" trouble which appeared so threatening in December and January.

These results are due to the skill and energy which have characterised in a marked degree the work of the Royal Army Medical Corps throughout the campaign, under the able supervision of Surgeon-General T.J. O'Donnell, D.S.O., Deputy Director-General, Medical Services. But much credit is also due to Divisional, Brigade, Regimental and Company Commanders for the close supervision which has been kept over the health of their men by seeing that the precautions laid down for the troops before entering and after leaving the trenches are duly observed, and by the establishment and efficient maintenance of bathing-places and wash-houses, and by the ingenious means universally employed throughout the Forces to maintain the cleanliness of the men, having regard both to their bodies and their clothing.

I have inspected most of these houses and establishments, and consider them models of careful organisation and supervision.

I would particularly comment upon the energy displayed by the Royal Army Medical Corps in the scientific efforts they have made to discover and check disease in its earliest stages by a system of experimental research, which I think has never before been so fully developed in the field.

In this work they have been ably assisted by those distinguished members of the medical profession who are now employed as Military Medical Officers, and whose invaluable services I gratefully acknowledge.

The actual strength of the Force in the field has been increased and the health of the troops improved by a system of "convalescent" hospitals.

In these establishments slight wounds and minor ailments are treated, and men requiring attention and rest are received.

By these means efficient soldiers, whose services would otherwise be lost for a long time, are kept in the country, whilst a large number of men are given immediate relief and rest when they require it without removing them from the area of operations.

This adds materially to the fighting efficiency of the Forces.

The principal convalescent hospital is at St. Omer. It was started and organised by Colonel A.F.L. Bate, Army Medical Service, whose zeal, energy and organising power have rendered it a model hospital of its kind, and this example has materially assisted in the efficient organisation of similar smaller establishments at every Divisional Headquarters.

8. I have already commented upon the number and severity of the casualties in action which have occurred in the period under report. Here once again I have to draw attention to the excellent work done by Surgeon-General O'Donnell and his officers. No organisation could excel the efficiency of the arrangements – whether in regard to time, space, care and comfort, or transport – which are made for the speedy evacuation of the wounded.

I wish particularly to express my deep sense of the loss incurred by the Army in General, and by the Forces in France in particular, in the death of Brigadier-General J.E. Gough, V.C., C.M.G., A.D.C., late Brigadier-General, General Staff, First Army, which occurred on 22nd February as a result of a severe wound received on the 20th February when inspecting the trenches of the 4th Corps.

I always regarded General Gough as one of our most promising military leaders of the future. His services as a Staff Officer throughout the campaign have been invaluable, and I had already brought his name before Your Lordship for immediate promotion.

I can well understand how deeply these casualties are felt by the nation at large, but each daily report shows clearly that they are being endured on at least an equal scale by all the combatants engaged throughout Europe, friends and foes alike.

In war as it is today between civilised nations, armed to the teeth with the present deadly rifle and machine-gun, heavy casualties are absolutely unavoidable. For the slightest undue exposure the heaviest toll is exacted.

The power of defence conferred by modern weapons is the main cause of the long duration of the battles of the present day, and it is this fact which mainly accounts for such loss and waste of life.

Both one and the other can, however, be shortened and lessened if attacks can be supported by the most efficient and powerful force of artillery available; but an almost unlimited supply of ammunition is necessary and a most liberal discretionary power as to its use must be given to the Artillery Commanders.

I am confident that this is the only means, by which great results can be obtained with a minimum of loss.

9. On the 15th February the Canadian Division began to arrive in this country. I inspected the Division, which was under the command of Lieutenant-General E.A.H. Alderson, C.B., on 20th February.

They presented a splendid and most soldier-like appearance on parade. The men were of good physique, hard and fit. I judged by what I saw of them that they were well trained, and quite able to take their places in the line of battle.

Since then the Division has thoroughly justified the good opinion I formed of it.

The troops of the Canadian Division were first attached for a few days by brigades for training in the 3rd Corps trenches under Lieutenant-General Sir William Pulteney, who gave me such an excellent report of their efficiency that I was able to employ them in the trenches early in March.

During the Battle of Neuve Chapelle they held a part of the line allotted to the First Army, and, although they were not actually engaged in the main attack, they rendered valuable help by keeping the enemy actively employed in front of their trenches.

All the soldiers of Canada serving in the Army under my command have so far splendidly upheld the traditions of the Empire, and will, I feel sure, prove to be a great source of additional strength to the forces in this country.

In former despatches I have been able to comment very favourably upon the conduct and bearing of the Territorial Forces throughout the operations in which they have been engaged.

As time goes on, and I see more and more of their work, whether in the trenches or engaged in more active operations, I am still further impressed with their value.

Several battalions were engaged in the most critical moments of the heavy fighting which occurred in the middle of March, and they acquitted themselves with the utmost credit.

Up till lately the troops of the Territorial Force in this country were only employed by battalions, but for some weeks past I have seen formed divisions working together, and I have every hope that their employment in the larger units will prove as successful as in the smaller. These opinions are fully borne out by the result of the close inspection which I have recently made of the North Midland Division, under Major-General Hon. Montagu-Stuart-Wortley, and the 2nd London Division, under Major-General Barter.

10. General Baron Von Kaulbars, of the Russian General Staff, arrived at my Headquarters on the 18th March. He was anxious to study our aviation system, and I gave him every opportunity of doing so.

The Bishop of London arrived here with his Chaplain on Saturday, March 27th, and left on Monday, April 5th.

During the course of his visit to the Army His Lordship was at the front every day, and I think I am right in saying that there was scarcely a unit in the command which was not at one time or another present at his services or addresses.

Personal fatigue and even danger were completely ignored by His Lordship. The Bishop held several services virtually under shell fire, and it was with difficulty that he could be prevented from carrying on his ministrations under rifle fire in the trenches.

I am anxious to place on record my deep sense of the good effect produced throughout the Army by this self-sacrificing devotion on the part of the Bishop of London, to whom I feel personally very deeply indebted.

I have once more to remark upon the devotion to duty, courage and contempt of danger which has characterised the work of the Chaplains of the Army throughout this campaign.

11. The increased strength of the Force and the gradual exhaustion of the local resources have necessitated a corresponding increase in our demands on the Line of Communications, since we are now compelled to import many articles which in the early stages could be obtained by local purchase. The Directorates concerned have, however, been carefully watching the situation,

and all the Administrative Services on the Line of Communication have continued to work with smoothness and regularity, in spite of the increased pressure thrown upon them. In this connection I wish to bring to notice the good service which has been rendered by the Staff of the Base Ports.

The work of the Railway Transport Department has been excellently carried out, and I take this opportunity of expressing my appreciation of the valuable service rendered by the French railway authorities generally, and especially by Colonel Ragueneau, late Directeur des Chemins de Fer, Lieutenant-Colonel Le Hénaff, Directeur des Chemins de Fer, Lieutenant-Colonel Dumont, Commissaire Militaire, Chemin de Fer du Nord, and Lieutenant-Colonel Frid, Commissaire Regulateur, Armée Anglaise.

The Army Postal Service has continued to work well, and at the present time a letter posted in London is delivered at General Headquarters or at the Headquarters of the Armies and Army Corps on the following evening, and reaches an addressee in the trenches on the second day after posting. The delivery of parcels has also been accelerated, and is carried out with regularity and despatch.

12. His Majesty the King of the Belgians visited the British lines on February 8th and inspected some of the units in reserve behind the trenches.

During the last two months I have been much indebted to His Majesty and his gallant Army for valuable assistance and co-operation in various ways.

13. His Royal Highness the Prince of Wales is the bearer of this despatch.

His Royal Highness continues to make most satisfactory progress. During the Battle of Neuve Chapelle he acted on my General Staff as a Liaison Officer. Reports from the General Officers Commanding Corps and Divisions to which he has been attached agree in commending the thoroughness in which he performs any work entrusted to him.

I have myself been very favourably impressed by the quickness with which His Royal Highness has acquired knowledge of the various branches of the service, and the deep interest he has always displayed in the comfort and welfare of the men.

His visits to the troops, both in the field and in hospitals, have been greatly appreciated by all ranks.

His Royal Highness did duty for a time in the trenches with the Battalion to which he belongs.

14. In connection with the Battle of Neuve Chapelle I desire to bring to Your Lordship's special notice the valuable services of General Sir Douglas Haig, K.C.B., K.C.I.E., K.C.V.O., A.D.C., Commanding the First Army.

I am also much indebted to the able and devoted assistance I have received from Lieutenant-General Sir William Robertson, K.C.B., K.C.V.O., D.S.O., Chief of the General Staff, in the direction of all the operations recorded in this despatch.

I have many other names to bring to notice for valuable, gallant and distinguished service during the period under review, and these will form the subject of a separate report at an early date.

I have the honour to be,
Your Lordship's most obedient Servant,
J.D.P. FRENCH,
Field-Marshal,
Commanding-in-Chief,
The British Army in the Field.

SIR JOHN FRENCH'S DESPATCH OF 15 JUNE 1915

Second Battle of Ypres, Battle of Aubers Ridge and Battle of Festubert

SATURDAY, 10 JULY, 1915

From the Field-Marshal Commanding-in-Chief, The British Army in the Field.

To the Secretary of State for War, War Office, London, S.W.

General Headquarters,
15th June, 1915.

MY LORD,

I have the honour to report that since the date of my last despatch (5th April, 1915) the Army in France under my command has been heavily engaged opposite both flanks of the line held by the British Forces.

1. In the North the town and district of Ypres have once more in this campaign been successfully defended against vigorous and sustained attacks made by large forces of the enemy, and supported by a mass of heavy and field artillery, which, not only in number, but also in weight and calibre, is superior to any concentration of guns which has previously assailed that part of the line.

In the South a vigorous offensive has again been taken by troops of the First Army, in the course of which a large area of entrenched and fortified ground has been captured from the enemy, whilst valuable support has been afforded to the attack which our Allies have carried on with such marked success against the enemy's positions to the east of Arras and Lens.

2. I much regret that during the period under report the fighting has been characterised on the enemy's side by a cynical and barbarous disregard of the well-known usages of civilised war and a flagrant defiance of the Hague Convention.

All the scientific resources of Germany have apparently been brought into play to produce a gas of so virulent and poisonous a nature that any human being brought into contact with it is first paralysed and then meets with a lingering and agonising death.

The enemy has invariably preceded, prepared and supported his attacks by a discharge in stupendous volume of these poisonous gas fumes whenever the wind was favourable.

Such weather conditions have only prevailed to any extent in the neighbourhood of Ypres, and there can be no doubt that the effect of these poisonous fumes materially influenced the operations in that theatre, until experience suggested effective counter-measures, which have since been so perfected as to render them innocuous.

The brain power and thought which has evidently been at work before this unworthy method of making war reached the pitch of efficiency which has been demonstrated in its practice shows that the Germans must have harboured these designs for a long time.

As a soldier I cannot help expressing the deepest regret and some surprise that an Army which hitherto has claimed to be the chief exponent of the chivalry of war should have stooped to employ such devices against brave and gallant foes.

3. On the night of Saturday, April 17th, a commanding hill which afforded the enemy excellent artillery observation toward the West and North-West was successfully mined and captured.

This hill, known as Hill 60, lies opposite the northern extremity of the line held by the 2nd Corps.

The operation was planned and the mining commenced by Major-General Bulfin before the ground was handed over to the troops under Lieutenant-General Sir Charles Fergusson, under whose supervision the operation was carried out.

The mines were successfully fired at 7 p.m. on the 17th instant, and immediately afterwards the hill was attacked and gained, without difficulty, by the 1st Battalion, Royal West Kent Regiment, and the 2nd Battalion, King's Own Scottish Borderers. The attack was well supported by the Divisional Artillery, assisted by French and Belgian batteries.

During the night several of the enemy's counter-attacks were repulsed with heavy loss, and fierce hand-to-hand fighting took place; but on the early morning of the 18th the enemy succeeded in forcing back the troops holding the right of the hill to the reverse slope, where, however, they hung on throughout the day.

On the evening of the 18th these two battalions were relieved by the 2nd Battalion, West Riding Regiment, and the 2nd Battalion, King's Own Yorkshire Light Infantry, who again stormed the hill undercover of heavy artillery fire, and the enemy was driven off at the point of the bayonet.

In this operation fifty-three prisoners were captured, including four officers.

On the 20th and following days many unsuccessful attacks by the enemy were made on Hill 60, which was continuously shelled by heavy artillery.

On May 1st another attempt to recapture Hill 60 was supported by great volumes of asphyxiating gas, which caused nearly all the men along a front of about 400 yards to be immediately struck down by its fumes.

The splendid courage with which the leaders rallied their men and subdued the natural tendency to panic (which is inevitable on such occasions), combined with the prompt intervention of supports, once more drove the enemy back.

A second and more severe "gas" attack, under much more favourable weather conditions, enabled the enemy to recapture this position on May 5th.

The enemy owes his success in this last attack entirely to the use of asphyxiating gas. It was only a few days later that the means, which have since proved so effective, of counter-acting this method, of making war were put into practice. Had it been otherwise, the enemy's attack on May 5th would most certainly have shared the fate of all the many previous attempts he had made.

4. It was at the commencement of the Second Battle of Ypres on the evening of the 22nd April, referred to in paragraph 1 of this report, that the enemy first made use of asphyxiating gas.

Some days previously I had complied with General Joffre's request to take over the trenches occupied by the French, and on the evening of the 22nd the troops holding the lines east of Ypres were posted as follows:-

> From Steenstraate to the east of Langemarck, as far as the Poelcappelle Road, a French Division.
>
> Thence, in a south-easterly direction toward the Passchendaele-Becelaere Road, the Canadian Division.
>
> Thence a Division took up the line in a southerly direction east of Zonnebeke to a point west of Becelaere, whence another Division continued the line south-east to the northern limit of the Corps on its right.

Of the 5th Corps there were four battalions in Divisional Reserve about Ypres; the Canadian Division had one battalion in Divisional Reserve and the 1st Canadian Brigade in Army Reserve. An Infantry Brigade, which had just been withdrawn after suffering heavy losses on Hill 60, was resting about Vlamertinghe.

Following a heavy bombardment, the enemy attacked the French Division at about 5 p.m., using asphyxiating gases for the first time. Aircraft reported that at about 5 p.m. thick yellow smoke had been seen issuing from the German trenches between Langemarck and Bixschoote. The French reported that two simultaneous attacks had been made east of the Ypres-Staden Railway, in which these asphyxiating gases had been employed.

What follows almost defies description. The effect of these poisonous gases was so virulent as to render the whole of the line held by the French Division mentioned above practically incapable of any action at all. It was at first impossible for anyone to realise what had actually happened. The smoke and fumes hid everything from sight, and hundreds of men were thrown into a comatose or dying condition, and within an hour the whole position had to be abandoned, together with about 50 guns.

I wish particularly to repudiate any idea of attaching the least blame to the French Division for this unfortunate incident.

After all the examples our gallant Allies have shown of dogged and tenacious courage in the many trying situations in which they have been placed throughout the course of this campaign it is quite superfluous for me to dwell on this aspect of the incident, and I would only express my firm conviction that, if any troops in the world had been able to hold their trenches in the face of such a treacherous and altogether unexpected onslaught, the French Division would have stood firm.

The left flank of the Canadian Division was thus left dangerously exposed to serious attack in flank, and there appeared to be a prospect of their being overwhelmed and of a successful attempt by the Germans to cut off the British troops occupying the salient to the East.

In spite of the danger to which they were exposed the Canadians held their ground with a magnificent display of tenacity and courage; and it is not too much to say that the bearing and conduct of these splendid troops averted a disaster which might have been attended with the most serious consequences.

They were supported with great promptitude by the reserves of the Divisions holding the salient and by a Brigade which had been resting in billets.

Throughout the night the enemy's attacks were repulsed, effective counter-attacks were delivered, and at length touch was gained with the French right, and a new line was formed. The 2nd London Heavy Battery, which had been attached to the Canadian Division, was posted behind the right of the French Division, and, being involved in their retreat, fell into the enemy's hands. It was recaptured by the Canadians in their counter-attack, but the guns could not be withdrawn before the Canadians were again driven back.

During the night I directed the Cavalry Corps and the Northumbrian Division, which was then in general reserve, to move to the west of Ypres, and placed these troops at the disposal of the General Officer Commanding the

Second Army. I also directed other reserve troops from the 3rd Corps and the First Army to be held in readiness to meet eventualities.

In the confusion of the gas and smoke the Germans succeeded in capturing the bridge at Steenstraate and some works south of Lizerne, all of which were in occupation by the French. The enemy having thus established himself to the west of the Ypres Canal, I was somewhat apprehensive of his succeeding in driving a wedge between the French and Belgian troops at this point. I directed, therefore, that some of the reinforcements sent north should be used to support and assist General Putz, should he find difficulty in preventing any further advance of the Germans west of the canal.

At about 10 o'clock on the morning of the 23rd connection was finally ensured between the left of the Canadian Division and the French right, about eight hundred yards east of the canal; but as this entailed the maintenance by the British troops of a much longer line than that which they had held before the attack commenced on the previous night, there were no reserves available for counter-attack until reinforcements, which were ordered up from the Second Army, were able to deploy to the east of Ypres.

Early on the morning of the 23rd I went to see General Foch, and from him I received a detailed account of what had happened, as reported by General Putz. General Foch informed me that it was his intention to make good the original line and regain the trenches which the French Division had lost. He expressed the desire that I should maintain my present line, assuring me that the original position would be re-established in a few days. General Foch further informed me that he had ordered up large French reinforcements, which were now on their way, and that troops from the North had already arrived to reinforce General Putz.

I fully concurred in the wisdom of the General's wish to re-establish our old line, and agreed to co-operate in the way he desired, stipulating, however, that if the position was not re-established within a limited time I could not allow the British troops to remain in so exposed a situation as that which the action of the previous twenty-four hours had compelled them to occupy. During the whole of the 23rd the enemy's artillery was very active, and his attacks all along the front were supported by some heavy guns which had been brought down from the coast in the neighbourhood of Ostend.

The loss of the guns on the night of the 22nd prevented this fire from being kept down, and much aggravated the situation. Our positions, however, were well maintained by the vigorous counter-attacks made by the 5th Corps.

During the day I directed two Brigades of the 3rd Corps, and the Lahore Division of the Indian Corps, to be moved up to the Ypres area and placed at the disposal of the Second Army.

In the course of these two or three days many circumstances combined to render the situation east of the Ypres Canal very critical and most difficult to deal with.

The confusion caused by the sudden retirement of the French Division, and the necessity for closing up the gap and checking the enemy's advance at all costs, led to a mixing up of units and a sudden shifting of the areas of command, which was quite unavoidable. Fresh units, as they came up from the South, had to be pushed into the firing line in an area swept by artillery fire which, owing to the capture of the French guns, we were unable to keep down. All this led to very heavy casualties; and I wish to place on record the deep admiration which I feel for the resource and presence of mind evinced by the leaders actually on the spot.

The parts taken by Major-General Snow and Brigadier-General Hull were reported to me as being particularly marked in this respect.

An instance of this occurred on the afternoon of the 24th when the enemy succeeded in breaking through the line at St. Julien.

Brigadier-General Hull, acting under the orders of Lieutenant-General Alderson, organised a powerful counter attack with his own Brigade and some of the nearest available units. He was called upon to control, with only his Brigade Staff, parts of battalions from six separate divisions which were quite new to the ground. Although the attack did not succeed in retaking St. Julien, it effectually checked the enemy's further advance.

It was only on the morning of the 25th that the enemy were able to force back the left of the Canadian Division from the point where it had originally joined the French line.

During the night, and the early morning of the 25th, the enemy directed a heavy attack against the Division at Broodseinde crossroads which was supported by a powerful shell fire, but he failed to make any progress.

During the whole of this time the town of Ypres and all the roads to the East and West were uninterruptedly subjected to a violent artillery fire, but in spite of this the supply of both food and ammunition was maintained throughout with order and efficiency.

During the afternoon of the 25th many German prisoners were taken, including some officers. The hand-to-hand fighting was very severe, and the enemy suffered heavy loss. During the 26th the Lahore Division and a Cavalry Division were pushed up into the fighting line, the former on the right of the French, the latter in support of the 5th Corps.

In the afternoon the Lahore Division, in conjunction with the French right, succeeded in pushing the enemy back some little distance toward the North, but their further advance was stopped owing to the continual employment by the enemy of asphyxiating gas.

On the right of the Lahore Division the Northumberland Infantry Brigade advanced against St. Julien and actually succeeded in entering, and for a time occupying, the southern portion of that village. They were, however, eventually driven back, largely owing to gas, and finally occupied a line a short way to the South. This, attack was most successfully and gallantly led by Brigadier-General Riddell, who, I regret to say, was killed during the progress of the operation.

Although no attack was made on the south-eastern side of the salient, the troops operating to the east of Ypres were subjected to heavy artillery fire from this direction which took some of the battalions, which were advancing North to the attack, in reverse.

Some gallant attempts made by the Lahore Division on the 27th, in conjunction with the French, pushed the enemy further North; but they were partially frustrated by the constant fumes of gas to which they were exposed. In spite of this, however, a certain amount of ground was gained.

The French had succeeded in retaking Lizerne, and had made some progress at Steenstraate and Het Sas; but up to the evening of the 28th no further progress had been made toward the recapture of the original line.

I sent instructions, therefore, to Sir Herbert Plumer, who was now in charge of the operation, to take preliminary measures for the retirement to the new line which had been fixed upon. On the morning of the 29th I had another interview with General Foch, who informed me that strong reinforcements were hourly arriving to support General Putz, and urged me to postpone issuing orders for any retirement until the result of his attack, which was timed to commence at daybreak on the 30th, should be known. To this I agreed, and instructed Sir Herbert Plumer accordingly.

No substantial advance having been made by the French, I issued orders to Sir Herbert Plumer at one o'clock on May 1st to commence his withdrawal to the new line.

The retirement was commenced the following night, and the new line was occupied on the morning of May 4th.

I am of opinion that this retirement, carried out deliberately with scarcely any loss, and in the face of an enemy in position, reflects the greatest possible credit on Sir Herbert Plumer and those who so efficiently carried out his orders.

The successful conduct of this operation was the more remarkable from the fact that on the evening of May 2nd, when it was only half completed, the enemy made a heavy attack, with the usual gas accompaniment, on St. Julien and the line to the west of it.

An attack on a line to the east of Fortuin was made at the same time under similar conditions.

In both cases our troops were at first driven from their trenches by gas fumes, but on the arrival of the supporting battalions and two brigades of a Cavalry Division, which were sent up in support from about Potijze, all the lost trenches were regained at night.

On the 3rd May, while the retirement was still going on, another violent attack was directed on the northern face of the salient. This was also driven back with heavy loss to the enemy. Further attempts of the enemy during the night of the 3rd to advance from the woods west of St. Julien were frustrated entirely by the fire of our artillery.

During the whole of the 4th the enemy heavily shelled the trenches we had evacuated, quite unaware that they were no longer occupied. So as soon as the retirement was discovered the Germans commenced to entrench opposite our new line and to advance their guns to new positions. Our artillery, assisted by aeroplanes, caused him considerable loss in carrying out these operations.

Up to the morning of the 8th the enemy made attacks at short intervals, covered by gas, on all parts of the line to the east of Ypres, but was everywhere driven back with heavy loss. Throughout the whole period since the first break of the line on the night of April 22nd all the troops in this area had been constantly subjected to violent artillery bombardment from a large mass of guns with an unlimited supply of ammunition. It proved impossible whilst under so vastly superior fire of artillery to dig efficient trenches, or to properly reorganise the line, after the confusion and demoralisation caused by the first great gas surprise and the subsequent almost daily gas attacks. Nor was it until after this date (May 8th) that effective preventatives had been devised and provided. In these circumstances a violent bombardment of nearly the whole of the 5th Corps front broke out at 7 a.m. on the morning of the 8th, which gradually concentrated on the front of the Division between north and south of Frezenberg. This fire completely obliterated the trenches and caused enormous losses.

The artillery bombardment was shortly followed by a heavy infantry attack, before which our line had to give way.

I relate what happened in Sir Herbert Plumer's own words:-

"The right of one Brigade was broken about 10.15 a.m.; then its centre, and then part of the left of the Brigade in the next section to the south. The Princess Patricia's Canadian Light Infantry, however, although suffering very heavily, stuck to their fire or support trenches throughout the day. At this time two battalions were moved to General Headquarters 2nd line astride the Menin road to support and cover the left of their Division.

"At 12.25 p.m. the centre of a Brigade further to the left also broke; its right battalion, however, the 1st Suffolks, which had been refused to cover a gap, still held on and were apparently surrounded and overwhelmed. Meanwhile, three more battalions had been moved up to reinforce, two other battalions were moved up in support to General Headquarters line, and an Infantry Brigade came up to the grounds of Vlamertinghe Chateau in Corps Reserve.

"At 11.30 a.m. a small party of Germans attempted to advance against the left of the British line, but were destroyed by the 2nd Essex Regiment.

"A counter attack was launched at 3.30 p.m. by the 1st York and Lancaster Regiment, 3rd Middlesex Regiment, 2nd East Surrey Regiment, 2nd Royal Dublin Fusiliers and the 1st Royal Warwickshire Regiment. The counter attack reached Frezenberg, but was eventually driven back and held up on a line running about north and south through Verlorenhoek, despite repeated efforts to advance. The 12th London Regiment on the left succeeded at great cost in reaching the original trench line, and did considerable execution with their machine gun.

"The 7th Argyll and Sutherland Highlanders and the 1st East Lancashire Regiment attacked in a north-easterly direction towards Wieltje, and connected the old trench line with the ground gained by the counter-attack, the line being consolidated during the night.

"During the night orders were received that two Cavalry Divisions would be moved up and placed at the disposal of the 5th Corps, and a Territorial Division would be moved up to be used if required.

"On the 9th the Germans again repeated their bombardment. Very heavy shell fire was concentrated for two hours on the trenches of the 2nd Gloucestershire Regiment and 2nd Cameron Highlanders, followed by an infantry attack which was successfully repulsed. The Germans again bombarded the salient, and a further attack in the afternoon succeeded in occupying 150 yards of trench. The Gloucesters counter-attacked, but suffered heavily, and the attack failed. The salient being very exposed to shell fire from both flanks, as well as in front, it was deemed advisable not to attempt to retake the trench at night, and a retrenchment was therefore dug across it.

"At 3 p.m. the enemy started to shell the whole front of the centre Division, and it was reported that the right Brigade of this Division was being heavily punished, but continued to maintain its line.

"The trenches of the Brigades on the left centre were also heavily shelled during the day and attacked by infantry. Both attacks were repulsed.

"On the 10th instant the trenches on either side of the Menin – Ypres Road were shelled very severely all the morning. The 2nd Cameron Highlanders, 9th Royal Scots, and the 3rd and 4th King's Royal Rifles, however, repulsed an attack made, under cover of gas, with heavy loss. Finally, when the trenches had been practically destroyed and a large number of the garrison buried, the 3rd King's Royal Rifles and 4th Rifle Brigade fell back to the trenches immediately west of Bellewaarde Wood. So heavy had been the shell fire that the proposal to join up the line with a switch through the wood had to be abandoned, the trees broken by the shells forming an impassable entanglement.

"After a comparatively quiet night and morning (10th-11th) the hostile artillery fire was concentrated on the trenches of the 2nd Cameron Highlanders and 1st Argyll and Sutherland Highlanders at a slightly more northern point than on the previous day. The Germans attacked in force and gained a footing in part of the trenches, but were promptly ejected by a supporting company of the 9th Royal Scots. After a second short artillery bombardment the Germans again attacked about 4.15 p.m., but were again repulsed by rifle and machine-gun fire. A third bombardment followed, and this time the Germans succeeded in gaining a trench – or rather what was left of it – a local counter-attack failing. However, during the night the enemy were again driven out. The trench by this time being practically non-existent, the garrison found it untenable under the very heavy shell fire the enemy brought to bear upon it, and the trench was evacuated. Twice more did the German snipers creep back into it, and twice more they were ejected. Finally, a retrenchment was made, cutting off the salient which had been contested throughout the day. It was won owing solely to the superior weight and number of the enemy's guns, but both our infantry and our artillery took a very heavy toll of the enemy, and the ground lost has proved of little use to the enemy.

"On the remainder of the front the day passed comparatively quietly, though most parts of the line underwent intermittent shelling by gun's of various calibres.

"With the assistance of the Royal Flying Corps the 31st Heavy Battery scored a direct hit on a German gun, and the North Midland Heavy Battery got on to some German howitzers with great success.

"With the exception of another very heavy burst of shell fire against the right Division early in the morning, the 12th passed uneventfully.

"On the night of the 12th-13th the line was re-organised, the centre Division retiring into Army Reserve to rest, and their places being taken in the trenches by the two Cavalry Divisions; the Artillery and Engineers of the centre Division forming with them what was known as the 'Cavalry Force' under the command of General De Lisle.

"On the 13th the various reliefs having been completed without incident, the heaviest bombardment yet experienced broke out at 4.30 a.m., and continued with little intermission throughout the day. At about 7.45 a.m. the

Cavalry Brigade astride the railway, having suffered very severely, and their trenches having been obliterated, fell back about 800 yards. The North Somerset Yeomanry on the right of the Brigade, although also suffering severely, hung on to their trenches throughout the day, and actually advanced and attacked the enemy with the bayonet. The Brigade on its right also maintained its position; as did also the Cavalry Division, except the left squadron which, when reduced to sixteen men, fell back. The 2nd Essex Regiment, realising the situation, promptly charged and retook the trench, holding it till relieved by the Cavalry. Meanwhile a counter-attack by two Cavalry Brigades was launched at 2.30 p.m., and succeeded in spite of very heavy shrapnel and rifle fire, in regaining the original line of trenches, turning out the Germans who had entered it, and in some cases pursuing them for some distance. But a very heavy shell fire was again opened on them, and they were again compelled to retire to an irregular line in rear, principally the craters of shell holes. The enemy in their counter-attack suffered very severe losses.

"The fighting in other parts of the line was little less severe. The 1st East Lancashire Regiment were shelled out of their trenches, but their support company and the 2nd Essex Regiment, again acting on their own initiative, won them back. The enemy penetrated into the farm at the north-east corner of the line, but the 1st Rifle Brigade, after a severe struggle, expelled them. The 1st Hampshire Regiment also repelled an attack, and killed every German who got within fifty yards of their trenches. The 5th London Regiment, despite very heavy casualties, maintained their position unfalteringly. At the southern end of the line the left Brigade was once again heavily shelled, as indeed was the whole front. At the end of a very hard day's fighting our line remained in its former position, with the exception of the short distance lost by one Cavalry Division. Later, the line was pushed forward, and a new line was dug in a less exposed position, slightly in rear of that originally held. The night passed quietly.

"Working parties of from 1,200 to 1,800 men have been found every night by a Territorial Division and other unit for work on rear lines of defence, in addition to the work performed by the garrisons in reconstructing the front line trenches which were, daily destroyed by shell fire.

"The work performed by the Royal Flying Corps has been invaluable. Apart from the hostile aeroplanes actually destroyed, our airmen have prevented a great deal of aerial reconnaissance by the enemy, and have registered a large number of targets with our artillery.

"There have been many cases of individual gallantry. As instances may be given the following:-

"During one of the heavy attacks made against our infantry gas was seen rolling forward from the enemy's trenches. Private Lynn of the 2nd Lancashire Fusiliers at once rushed to the machine gun without waiting to adjust his respirator. Single-handed he kept his gun in action the whole time the gas was rolling over, actually hoisting it on the parapet to get a better field of fire. Although nearly suffocated by the gas, he poured a stream of lead into the advancing enemy and checked their attack. He was carried to his dug-out, but, hearing another attack was imminent, he tried to get back to his gun. Twenty-four hours later he died in great agony from the effects of the gas.

"A young subaltern in a cavalry regiment went forward alone one afternoon to reconnoitre. He got into a wood, 1,200 yards in front of our lines, which he found occupied by Germans, and came back with the information that the enemy had evacuated a trench and were digging another – information which proved most valuable to the artillery as well as to his own unit.

"A patrol of two officers and a non-commissioned officer of the 1st Cambridgeshires went out one night to reconnoitre a German trench 350 yards away. Creeping along the parapet of the trench, they heard sounds indicating the presence of six or seven of the enemy. Further on they heard deep snores, apparently proceeding from a dug-out immediately beneath them. Although they knew that the garrison of the trench outnumbered them, they decided to procure an identification. Unfortunately, in pulling out a clasp knife with which to cut off the sleeper's identity disc, one of the officer's revolvers went off. A conversation in agitated whispers broke out in the German trench, but the patrol crept safely away, the garrison being too startled to fire.

"Despite the very severe shelling to which the troops had been subjected, which obliterated trenches and caused very many casualties, the spirit of all ranks remains excellent. The enemy's losses, particularly on the 10th and 13th, have unquestionably been serious. On the latter day they evacuated trenches (in face of the cavalry counter-attack) in which were afterwards found quantities of equipment and some of their own wounded. The enemy have been seen stripping our dead, and on three occasions men in khaki have been seen advancing."

The fight went on by the exchange of desultory shell and rifle fire, but without any remarkable incident until, the morning of May 24th. During this period, however, the French on our left had attained considerable success. On the 15th instant they captured Steenstraate and the trenches in Het Sas, and on the 16th they drove the enemy headlong over the canal, finding two thousand German dead. On the 17th they made a substantial advance on the east side of the canal, and on the 20th they repelled a German counter-attack, making a further advance in the same direction, and taking one hundred prisoners.

On the early morning of the 24th a violent outburst of gas against nearly the whole front was followed by heavy shell fire, and the most determined attack was delivered against our position east of Ypres.

The hour the attack commenced was 2.45 a.m. A large proportion of the men were asleep, and the attack was too sudden to give them time to put on their respirators.

The 2nd Royal Irish and the 9th Argyll and Sutherland Highlanders, overcome by gas fumes, were driven out of a farm held in front of the left Division, and this the enemy proceeded to hold and fortify.

All attempts to retake this farm during the day failed, and during the night of the 24th-25th the General Officer Commanding the left Division decided to take up a new line which, although slightly in rear of the old one, he considered to be a much better position. This operation was successfully carried out.

Throughout the day the whole line was subjected to one of the most violent artillery attacks which it had ever undergone; and the 5th Corps and the Cavalry Divisions engaged had to fight hard to maintain their positions. On the following day, however, the line was consolidated, joining the right of the French at the same place as before, and passing through Wieltje (which was strongly fortified) in a southerly direction on to Hooge, where the Cavalry have since strongly occupied the chateau, and pushed our line further east.

5. In pursuance of a promise which I made to the French Commander-in-Chief to support an attack which his troops were making on the 9th May between the right of my line and Arras, I directed Sir Douglas Haig to carry out on that date an attack on the German trenches in the neighbourhood of Rougebanc (northwest of Fromelles) by the 4th Corps, and between Neuve Chapelle and Givenchy, by the 1st and Indian Corps.

The bombardment of the enemy's positions commenced at 5 a.m.

Half-an-hour later the 8th Division of the 4th Corps captured the first line of German trenches about Rougebanc, and some detachments seized a few localities beyond this line. It was soon found, however, that the position was much stronger than had been anticipated, and that a more extensive artillery preparation was necessary to crush the resistance offered by his numerous fortified posts.

Throughout the 9th and 10th repeated efforts were made to make further progress. Not only was this found to be impossible, but the violence of the enemy's machine-gun fire from his posts on the flanks rendered the captured trenches so difficult to hold that all the units of the 4th Corps had to retire to their original position by the morning of the 10th.

The 1st and Indian Divisions south of Neuve Chapelle met with no greater success, and on the evening of the 10th I sanctioned Sir Douglas Haig's proposal to concentrate all our available resources on the southern point of attack.

The 7th Division was moved round from the 4th Corps area to support this attack, and I directed the General Officer Commanding the First Army to delay it long enough to ensure a powerful and deliberate artillery preparation.

The operations of the 9th and 10th formed part of a general plan of attack which the Allies were conjointly conducting on a line extending from the north of Arras to the south of Armentieres; and, although immediate progress was not made during this time by the British forces, their attack assisted in securing the brilliant successes attained by the French forces on their right, not only by holding the enemy in their front but by drawing off a part of the German reinforcements which were coming up to support their forces east of Arras.

It was decided that the attack should be resumed on the night of the 12th instant, but the weather continued very dull and misty, interfering much with artillery observation. Orders were finally issued, therefore, for the action to commence on the night of the 15th instant.

On the 15th May I moved the Canadian Division into the 1st Corps area and placed them at the disposal of Sir Douglas Haig.

The infantry of the Indian Corps and the 2nd Division of the 1st Corps advanced to the attack of the enemy's trenches which extended from Richebourg L'Avoué in a south-westerly direction.

Before daybreak the 2nd Division had succeeded in capturing two lines of the enemy's trenches, but the Indian Corps were unable to make any progress owing to the strength of the enemy's defences in the neighbourhood of Richebourg L'Avoué.

At daybreak the 7th Division, on the right of the 2nd, advanced to the attack, and by 7 a.m. had entrenched themselves on a line running nearly North and South, half-way between their original trenches and La Quinque Rue, having cleared and captured several lines of the enemy's trenches, including a number of fortified posts.

As it was found impossible for the Indian Corps to make any progress in face of the enemy's defences Sir Douglas Haig directed the attack to be suspended at this point and ordered the Indian Corps to form a defensive flank.

The remainder of the day was spent in securing and consolidating positions which had been won, and endeavouring to unite the inner flanks of the 7th and 2nd Divisions, which were separated by trenches and posts strongly held by the enemy.

Various attempts which were made throughout the day to secure this object had not succeeded at nightfall in driving the enemy back.

The German communications leading to the rear of their positions were systematically shelled throughout the night.

About two hundred prisoners were captured on the 16th instant.

Fighting was resumed at daybreak; and by 11 o'clock the 7th Division had made a considerable advance, capturing several more of the enemy's trenches. The task allotted to this Division was to push on in the direction of Rue D'Ouvert, Chateau St. Roch and Canteleux.

The 2nd Division was directed to push off when the situation permitted towards the Rue de Marais and Violaines.

The Indian Division was ordered to extend its front far enough to enable it to keep touch with the left of the 2nd Division when they advanced.

On this day I gave orders for the 51st (Highland) Division to move into the neighbourhood of Estaires to be ready to support the operations of the First Army.

At about noon the enemy was driven out of the trenches and posts which he occupied between the two Divisions, the inner flanks of which were thus enabled to join hands.

By nightfall the 2nd and 7th Divisions had made good progress, the area of captured ground being considerably extended to the right by the successful operations of the latter.

The state of the weather on the morning of the 18th much hindered an effective artillery bombardment, and further attacks had, consequently, to be postponed.

Infantry attacks, were made throughout the line in the course of the afternoon and evening; but, although not very much progress was made, the line was advanced to the La Quinque Rue – Bethune Road before nightfall.

On the 19th May the 7th and 2nd Divisions were drawn out of the line to rest. The 7th Division was relieved by the Canadian Division and the 2nd Division by the 51st (Highland) Division.

Sir Douglas Haig placed the Canadian and 51st Divisions, together with the artillery of the 2nd and 7th Division, under the command of Lieutenant-General Alderson, whom he directed to conduct the operations which had hitherto been carried on by the General Officer Commanding First Corps; and he directed the 7th Division to remain in Army Reserve. During the night of the 19th-20th a small post of the enemy in front of La Quinque Rue was captured.

During the night of the 20th-21st the Canadian Division brilliantly carried on the excellent progress made by the 7th Division by seizing several of the enemy's trenches and pushing forward their whole line several hundred yards. A number of prisoners and some machine guns were captured.

On the 22nd instant the 51st (Highland) Division was attached to the Indian Corps, and the General Officer Commanding the Indian Corps took charge of the operations at La Quinque Rue, Lieutenant-General Alderson with the Canadians conducting the operations to the north of that place.

On this day the Canadian Division extended their line slightly to the right and repulsed three very severe hostile counter attacks.

On the 24th and 25th May the 47th Division (2nd London Territorial) succeeded in taking some more of the enemy's trenches and making good the ground gained to the east and north. I had now reason to consider that the battle, which was commenced by the First Army on the 9th May and renewed on the 16th, having attained for the moment the immediate object I had in view, should not be further actively proceeded with; and I gave orders to Sir Douglas Haig to curtail his artillery attack and to strengthen and consolidate the ground he had won.

In the battle of Festubert above described the enemy was driven from a position which was strongly entrenched and fortified, and ground was won on a front of four miles to an average depth of 600 yards.

The enemy is known to have suffered very heavy losses, and in the course of the battle 785 prisoners and 10 machine guns were captured. A number of machine guns were also destroyed by our fire.

During the period under report the Army under my command has taken over trenches occupied by some other French Divisions.

I am much indebted to General D'Urbal, commanding the 10th French Army, for the valuable and efficient support received throughout the battle of Festubert from three groups of French 75 centimetre guns.

In spite of very unfavourable weather conditions, rendering observation most difficult, our own artillery did excellent work throughout the battle.

6. During the important operations described above, which were carried on by the First and Second Armies, the 3rd Corps was particularly active in making demonstrations with a view to holding the enemy in its front and preventing reinforcements reaching the threatened areas. As an instance of the successful attempts to deceive the enemy in this respect it may be mentioned that on the afternoon of the 24th instant a bombardment of about an hour was carried out by the 6th Division with the object of distracting attention from the Ypres salient. Considerable damage was done to the enemy's parapets and wire; and that the desired impression was produced on the

enemy is evident from the German wireless news on that day, which stated "West of Lille the English attempts to attack were nipped in the bud." In previous reports I have drawn attention to the enterprise displayed by the troops of the 3rd Corps in conducting night reconnaissances, and to the courage and resource shown by officers' and other patrols in the conduct of these minor operations.

Throughout the period under report this display of activity has been very marked all along the 3rd Corps front, and much valuable information and intelligence have been collected.

7. I have much pleasure in again expressing my warm appreciation of the admirable manner in which all branches of the Medical Services now in the field, under the direction of Surgeon-General Sir Arthur Sloggett, have met and dealt with the many difficult situations resulting from the operations during the last two months.

The medical units at the front were frequently exposed to the enemy's fire, and many casualties occurred amongst the officers of the regimental Medical Service. At all times the officers, non-commissioned officers and men, and nurses carried out their duties with fearless bravery and great devotion to the welfare of the sick and wounded.

The evacuation of casualties from the front to the Base and to England was expeditiously accomplished by the Administrative Medical Staffs at the front and on the Lines of Communication. All ranks employed in units of evacuation and in Base Hospitals have shown the highest skill and untiring zeal and energy in alleviating the condition of those who passed through their hands.

The whole organisation of the Medical Services reflects the highest credit on all concerned.

8. I have once more to call your Lordship's attention to the part taken by the Royal Flying Corps in the general progress of the campaign, and I wish particularly to mention the invaluable assistance they rendered in the operations described in this report, under the able direction of Major-General Sir David Henderson.

The Royal Flying Corps is becoming more and more an indispensable factor in combined operations. In co-operation with the artillery, in particular, there has been continuous improvement both in the methods and in the technical material employed. The ingenuity and technical skill displayed by the officers of the Royal Flying Corps, in effecting this improvement, have been most marked.

Since my last despatch there has been a considerable increase both in the number and in the activity of German aeroplanes in our front. During this period there have been more than sixty combats in the air, in which not one

British aeroplane has been lost. As these fights take place almost invariably over or behind the German lines, only one hostile aeroplane has been brought down in our territory. Five more, however, have been definitely wrecked behind their own lines, and many have been chased down and forced to land in most unsuitable ground.

In spite of the opposition of hostile aircraft, and the great number of anti-aircraft guns employed by the enemy, air reconnaissance has been carried out with regularity and accuracy. I desire to bring to your Lordship's notice the assistance given by the French Military Authorities, and in particular by General Hirschauer, Director of the French Aviation Service, and his assistants, Colonel Bottieaux and Colonel Stammler, in the supply of aeronautical material, without which the efficiency of the Royal Flying Corps would have been seriously impaired.

9. In this despatch I wish again to remark upon the exceptionally good work done throughout this campaign by the Army Service Corps and by the Army Ordnance Department, not only in the field, but also on the Lines of Communication and at the Base Ports.

To foresee and meet the requirements in the matter of Ammunition, Stores, Equipment, Supplies and Transport has entailed on the part of the officers, non-commissioned officers and men of these Services a sustained effort which has never been relaxed since the beginning of the war, and which has been rewarded by the most conspicuous success.

The close co-operation of the Railway Transport Department, whose excellent work, in combination with the French Railway Staff, has ensured the regularity of the maintenance services, has greatly contributed to this success.

The degree of efficiency to which these Services have been brought was well demonstrated in the course of the Second Battle of Ypres.

The roads between Poperinghe and Ypres, over which transport, supply and ammunition columns had to pass, were continually searched by hostile heavy artillery during the day and night; whilst the passage of the canal through the town of Ypres, and along the roads east of that town, could only be effected under most difficult and dangerous conditions as regards hostile shell fire. Yet, throughout the whole five or six weeks during which these conditions prevailed the work was carried on with perfect order and efficiency.

10. Since the date of my last report some Divisions of the "New" Army have arrived in this country.

I made a close inspection of one Division, formed up on parade, and have at various times seen several units belonging to others.

These Divisions have as yet had very little experience in actual fighting; but, judging from all I have seen, I am of opinion that they ought to prove a valuable addition to any fighting force. As regards the Infantry, their physique is excellent, whilst their bearing and appearance on parade reflects great credit on the officers and staffs responsible for their training. The units appear to be thoroughly well officered and commanded. The equipment is in good order and efficient.

Several units of artillery have been tested in the firing line behind the trenches, and I hear very good reports of them. Their shooting has been extremely good, and they are quite fit to take their places in the line.

The Pioneer Battalions have created a very favourable impression, the officers being keen and ingenious and the men of good physique and good diggers. The equipment is suitable. The training in field works has been good, but, generally speaking, they require the assistance of Regular Royal Engineers as regards laying out of important works. Man for man in digging the battalions should do practically the same amount of work as an equivalent number of sappers, and in rivetting, entanglement, etc., a great deal more than the ordinary infantry battalions.

11. During the months of April and May several divisions of the Territorial Force joined the Army under my command.

Experience has shown that these troops have now reached a standard of efficiency which enables them to be usefully employed in complete divisional units.

Several divisions have been so employed; some in the trenches, others in the various offensive and defensive operations reported in this despatch.

In whatever kind of work these units have been engaged, they have all borne an active and distinguished part, and have proved themselves thoroughly reliable and efficient.

The opinion I have expressed in former despatches as to the use and value of the Territorial Force has been fully justified by recent events.

12. The Prime Minister was kind enough to accept an invitation from me to visit the Army in France, and arrived at my Headquarters on the 30th May.

Mr. Asquith made an exhaustive tour of the front, the hospitals and all the administrative arrangements made by Corps Commanders for the health and comfort of men behind the trenches.

It was a great encouragement to all ranks to see the Prime Minister amongst them; and the eloquent words which on several occasions he addressed to the troops had a most powerful and beneficial effect.

As I was desirous that the French Commander-in-Chief should see something of the British troops, I asked General Joffre to be kind enough to inspect a division on parade.

The General accepted my invitation, and on the 27th May he inspected the 7th Division, under the command of Major-General H. de la P. Gough, C.B., which was resting behind the trenches.

General Joffre subsequently expressed to me in a letter the pleasure it gave him to see the British troops, and his appreciation of their appearance on parade. He requested me to make this known to all ranks.

The Moderator of the Church of Scotland, the Right Reverend Dr. Wallace Williamson, Dean of the Order of the Thistle, visited the Army in France between the 7th and 17th May, and made a tour of the Scottish regiments with excellent results.

13. In spite of the constant strain put upon them by the arduous nature of the fighting which they are called upon to carry out daily and almost hourly, the spirit which animates all ranks of the Army in France remains high and confident.

They meet every demand made upon them with the utmost cheerfulness.

This splendid spirit is particularly manifested by the men in hospital, even amongst those who are mortally wounded.

The invariable question which comes from lips hardly able to utter a sound is, "How are things going on at the front?"

14. In conclusion, I desire to bring to Your Lordship's special notice the valuable services rendered by General Sir Douglas Haig in his successful handling of the troops of the First Army throughout the Battle of Festubert, and Lieutenant-General Sir Herbert Plumer for his fine defence of Ypres throughout the arduous and difficult operations during the latter part of April and the month of May.

I have the honour to be,
Your Lordship's most obedient Servant,
J.D.P. FRENCH,
Field-Marshal, Commanding-in-Chief,
The British Army in the Field.

SIR JOHN FRENCH'S DESPATCH OF 15 OCTOBER 1915

The Battle of Loos

War Office,
1st November, 1915.

The following despatch has been received by the Secretary of State for War from the Field-Marshal Commanding-in-Chief, The British Army in France:-

General Headquarters,
British Army in France.
15*th October,* 1915.

MY LORD,

I have the honour to report the operations of the Forces under my command since the date of those described in my last despatch dated 15th June, 1915.

1. Those of the greatest importance took place during the last days of the period under report. Nevertheless, the Army under my command was constantly engaged throughout the whole time in enterprises which, although not securing the same important results, have yet had considerable influence on the course of events.

2. On 2nd June the enemy made a final offensive in the Ypres salient with the object of gaining our trenches and position at Hooge. The attack was most determined and was preceded by a severe bombardment. A gallant defence was made by troops of the 3rd Cavalry Division and 1st Indian Cavalry Division, and our position was maintained throughout. During the first weeks of June the front of the Second Army was extended to the North as far as the village of Boesinghe.

3. After the conclusion of the Battle of Festubert the troops of the First Army were engaged in several minor operations.

By an attack delivered on the evening of 15th June after a prolonged bombardment the 1st Canadian Brigade obtained possession of the German front line trenches north-east of Givenchy, but were unable to retain them owing to their flanks being too much exposed.

4. On 16th June an attack was carried out by the 5th Corps on the Belle-waarde Ridge, east of Ypres.

The enemy's front line was captured, many of his dead and wounded being found in the trenches.

The troops, pressing forward, gained ground as far East as the Bellewaarde Lake, but found themselves unable to maintain this advanced position. They were, however, successful in securing and consolidating the ground won during the first part of the attack, on a front of a thousand yards, including the advanced portion of the enemy's salient north of the Ypres – Menin Road.

During this action the fire of the artillery was most effective, the prisoners testifying to its destructiveness and accuracy. It also prevented the delivery of counter attacks, which were paralysed at the outset.

Over two hundred prisoners were taken, besides some machine-guns, trench material and gas apparatus.

Holding attacks by the neighbouring 2nd and 6th Corps were successful in helping the main attack, whilst the 36th French Corps co-operated very usefully with artillery fire on Pilkem. Near Hill 60 the 15th Infantry Brigade made four bombing atacks, gaining and occupying about fifty yards of trench.

On 6th July a small attack was made by the 11th Infantry Brigade on a German salient between Boesinghe and Ypres, which resulted in the capture of a frontage of about 500 yards of trench and a number of prisoners.

In the course of this operation it was necessary to move a gun of the 135th Battery, Royal Field Artillery, into the front line to destroy an enemy sap-head. To reach its position the gun had to be taken over a high canal embankment, rafted over the canal under fire, pulled up a bank with a slope of nearly 45 degrees, and then dragged over three trenches and a sky line to its position seventy yards from the German lines. This was carried out without loss.

This incident is of minor importance in itself, but I quote it as an example of the daily difficulties which officers and men in the trenches are constantly called upon to overcome, and of the spirit of initiative and resource which is so marked a feature amongst them. From the 10th to the 12th July the enemy made attempts, after heavy shelling, to recapture the lost portion of their line; but our artillery, assisted by that of the French on our left, prevented any serious assault from being delivered. Minor attacks were constant, but were easily repulsed by the garrison of our trenches.

On 19th July an enemy's redoubt at the western end of the Hooge defences was successfully mined and destroyed, and a small portion of the enemy's trenches was captured.

5. Since my last despatch a new device has been adopted by the enemy for driving burning liquid into our trenches with a strong jet.

Thus supported, an attack was made on the trenches of the Second Army at Hooge, on the Menin Road, early on 30th July. Most of the infantry occupying these trenches were driven back, but their retirement was due far more to the surprise and temporary confusion caused by the burning liquid than to the actual damage inflicted.

Gallant endeavours were made by repeated counter attacks to recapture the lost section of trenches. These, however, proving unsuccessful and costly, a new line of trenches was consolidated a short distance further back.

Attacks made by the enemy at the same time west of Bellewaarde Lake were repulsed.

On 9th August these losses were brilliantly regained; owing to a successful attack carried out by the 6th Division. This attack was very well executed and resulted in the recapture, with small casualties, not only of the whole of the lost trenches, but, in addition, of four hundred yards of German trench north of the Menin Road.

At the end of this engagement it was estimated that between four and five hundred German dead were lying on the battlefield.

Valuable help was rendered by two batteries of French artillery lent by General Hely d'Oissel, commanding 36th French Corps.

6. From the conclusion of the above-mentioned operations until the last week in September there was relative quiet along the whole of the British line, except at those points where the normal conditions of existence comprised occasional shelling or constant mine and bomb warfare. In these trying forms of encounter all ranks have constantly shown the greatest enterprise and courage, and have consistently maintained the upper hand.

The close accord and co-operation which has always existed between the Commander-in-Chief of our Allies and myself has been maintained, and I have had constant meetings with General Joffre, who has kept me informed of his views and intentions, and explained the successive methods by which he hopes to attain his ultimate object.

After full discussion of the military situation a decision was arrived at for joint action, in which I acquiesced.

It was arranged that we should make a combined attack from certain points of the Allied line during the last week in September.

The reinforcements I have received enabled me to comply with several requests which General Joffre has made that I should take over additional portions of the French line.

7. In fulfilment of the rôle assigned to it in these operations the Army under my command attacked the enemy on the morning of the 25th September.

The main attack was delivered by the 1st and 4th Corps between the La Bassée Canal on the north and a point of the enemy's line opposite the village of Grenay on the south.

At the same time a secondary attack, designed with the object of distracting the enemy's attention and holding his troops to their ground, was made by the 5th Corps on Bellewaarde Farm, situated to the east of Ypres. Subsidiary attacks with similar objects were delivered by the 3rd and Indian Corps north of the La Bassée Canal and along the whole front of the Second Army.

The object of the secondary attack by the 5th Corps was most effectively achieved, for not only was the enemy contained on that front, but we have reason to believe that reserves were hurried toward that point of the line.

The attack was made at daybreak by the 3rd and 14th Divisions, and at first the greater part of the enemy's front line was taken; but, owing to the powerful artillery fire concentrated against them, the troops were unable to retain the ground, and had to return to their original trenches toward nightfall. The 5th Corps succeeded, however, in capturing two officers and 138 other prisoners.

Similar demonstrations with equally good results were made along the whole front of the Second Army.

With the same object in view, those units of the First Army occupying the line north of the Bethune – La Bassée Canal were detailed to carry out some minor operations.

Portions of the 1st Corps assaulted the enemy's trenches at Givenchy. The Indian Corps atacked the Moulin du Piétre; while the 3rd Corps was directed against the trenches at Le Bridoux.

These attacks started at daybreak and were at first successful all along the line. Later in the day the enemy brought up strong reserves, and after hard fighting and variable fortunes the troops engaged in this part of the line reoccupied their original trenches at nightfall. They succeeded admirably, however, in fulfilling the rôle allotted to them, and in holding large numbers of the enemy away from the main attack.

The 8th Division of the 3rd Corps and the Meerut Division of the Indian Corps were principally engaged in this part of the line.

On the front of the Third Army subsidiary operations of a similar nature were successfully carried out.

The Wing of the Royal Flying Corps attached to this Army performed valuable work by undertaking distant flights behind the enemy's lines and by successfully blowing up railways, wrecking trains and damaging stations on his line of communication by means of bomb attacks.

Valuable assistance was rendered by Vice-Admiral Bacon and a squadron of His Majesty's ships operating off Zeebrugge and Ostend.

8. The general plan of the main attack on the 25th September was as follows:-

In co-operation with an offensive movement by the 10th French Army on our right, the 1st and 4th Corps were to attack the enemy from a point opposite the little mining village of Grenay on the south to the La Bassée Canal on the north. The Vermelles – Hulluch Road was to be the dividing line between the two Corps, the 4th Corps delivering the right attack, the 1st Corps the left.

In view of the great length of line along which the British troops were operating it was necessary to keep a strong reserve in my own hand. The 11th Corps, consisting of the Guards, the 21st and the 24th Divisions, were detailed for this purpose.

This reserve was the more necessary owing to the fact that the 10th French Army had to postpone its attack until one o'clock in the day; and, further, that the Corps operating on the French left had to be directed in a more or less south-easterly direction, involving, in case of our success, a considerable gap in our line.

To ensure, however, the speedy and effective support to the 1st and 4th Corps in the case of their success, the 21st and 24th Divisions passed the night of the 24th/25th on the line Beuvry (to the east of Bethune) – Noeux les Mines. The Guards Division was in the neighbourhood of Lillers on the same night.

I also directed the General Officer Commanding Second Army to draw the 28th Division back to Bailleul and to hold it in readiness to meet unexpected eventualities.

The British Cavalry Corps, less 3rd Cavalry Division, under General Fanshawe, was posted in the neighbourhood of St. Pol and Bailleul les Pernes; and the Indian Cavalry Corps, under General Rimington, at Doullens; both in readiness to co-operate with the French Cavalry in exploiting any success which might be attained by the combined French and British Forces. Plans for effective co-operation were fully arranged between the Cavalry Commanders of both Armies.

The 3rd Cavalry Division, less one brigade, was assigned to the General Officer Commanding First Army as a reserve, and moved into the area of the 4th Corps on the 21st and 22nd September.

9. Opposite the front of the main line of attack the distance between the enemy's trenches and our own varied from about 100 to 500 yards.

The country over which the advance took place is open and overgrown with long grass and self-sown crops.

From the canal southward our trenches and those of the enemy ran, roughly, parallel up an almost imperceptible rise to the south-west.

A portrait of John French, 1st Earl of Ypres. He became Chief of the Imperial General Staff on 15 March 1912, and was promoted to Field Marshal on 3 June 1913. (*US Library of Congress*)

Field Marshal Sir John French pictured with ADCs at his General Headquarters. French died on 22 May 1925, aged 72. An estimated 7,000 people filed past his coffin during the first two hours it lay in state, many of them veterans of the retreat from Mons. Haig, Robertson, Hamilton and Smith-Dorrien were pall bearers at his funeral at Westminster Abbey – the first of a major First World War leader. (*HMP*)

A portrait of Field Marshal Douglas Haig. Earl Haig died in 1928 and was accorded a state funeral in Westminster Abbey. Many men who had served under him in the First World War volunteered to line the route of the funeral procession. He was then buried at Dryburgh Abbey, close to Bemersyde. (*HMP*)

Field Marshal Haig reviewing troops in Canterbury, Kent. Statues of Earl Haig on horseback can be found in Whitehall in London, on the Castle Esplanade in Edinburgh and at Montreuil in France, where once he had his headquarters. (*Courtesy of the James Luto Collection*)

The men of 'A' Company, 4th Battalion, Royal Fusiliers (9th Brigade, 3rd Division) pictured resting in Grand Place at Mons, Belgium, on 22 August 1914 – the day before the Battle of Mons. Shortly after this picture was taken the company moved into position at Nimy on the bank of the Mons-Condé Canal. (*HMP*)

The so-called 'First Shot' Memorial near Mons. On 22 August 1914, at this spot on the main Brussels-Mons Road, four and a half miles north-east of Mons, the first crack of a British rifle fired in anger during the First World War was heard. It is often stated that the first shot was fired by Trooper E. Thomas, of 'C' Squadron 4th (Royal Irish) Dragoon Guards. (*HMP*)

The standard Commonwealth War Graves Commission headstone of Private John Parr of the 4th Battalion Middlesex Regiment in St Symphorien Military Cemetery near Mons, Belgium. Private Parr was the first British soldier to die in the First World War. It is stated that Parr was born in 1898 in Church End, North London, and was therefore only sixteen at the time of his death. (*HMP*)

An artist's depiction of 24-year-old Lance Corporal Frederick William Holmes, of the 2nd Battalion, The King's Own Yorkshire Light Infantry, during the action for which he was awarded the Victoria Cross in the fighting at Le Cateau on 26 August 1914. Under very heavy fire Lance Corporal Holmes carried a wounded man from the hastily dug trenches, and later mounted one of the leading horses of a gun team, when the driver had been wounded, to assist in driving the gun out of action. (*HMP*)

A photograph of the ruined battlefield of Festubert which was taken in the spring of 1919. Despite the time that has passed since the battle fought here in 1915, the ground still shows the scars from the heavy fighting. (*HMP*)

Men of the 7th (City of London) Battalion London Regiment ('The Shiny Seventh'), being led forward by Sergeant Hayward during the afternoon of Sunday, 16 May 1915, the second day of the Battle of Festubert. Hayward had received orders to reinforce a communication trench captured from the Germans near Festubert earlier in the day. On reaching the trench the British soldiers proceeded along it for about a mile, at which point orders were then given to attack a neighbouring farmhouse and occupy an orchard adjoining it. As they emerged from cover the Germans opened fire upon them with machine-guns, besides hurling grenades. In spite of the heavy fire, Hayward and his men crossed the orchard until further advance was held up by barbed wire. Taking cover, they held their ground for some time, but were eventually obliged to retire. Hayward was awarded the DCM. (*HMP*)

British troops advancing across No Man's Land through a cloud of poison gas, as viewed from the trench they have just left, during the Battle of Loos, 25 September 1915. This remarkable photograph was taken by a soldier of the London Rifle Brigade from a front line trench during the first British use of poison gas. The wind blew back some of the gas towards the British trenches. (*HMP*)

Fighting in the Ypres Salient. The men of the Liverpool Scottish and the Honourable Artillery Company (HAC) during the attack on Y Wood, 16 June 1915. The First Attack on Bellewaarde, sometimes referred to as The Battle of Hooge or Menin Road, was fought in an area between the Menin Road and the Ypres-Roulers railway line. The German front line of the Ypres Salient ran along the edge of Y Wood. The action began with a highly accurate artillery bombardment which commenced at 02.50 hours on 16 June. When it stopped at 04.15 hours, 7th Brigade advanced on the German line. This image was taken by F.A. Fyfe, a bomber with the 10th Liverpool Scottish, at 06.00 hours on the 16th. It shows a detachment of the 1st Battalion HAC taking cover under the parapet of the German front line trench. The flag in the centre is one of those put up to show that the enemy trench had been captured and that the troops were going on. (*HMP*)

The original caption to this picture states that it shows 'men of the New Army resting whilst en route to the front'. Also referred to as 'Kitchener's Army', this was an (initially) all-volunteer army formed in the United Kingdom following the outbreak of hostilities in the First World War. It was created on the recommendation of Lord Kitchener, the then Secretary of State for War. (*HMP*)

The calm before the storm. Troops pictured waiting, some still asleep, in a support trench shortly before Zero Hour near Beaumont Hamel on the first day of the Battle of the Somme. (*HMP*)

The 103rd (Tyneside Irish) Brigade, part of the 34th Division, pictured advancing from the Tara-Usna Line to attack the village of La Boisselle on the morning of 1 July 1916. The 34th Division suffered heavier losses than any other British division that day. *(HMP)*

One of the trenches with which the fighting on the Western Front has become synonymous. Here, soldiers of 'A' Company, 11th Battalion, the Cheshire Regiment, occupy a captured German trench at Ovillers-la-Boisselle on the Somme during July 1916. In this photograph one man keeps sentry duty, looking over the parados and using an improvised fire step cut into the back slope of the trench, while his comrades rest. *(HMP)*

From the Vermelles – Hulluch Road southward the advantage of height is on the enemy's side as far as the Bethune – Lens Road. There the two lines of trenches cross a spur in which the rise culminates, and thence the command lies on the side of the British trenches.

Due east of the intersection of spur and trenches, and a short mile away, stands Loos.

Less than a mile further south-east is Hill 70, which is the summit of the gentle rise in the ground.

Other notable tactical points in our front were:-

"Fosse 8" (a thousand yards south of Auchy), which is a coal mine with a high and strongly defended slag heap.

"The Hohenzollern Redoubt." – A strong work thrust out nearly five hundred yards in front of the German lines and close to our own. It is connected with their front line by three communication trenches abutting into the defences of Fosse 8.

Cité St. Elie. – A strongly defended mining village lying fifteen hundred yards south of Haisnes.

"The Quarries." – Lying half way to the German trenches west of Cité St. Elie.

Hulluch. – A village strung out along a small stream, lying less than half a mile south-east of Cité St. Elie and 3,000 yards north-east of Loos.

Half a mile north of Hill 70 is *"Puits* 14 *bis,"* another coal mine, possessing great possibilities for defence when taken in conjunction with a strong redoubt situated on the northeast side of Hill 70.

10. The attacks of the 1st and 4th Corps were delivered at 6.30 a.m. and were successful all along the line, except just south of the La Bassée Canal.

The enemy met the advance by wild infantry fire of slight intensity, but his artillery fire was accurate and caused considerable casualties.

The 47th Division on the right of the 4th Corps rapidly swung its left forward and occupied the southern outskirts of Loos and a big double slag heap opposite Grenay, known as the Double Crassier. Thence it pushed on, and, by taking possession of the cemetery, the enclosures and chalk pits south of Loos, succeeded in forming a strong defensive flank.

This London Territorial Division acquitted itself most creditably. It was skilfully led and the troops carried out their task with great energy and determination. They contributed largely to our success in this part of the field.

On the left of the 47th Division a Scottish Division of the New Armies (15th Division) assaulted Loos, Hill 70 and Fosse 14 bis.

The attack was admirably delivered, and in a little more than an hour parts of the division occupied Loos and its northern outskirts, Puits 14 bis and

Hill 70, whilst some units had pushed on as far as Cité St. Auguste, a mile east of Hill 70.

The 15th Division carried out its advance with the greatest vigour, in spite of its left flank being exposed, owing to the 1st Division on its left having been checked.

About 1 p.m. the enemy brought up strong reserves, and the advanced portions of the division at Fosse 14 bis and on the far side of Hill 70 were driven in. We had, however, secured the very substantial gain of Loos and the western portion of Hill 70.

11. At 9.30 a.m. I placed the 21st and 24th Divisions at the disposal of the General Officer commanding First Army, who at once ordered the General Officer commanding the 11th Corps to move them up in support of the attacking troops.

Between 11 a.m. and 12 noon the central brigades of these divisions filed past me at Bethune and Noeux les Mines respectively. At 11.30 a.m. the heads of both divisions were within three miles of our original trench line.

As the success of the 47th Division on the right of the 4th Corps caused me less apprehension of a gap in our line near that point, I ordered the Guards Division up to Noeux les Mines, and the 28th Division to move in a southerly direction from Bailleul.

12. The 1st Division, attacking on the left of the 15th, was unable at first to make any headway with its right brigade.

The brigade on its left (the 1st) was, however, able to get forward and penetrated into the outskirts of the village of Hulluch, capturing some gun positions on the way.

The determined advance of this brigade, with its right flank dangerously exposed, was most praiseworthy, and, combined with the action of divisional reserves, was instrumental in causing the surrender of a German detachment some 500 strong which was holding up the advance of the right brigade in the front system of trenches.

The inability of the right of this division to get forward had, however, caused sufficient delay to enable the enemy to collect local reserves behind the strong second line.

The arrangements, the planning and execution of the attack, and the conduct of the troops of the 4th Corps were most efficient and praiseworthy.

13. In the attack of the 1st Corps the 7th Division was directed on the Quarries. The 9th Division was to capture the Hohenzollern Redoubt and then to push on to Fosse 8.

The assault of the 7th Division succeeded at once, and in a very short time they had reached the western edge of the Quarries, Cité St. Elie and even the village of Haisnes, the tendency of the action having been to draw the troops northward.

On the right of the 9th Division the 26th Brigade secured Fosse 8 after heavy fighting, and the 28th Brigade captured the front line of the German trenches east of Vermelles railway. At the latter point the fighting was extremely severe; and this brigade, suffering considerable losses, was driven back to its own trenches.

At nightfall, after a heavy day's fighting and numerous German counter attacks, the line was, roughly, as follows:-

> From the Double Crassier, south of Loos, by the western part of Hill 70, to the western exit of Hulluch; thence by the Quarries and western end of Cité St. Elie, east of Fosse 8, back to our original line.

> Throughout the length of the line heavy fighting was in progress, and our hold on Fosse 8, backed as it is by the strong defences and guns of Auchy, was distinctly precarious.

> Heavy rain fell throughout the day, which was very detrimental to efficient observation of fire and reconnaissance by aircraft.

> In the course of the night 25th/26th September the enemy delivered a series of heavy counter attacks along most of our new front. The majority of these were repulsed with heavy loss; but in parts of the line, notably near the Quarries, our troops were driven back a certain distance. At 6 p.m. the Guards Division arrived at Noeux les Mines, and on the morning of the 26th I placed them at the disposal of the General Officer commanding First Army.

14. The situation at the Quarries, described above, was re-adjusted by an attack of the 7th Division on the afternoon of September 26th; and on that evening very heavy attacks delivered by the enemy were repulsed with severe loss.

On the 4th Corps front attacks on Hulluch and on the redoubt on the east side of Hill 70 were put in operation, but were anticipated by the enemy organising a very strong offensive from that direction. These attacks drove in the advanced troops of the 21st and 24th Divisions, which were then moving forward to attack.

Reports regarding this portion of the action are very conflicting, and it is not possible to form an entirely just appreciation of what occurred in this part of the field.

At nightfall there was no change up to Hill 70, except for a small gain of ground south of Loos. From Hill 70 the line bent sharply back to the north-west as far as Loos – La Bassée Road, which it followed for a thousand yards, bearing thence north-eastward to near the west end of Hulluch. Thence northward it was the same as it had been on the previous night. The night of September 26th/27th was as disturbed as the previous night, for many further counter attacks were made and constant pressure was maintained by the enemy.

A dismounted cavalry brigade was thrown into Loos to form a garrison.

On this day I placed the 28th Division at the disposal of the General Officer commanding First Army.

I regret to say that Major-General Sir Thompson Capper, K.C.M.G., C.B., D.S.O., commanding 7th Division, was severely wounded on the 26th, and died on the morning of the 27th. He was a most distinguished and capable leader, and his loss will be severely felt.

15. Soon after dawn on the 27th it became apparent that the brigade holding Fosse 8 was unable to maintain its position, and eventually it was slowly forced back until at length our front at this point coincided with the eastern portion of the Hohenzollern Redoubt.

I regret to say that during this operation Major-General G.H. Thesiger, C.B., C.M.G., A.D.C., commanding the 9th Division, was killed whilst most gallantly endeavouring to secure the ground which had been won.

In the afternoon of this day the Guards Division, which had taken over part of the line to the north of the 4th Corps, almost restored our former line, bringing it up parallel to and slightly west of the Lens – La Bassée Road.

This Division made a very brilliant and successful attack on Hill 70 in the afternoon. They drove the Germans off the top of the hill, but could not take the redoubt, which is on the north-east slopes below the crest. They also took the Chalk Pit which lies north of Puits 14, and all the adjacent woods, but were unable to maintain themselves in the Puits itself, which was most effectively commanded by well-posted machine-guns.

The 47th Division on the right of the Guards captured a wood further to the south and repulsed a severe hostile counter attack.

The 28th was passed in consolidating the ground gained and in making a certain number of internal moves of divisions, in order to give the troops rest and to enable those units whose casualties had been heavy to refill their ranks with reinforcements.

The 47th Division made a little more ground to the south, capturing one field gun and a few machine-guns.

On the evening of this day the situation remained practically unchanged.

16. The line occupied by the troops of the First Army south of the canal became now very much extended by the salient with which it indented the enemy's line.

The French 10th Army had been very heavily opposed, and I considered that the advance they were able to make did not afford sufficient protection to my right flank.

On representing this to General Joffre he was kind enough to ask the Commander of the northern group of French Armies to render me assistance.

General Foch met these demands in the same friendly spirit which he has always displayed throughout the course of the whole campaign, and expressed his readiness to give me all the support he could.

On the morning of the 28th we discussed the situation, and the General agreed to send the 9th French Corps to take over the ground occupied by us extending from the French left up to and including that portion of Hill 70 which we were holding, and also the village of Loos. This relief was commenced on the 30th September, and completed on the two following nights.

17. During the 29th and 30th September and the first days of October fighting was almost continuous along the northern part of the new line, particularly about the Hohenzollern Redoubt and neighbouring trenches, to which the enemy evidently attached great value. His attacks, however, invariably broke down with very heavy loss under the accurate fire of our infantry and artillery.

The Germans succeeded in gaining some ground in and about the Hohenzollern Redoubt but they paid heavily for it in the losses they suffered.

Our troops all along the front were busily engaged in consolidating and strengthening the ground won, and the efficient and thorough manner in which this work was carried out reflects the greatest credit upon all ranks. Every precaution was made to deal with the counter attack which was inevitable.

During these operations the weather has been most unfavourable, and the troops have had to fight in rain and mud and often in darkness. Even these adverse circumstances have in no way affected the magnificent spirit continually displayed alike by officers and men. In the Casualty Clearing and Dressing Stations, of which I visited a great number during the course of the action, I found nothing but the most cheery optimism among the wounded.

I have to deplore the loss of a third most valuable and distinguished General of Division during these operations.

On the afternoon of 2nd October Major-General F.D.V. Wing, C.B., commanding the 12th Division, was killed.

18. On the afternoon of 8th October our expectations in regard to a counter attack were fulfilled. The enemy directed a violent and intense attack all along the line from Fosse 8 on the north to the right of the French 9th Corps on the south. The attack was delivered by some twenty-eight battalions in first line, with larger forces in support, and was prepared by a very heavy bombardment from all parts of the enemy's front.

At all parts of the line except two the Germans were repulsed with tremendous loss, and it is computed on reliable authority that they left some eight to nine thousand dead lying on the battlefield in front of the British and French trenches.

On the right the attack succeeded in making a small and unimportant lodgment on the Double Crassier held by the French; whilst on the left the trench held by troops of the Guards Division to the north-east of the Hohenzollern Redoubt was temporarily captured. The latter was, however, speedily retaken, and at midnight on the 9th October the line held by the First Army was identically the same as that held before the enemy's attack started.

The main enemy attacks on the front held by our troops had been against the 1st Division in the neighbourhood of the Chalk Pit and the Guards Division in the neighbourhood of the Hohenzollern Redoubt. Both attacks were repulsed, and the enemy lost heavily from machine-gun and artillery fire.

From subsequent information it transpired that the German attack was made by about twelve battalions against the line Loos-Chalk Pit, and that a subsidiary attack by six to eight battalions was made from the direction of the Hohenzollern Redoubt against the Guards Division.

Some eight or ten German battalions were directed against the French 9th Corps.

19. The position assaulted and carried with so much brilliancy and dash by the 1st and 4th Corps on 25th September was an exceptionally strong one. It extended along a distance of some 6,500 yards, consisted of a double line, which included works of considerable strength, and was a network of trenches and bomb-proof shelters. Some of the dug-outs and shelters formed veritable caves thirty feet below the ground, with almost impenetrable head cover. The enemy had expended months of labour upon perfecting these defences.

The total number of prisoners captured during these operations amounted to 57 officers and 3,000 other ranks. Material which fell into our hands included 26 field-guns, 40 machine-guns and 3 minenwerfer.

I deeply regret the heavy casualties which were incurred in this battle, but in view of the great strength of the position, the stubborn defence of the enemy and the powerful artillery by which he was supported, I do not think they were excessive. I am happy to be able to add that the proportion of slightly wounded is relatively very large indeed.

20. Since the date of my last despatch the Army has received strong reinforcements, and every reinforcement has had its quota of Field Artillery. In addition, numerous batteries of heavy guns and howitzers have been added to the strength of the heavy artillery. The arrival of these reinforcements in the field has tested the capacity of the Artillery as a whole to expand to meet the requirements of the Army, and to maintain the high level of efficiency that has characterised this arm throughout the campaign. Our enemy may have hoped, not perhaps without reason, that it would be impossible for us, starting from such small beginnings, to build up an efficient Artillery to provide for the very large expansion of the Army. If he entertained such hopes, he has now good reason to know that they have not been justified by the result.

The efficiency of the Artillery of the New Armies has exceeded all expectations, and during the period under review excellent services have been rendered by the Territorial Artillery. The necessity to denude the old batteries of Regular Horse and Field Artillery of officers and non-commissioned officers, in order to provide for the expansion referred to, has not in any way impaired their efficiency, and they continue to set an example to all by their high standard and devotion to duty.

I must give a special word of praise to the officers and rank and file of the Royal Garrison Artillery for the admirable way in which they have accustomed themselves to the conditions of active service in the field, to which for the most part they were unaccustomed, and for the manner in which they have applied their general knowledge of gunnery to the special problems arising in trench warfare. The excellence of their training and the accuracy of their shooting have, I feel sure, made a marked impression on the enemy.

21. The work of the Artillery during the daily life in the trenches calls for increasing vigilance and the maintenance of an intricate system of communications in a thorough state of efficiency, in order that the guns may be ever ready to render assistance to the Infantry when necessity arises. A high standard of initiative is also required in order to maintain the moral ascendancy over the enemy, by impeding his working parties, destroying his works and keeping his artillery fire under control.

To the many calls upon them the Artillery has responded in a manner that is altogether admirable.

In the severe offensive actions that have taken place it is not too much to say that the first element of success has been the artillery preparation of the attack. Only when this preparation has been thorough have our attacks succeeded. It is impossible to convey in a despatch an adequate impression of the amount of care and labour involved in the minute and exact preparations that are the necessary preliminaries of a bombardment preparatory to an attack in a modern battle.

The immense number of guns that it is necessary to concentrate, the amount of ammunition to be supplied to them, and the diversity of the tasks to be carried out, demand a very high order of skill in organisation and technical professional knowledge.

22. The successful attacks at Hooge on 9th August and of the First Army on 25th September show that our Artillery officers possess the necessary talents and the rank and file the necessary skill and endurance to ensure success in operations of this character.

Moreover, the repulse of the enemy's attack on 8th October in the neighbourhood of Loos and Hulluch with such heavy losses shows the capacity of the Artillery to concentrate its fire promptly and effectively at a moment's notice for the defence of the front.

I cannot close these remarks on the Artillery without expressing my admiration for the work of the observing officers and the men who work with them. Carrying out their duties, as they do, in close proximity to the front line in observing stations that are the special mark of the enemy's guns, they are constantly exposed to fire, and are compelled to carry on their work, involving the use of delicate instruments and the making of nice calculations, in circumstances of the greatest difficulty and danger. That they have never failed in their duties, and that they have suffered very heavy casualties in performing them, are to their lasting credit and honour.

The work of the Artillery in co-operation with the Royal Flying Corps continues to make most satisfactory progress, and has been most highly creditable to all concerned.

The new weapons that have been placed in the field during the period under review have more than fulfilled expectations, and the enemy must be well aware of their accuracy and general efficiency.

23. I have on previous occasions called your Lordship's attention to the admirable work of the Corps of the Royal Engineers.

This work covers a very wide field, demanding a high standard of technical knowledge and skill, as well as unflagging energy; and throughout the supreme test of war these qualities have never been found wanting, thus reflecting the greatest credit on the organisation of the Corps as a whole, and on the training of the officers and men individually.

The spirit which is imbued in all ranks from the base ports to the front trenches and beyond is the same.

No matter where or how the personnel of the Corps has been employed, devotion to duty and energy have been ever present.

In this despatch I wish particularly to draw attention to the work of the Field Units and Army Troops Companies, which must almost invariably be performed under the most trying circumstances by night as well as by day. Demanding qualities of whole-hearted courage and self-sacrifice, combined with sound judgment and instant action, the work of officers, non-commissioned officers and men has been beyond all praise.

The necessity for skilled labour at the front has been so continuous that Royal Engineer units have frequently been forced to forego those periods of rest which at times it has been possible to grant to other troops; but, in spite of this, they have responded loyally to every call on their services.

Notwithstanding the heavy casualties sustained by all ranks, the esprit de corps of the Royal Engineers is such that the new material is at once animated by the same ideals, and the same devotion to duty is maintained.

24. I desire to call your Lordship's attention to the splendid work carried out by the Tunnelling Companies. These companies, officered largely by mining engineers, and manned by professional miners, have devoted themselves whole-heartedly to the dangerous work of offensive and defensive mining, a task ever accompanied by great and unseen dangers.

It is impossible within the limits of a despatch to give any just idea of the work of these units, but it will be found, when their history comes to be written, that it will present a story of danger, of heroism, and of difficulties surmounted worthy of the best traditions of the Royal Engineers, under whose general direction their work is carried out.

25. Owing to the repeated use by the enemy of asphyxiating gases in their attacks on our positions, I have been compelled to resort to similar methods; and a detachment was organised for this purpose, which took part in the operations commencing on the 25th September for the first time.

Although the enemy was known to have been prepared for such reprisals, our gas attack met with marked success, and produced a demoralising effect in some of the opposing units, of which ample evidence was forthcoming in the captured trenches.

The men who undertook this work carried out their unfamiliar duties during a heavy bombardment with conspicuous gallantry and coolness; and I feel confident in their ability to more than hold their own should the enemy again resort to this method of warfare.

26. I would again call your Lordship's attention to the work of the Royal Flying Corps. Throughout the summer, notwithstanding much unfavourable

weather, the work of cooperating with the Artillery, photographing the positions of the enemy, bombing their communications and reconnoitring far over hostile territory has gone on unceasingly.

The volume of work performed steadily increases; the amount of flying has been more than doubled during this period. There have been more than 240 combats in the air, and in nearly every case our pilots have had to seek the enemy behind his own lines, where he is assisted by the fire of his movable anti-aircraft guns; and in spite of this they have succeeded in bringing down four of the German machines behind our trenches and at least twelve in the enemy's lines, and many more have been seen to dive to earth in a damaged condition or to have retired from the fight. On one occasion an officer of the Royal Flying Corps engaged four enemy machines and drove them off, proceeding on his reconnaissance. On another occasion two officers engaged six hostile machines and disabled at least one of them. Artillery observation and photography are two of the most trying tasks the Royal Flying Corps is called upon to perform, as our airmen must remain for long periods within easy range of the enemy's anti-aircraft guns.

The work of observation for the guns from aeroplanes has now become an important factor in artillery fire, and the personnel of the two arms work in the closest co-operation.

As evidence of the dangers our flying officers are called upon to face I may state that on one occasion a machine was hit in no fewer than 300 places soon after crossing the enemy's lines, and yet the officer successfully carried out his mission.

The Royal Flying Corps has on several occasions carried out a continuous bombing of the enemy's communications, descending to 500 feet and under in order to hit moving trains on the railway. This has in some cases been kept up day after day; and, during the operations at the end of September, in the space of five days nearly six tons of explosives were dropped on moving trains, and are known to have practically wrecked five, some containing troops, and to have damaged the main railway line in many different places.

For the valuable work carried out by the Royal Flying Corps I am greatly indebted to their commander, Brigadier-General H.M. Trenchard, C.B., D.S.O., A.D.C.

27. Throughout the campaign the financial requirements of the Army have been successfully met by the Army Pay Department. The troops have been paid, and all claims against the Army discharged, with unbroken regularity, and the difficulties inseparable from a foreign banking system and a strange currency have been overcome.

The work of the department has been greatly assisted by the Bank of France, the administration of which has spared no effort to help.

28. While the circumstances of this campaign have brought no exceptional strain on horses, great credit is due to all concerned for the excellent arrangements in the Remount Depôts and Veterinary Hospitals.

29. I am pleased to be able once more to report very favourably on the divisions of the New Armies which have arrived in this country since the date of my last report.

It is evident that great trouble and much hard work have been expended on these units during their training at home, and it is found that they have received such sound teaching that a short period of instruction in trench life under fire soon enables them to take their places with credit beside their acclimatised comrades of the older formations.

30. The Territorial Force units have continued to merit the favourable remarks I have made on them in previous despatches, and have taken a prominent part in many of the active operations in which the Army has been engaged.

31. A new Division has been sent from Canada and has joined the Army in the field. The material of which it is composed is excellent; and this Division will, I am convinced, acquit itself as well in face of the enemy as the 1st Canadian Division has always done.

32. During the period under report I have been very glad once more to receive the Prime Minister at my Headquarters, as well as the Secretary of State for War.

The Prime Minister of Canada and the Minister of Militia and Defence of Canada also came to France for a few days and visited the troops of the Canadian Contingent.

The Chief Rabbi paid a short visit to the front and interested himself in the members of the large Jewish community now serving with the Army in the Field.

33. I cannot conclude the account of these operations without expressing the deep admiration felt by all ranks of the Army under my command for the splendid part taken by our French Allies in the battle which opened on 25th September. Fortified positions of immense strength, upon which months of skill and labour had been expended, and which extended for many miles, were stormed and captured by our French comrades with a bravery and determination which went far to instil hope and spirit into the Allied Forces.

The large captures of men and material which fell into their hands testified to the completeness of their victory.

The close co-operation between the two Armies of the Allied Powers, which has been so marked a feature throughout the whole campaign, has been as prominent as ever in the work of the last three weeks.

I have already referred to the cordial and willing help rendered by General Foch in the support of the 9th French Corps, and I have also once again to express my deep indebtedness to General d'Urbal, commanding the 10th French Army, operating on my right; and to General Hely d'Oissel, commanding the French Forces in the North.

34. The part taken by the troops of His Majesty the King of the Belgians was very effective in holding the enemy in front of them to his positions.

35. I have many names to bring to your Lordship's notice for valuable, gallant and distinguished service during the period under review, and these will form the subject of a separate report at an early date.

> I have the honour to be,
> Your Lordship's most obedient Servant,
> J.D.P. FRENCH,
> Field-Marshal, Commanding-in-Chief,
> The British Army in the Field.

SIR JOHN FRENCH'S DESPATCH OF 31 JULY 1916

Final Stages of the Battle of Loos

War Office, S.W.,
21st August, 1916.

The Secretary of State for War has received the following despatch from Field-Marshal Viscount French:-

General Headquarters,
Home Forces,
Whitehall, S.W.,
31st July, 1916.

SIR,

I have the honour to forward a despatch covering the operation of the military forces under my command in France between the date of my last despatch (15th October) and 19th December, the date upon which I left France and assumed the command of the Forces in the United Kingdom.

The exhaustion in men and material, which results after a great battle, necessarily leads up to a time of comparative inactivity, and the period under review was, therefore, somewhat barren in incidents of military importance.

Up to the end of October the most important operation was an attack, which commenced about noon of the 13th, by troops of the 11th and 4th Corps against Fosse No. 8, the Quarries, and the German trenches on the Lens – La Bassee Road.

The Divisions chiefly engaged were the 1st Division (4th Corps) and the 12th and 46th Divisions (11th Corps).

Speaking generally, the objective of the 1st Division was the enemy's trenches on the Lens – La Bassee Road; that of the 12th Division was the Quarries; whilst the troops of the 46th Division attacked the Hohenzollern Redoubt and Fosse No. 8.

The day's fighting commenced with an artillery bombardment of the objectives of the attack, and in this bombardment the French artillery on our right collaborated.

Shortly before the attack was launched at 2 p.m. smoke was turned on all along our front from the Bethune – La Bassee Road southwards, and under cover of this smoke the attack was delivered. At the same time the heavy artillery lifted to further objectives while the enemy's front trench system was subjected to shrapnel fire.

At 2.10 p.m. it was reported that our infantry had passed the Hohenzollern Redoubt and were bombing up a trench towards the dump of Fosse 8; they were, however, opposed by heavy machine-gun fire from that point and such success as the original attack gained at the Fosse was only of a temporary nature.

At 2.45 p.m. the 4th Corps reported having captured 1,200 yards of trenches on the Lens – La Bassee Road, but as the left battalion of this corps had failed to get possession of the enemy's trenches the General Officer Commanding did not think it practicable to undertake any further offensive towards Hulluch.

The information received during the remainder of the day was very conflicting, and at nightfall the General Officer Commanding 1st Army was unable to define the exact position of the leading troops of the 1st Division.

One Battalion of the 12th Division had gained the south-westerly edge of the Quarries.

The fight for the Hohenzollern Redoubt and Fosse No. 8 was still proceeding with varying fortunes, but it appeared clear that none of our troops were in the Fosse or on the dump.

In the course of the next two days the whole attack died down without attaining the objective aimed at, and the situation in that part of the line remained much the same throughout the period covered by the present despatch.

During the night of October 16th-17th the enemy made two bombing attacks against the Guards Division in the vicinity of the Hohenzollern Redoubt. Both these attacks were easily repulsed. On 19th October the enemy was seen to be massing in the Quarries near the Hohenzollern Redoubt, and after artillery preparation made a determined attack against our lines to the south-west of the former place. This attack was repulsed with heavy loss to the enemy.

A bombing attack of two hours' duration in the same vicinity met with a similar fate. On 16th November the 2nd Canadian Infantry Brigade carried out a brilliant little operation near La Petite Douve Farm in raiding the enemy's trenches with bombing parties. They caused considerable damage to the enemy, brought away 12 prisoners, and only suffered one accidental casualty themselves.

On 25th November the Royal Flying Corps carried out an effective raid on the enemy's cantonments at Achiet Le Grand, and this was followed a few days later by a similar raid on Don Station and the adjoining stores, in the course of which several fires and an explosion were observed.

Another air raid against the quay and stores near Miraumont was also reported as having been effective on 30th November.

Throughout the period under review mining activity was constant on both sides; this, as well as almost continuous shelling of varying intensity, has become a practically permanent condition of warfare along the entire length of the line which we now occupy. I do not propose, in this short despatch, written only in order that the official published narrative of the war may be continuous, to make special mention of the services of individuals under my command, other than those which have already appeared.

The encomiums passed in my despatch of 15th October are proved to be more than justified by the conduct of all ranks of the Army in France up to the time of my handing over the command.

> I have the honour to be,
> Sir,
> Your most obedient Servant,
> FRENCH,
> Field-Marshal,
> Commanding-in-Chief.

SIR DOUGLAS HAIG'S DESPATCH OF 19 MAY 1916

Ypres Salient, Actions at the Bluff, German Gas Attacks and St Eloi

> *War Office,*
> *London, S.W.,*
> *29th May,* 1916.

The following Despatch has been received by the Secretary of State for War from General Sir Douglas Haig, G.C.B., Commanding-in-Chief, the British Forces in France:-

> *General Headquarters,*
> *19th May,* 1916.

MY LORD,

1. I have the honour to report the operations of the British Forces serving in France and Belgium since 19th December, 1915, on which date, in accordance with the orders of His Majesty's Government, I assumed the Chief Command.

During this period, the only offensive effort made by the enemy on a great scale was directed against our French Allies near Verdun. The fighting in that area has been prolonged and severe. The results have been worthy of the high traditions of the French Army and of great service to the cause of the Allies. The efforts made by the enemy have cost him heavy losses both in men and in prestige, and he has made these sacrifices without gaining any advantage to counterbalance them.

During this struggle my troops have been in readiness to co-operate as they might be needed, but the only assistance asked for by our Allies was of an indirect nature – viz., the relief of the French troops on a portion of their defensive front. This relief I was glad to be able to afford.

Its execution on a considerable front, everywhere in close touch with the enemy, was a somewhat delicate operation, but it was carried out with complete success, thanks to the cordial co-operation and goodwill of all ranks concerned and to the lack of enterprise shown by the enemy during the relief.

2. On the British front no action on a great scale, such as that at Verdun, has been fought during the past five months, nevertheless our troops have been far from idle or inactive. Although the struggle, in a general sense, has not

been intense, it has been everywhere continuous, and there have been many sharp local actions.

The maintenance and repair of our defences alone, especially in winter, entails constant heavy work. Bad weather and the enemy combine to flood and destroy trenches, dug-outs and communications; all such damages must be repaired promptly, under fire, and almost entirely by night.

Artillery and snipers are practically never silent, patrols are out in front of the lines every night, and heavy bombardments by the artillery of one or both sides take place daily in various parts of the line. Below ground there is continual mining and counter-mining, which, by the ever-present threat of sudden explosion and the uncertainty as to when and where it will take place, causes perhaps a more constant strain than any other form of warfare. In the air there is seldom a day, however bad the weather, when aircraft are not busy reconnoitring, photographing, and observing fire. All this is taking place constantly at any hour of the day or night, and in any part of the line.

3. In short, although there has been no great incident of historic importance to record on the British front during the period under review, a steady and continuous fight has gone on, day and night, above ground and below it. The comparative monotony of this struggle has been relieved at short intervals by sharp local actions, some of which, although individually almost insignificant in a war on such an immense scale, would have been thought worthy of a separate despatch under different conditions, while their cumulative effect, though difficult to appraise at its true value now, will doubtless prove hereafter to have been considerable.

One form of minor activity deserves special mention, namely, the raids or "cutting out parties" which are made at least twice or three times a week against the enemy's line. They consist of a brief attack, with some special object, on a section of the opposing trenches, usually carried out at night by a small body of men. The character of these operations – the preparation of a road through our own and the enemy's wire – the crossing of the open ground unseen – the penetration of the enemy's trenches – the hand-to-hand fighting in the darkness and the uncertainty as to the strength of the opposing force – give peculiar scope to the gallantry, dash and quickness of decision of the troops engaged; and much skill and daring are frequently displayed in these operations.

The initiative in these minor operations was taken, and on the whole has been held, by us; but the Germans have recently attempted some bold and well-conceived raids against our lines, many of which have been driven back, although some have succeeded in penetrating, as has been reported by me from time to time.

4. Of the numerous local actions alluded to, the total number, omitting the more minor raids, amounts to over 60 since December 19th, of which the most important have been:-

The operations at The Bluff, the Hohenzollern Redoubt, and at St. Eloi; the mining operations and crater fighting in the Loos salient and on the Vimy Ridge; and the hostile gas attacks north of Ypres in December, and opposite Hulluch and Messines in April.

The most recent local operations worthy of mention are the capture of some 500 yards of our trenches by the Germans at the Kink, on the 11th May, and the capture by us of 250 yards of their trenches near Cabaret Rouge, on the night of the 15th/16th May.

5. As an illustration of the nature of these local operations, it will suffice to describe two or three of the most important.

Ypres Salient and The Bluff, 8th February to 2nd March, 1916.
During the period 8th to 19th February the enemy displayed increased activity in the Ypres salient, and carried out a series of infantry attacks, preceded, as a rule, by intense bombardment, and by the explosion of mines. These attacks may, no doubt, be regarded as a subsidiary operation, designed partly to secure local points of vantage, but probably also to distract attention from the impending operations near Verdun, which began on the 21st February. After several days' heavy shelling over the whole of our line in this area, the first attack took place on 12th February at the extreme left of our line to the north of Ypres. A bombing attack was launched by the Germans in the early morning, and they succeeded in capturing our trenches. Our counter-attack, however, which was immediately organised, enabled us to clear our trenches of the enemy, and to pursue him to his own. After a period of further bombardment on both sides, the German fire again increased in intensity against our trenches and the French line beyond them; and in the evening a second attempt was made to rush our extreme left – this time entirely without success. Smaller attempts against other trenches in the neighbourhood were made at the same time, but were immediately repulsed by rifle and machine-gun fire. Throughout the operations our position in this part of the line remained intact, except that two isolated trenches of no tactical importance were captured by the enemy a day or two later; they were subsequently obliterated by our artillery fire. Throughout this fighting the French on our immediate left rendered us the prompt and valuable assistance which we have at all times received from them.

Another series of German attacks was launched about the same time in the neighbourhood of Hooge to the east of Ypres. The enemy had pushed out several saps in front of his trenches, and connected them up into a firing line some 150 yards from our lines. During the whole of the 13th February he heavily bombarded our front-line trenches in this neighbourhood, and completely destroyed them. On the following afternoon an intense bombardment of our line began, and the enemy exploded a series of mines in front of our trenches, simultaneously launching infantry attacks against Hooge and the northern and southern ends of Sanctuary Wood. Each of these attacks was repulsed by artillery, machine-gun and rifle fire.

Further to the South, however, the enemy was more successful. On the northern bank of the Ypres – Comines Canal there is a narrow ridge, 30 to 40 feet high, covered with trees – probably the heap formed by excavation when the canal was dug – which forms a feature of the flat-wooded country at the southern bend of the Ypres salient. It runs outward through our territory almost into the German area, so that our trenches pass over the eastern point of it, which is known as The Bluff. Here also our trenches were almost obliterated by the bombardment on the afternoon of the 14th, following which a sudden rush of hostile infantry was successful in capturing these and other front-line trenches immediately north of The Bluff – some 600 yards in all. Two of these trenches were at once regained, but the others were held by the enemy, in the face of several counter-attacks. On the night of the 15th-16th we made an unsuccessful counterattack, with the object of regaining the lost trenches. An advance was begun across the open on the north side of the canal, combined with grenade attacks along the communication trenches immediately north of The Bluff. The night was very dark, and heavy rain had turned the ground into a quagmire, so that progress was difficult for the attacking force, which was unable to consolidate its position in the face of heavy machine-gun and rifle fire. After the failure of this attack it was decided to adopt slower and more methodical methods of re-capturing the lost trenches, and nothing of special importance occurred in the Ypres salient during the rest of the month, although both sides displayed rather more than the usual activity.

The re-capture of The Bluff took place after the enemy had held it for seventeen days. After several days preliminary bombardment by our artillery, the assault was carried out at 4.29 a.m. on the 2nd March. Measures taken to deceive the enemy were successful, and our infantry effected a complete surprise, finding the enemy with their bayonets unfixed, and many of them without rifles or equipment. About 50 Germans took refuge in a crater at the eastern end of The Bluff, and these put up a brief, resistance before taking refuge in the tunnels they had constructed, in which they were captured at leisure. Otherwise our right hand attacking party, whose objective was The Bluff met with little opposition.

The front line of the centre attack, reaching its assigned objective without much opposition, swept on past it and seized the German Third Line at the eastern side of the salient. This line was not suitable to hold permanently, but it proved useful as a temporary covering position while the captured trenches in rear were being consolidated, and at nightfall the covering party was withdrawn unmolested. The later waves of our centre attack met and captured after some fighting, several Germans coming out of their dug-outs.

The left attacking party, at the first attempt, failed to reach the German trenches, but those who had penetrated to the German line on the right realised the situation and brought a Lewis gun to bear on the enemy's line of resistance, completely enfilading his trenches, and thus enabling the left company, to reach its goal.

Thus our objective, which included a part of the German line, as well as the whole of the front lost by us on the 14th February, was captured, and is still held by us. Several counter-attacks were destroyed by our fire. The enemy's trenches were found full of dead as a result of our bombardment, and five officers and 251 other ranks were captured.

The support of the Heavy and Field Artillery, and a number of trench mortars, contributed largely to the success of the operation.

St.Eloi

6. On the 27th March our troops made an attack with the object of straightening out the line at St. Eloi, and cutting away the small German salient which encroached on the semicircle of our line in the Ypres salient to a depth of about 100 yards over a front of some 600 yards. The operation was begun by the firing of six very large mines; the charge was so heavy that the explosion was felt in towns several miles behind the lines, and large numbers of the enemy were killed. Half a minute after the explosion our infantry attack was launched aiming at the German Second Line. The right attack met with little opposition, and captured its assigned objective; but the left attack was not so successful, and a gap was left in possession of the Germans, through which they entered one of the craters. The following days were spent by both sides in heavy bombardment and in unsuccessful attacks, intended on our part to capture the remaining trenches, and on the part of the Germans to drive us from the positions we had occupied. In the very early morning of April 3rd we succeeded in recapturing the crater and the trenches still held by the enemy, thereby securing the whole of our original objective. We had, moreover, captured five officers and 195 men in the first attack on March 27th, and five officers and 80 men in the attack on April 3rd. The work of consolidating our new position, however, proved extremely difficult, owing to the wet soil, heavy shelling and mine explosions; though pumps were brought up and

efforts at draining were instituted, the result achieved was comparatively small. By dint of much heavy work the Brigade holding these trenches succeeded in reducing the water in the trenches by 2 feet by the morning of the 5th. This state of affairs could not, even so, be regarded as satisfactory; and during the 5th the enemy's bombardment increased in intensity, and the new trenches practically ceased to exist. On the morning of the 6th the enemy attacked with one battalion supported by another; he penetrated our new line, and gained the two western most craters. It is difficult to follow in detail the fighting of the next three weeks, which consisted in repeated attacks by both sides on more or less isolated mine craters, the trench lines having been destroyed by shell fire. Great efforts were made to maintain communication with the garrisons of these advanced posts, and with considerable success. But there were periods of uncertainty, and some misconception as to the state of affairs arose. On the 11th it was reported to me that we had recaptured all that remained of the position won by us on the 27th March and 3rd April. This report, probably due to old craters having been mistaken for new ones, was subsequently found to be incorrect. The new craters, being exposed to the enemy's view and to the full weight of his artillery fire, have proved untenable, and at the present time our troops are occupying trenches roughly in the general line which was held by them before the 27th.

German Gas Attacks, 27th/30th April.

7. On the night of the 29th/30th April the enemy carried out a gas attack on a considerable scale near Wulverghem, on a front of 3,500 yards. The operation was opened by heavy rifle and machine-gun fire under cover of which the gas was released. Immediately afterwards a heavy "barrage," or curtain of artillery fire, was placed on three parts of this area, and eight infantry attacks were launched. Of these attacks only two penetrated our trenches; one was immediately repelled, while the other was driven out by a counter-attack after about 40 minutes occupation. The enemy's object would appear to have been the destruction of mine shafts, as a charge of guncotton was found unexploded in a disused shaft, to which the enemy had penetrated. But if this was his object he was completely unsuccessful.

Similar attacks were made by the Germans in front of Vermelles, to the south of La Bassee, on the 27th and 29th April, the discharge of a highly concentrated gas being accompanied by bombardment with lachrymatory and other shells and the explosion of a mine. On the first occasion two minor infantry attacks penetrated our trenches, but were driven out almost immediately; on the second occasion a small attack was repulsed, but the more serious advance which appears to have been intended was probably rendered impossible by the fact that a part of the enemy's gas broke back over his own lines, to the visible confusion of his troops, who were massing for the attack.

8. While many other units have done excellent work during the period under review, the following have been specially brought to my notice for good work in carrying out or repelling local attacks and raids:-

3rd Divisional Artillery.
17th Divisional Artillery.
1st Canadian Divisional Artillery.
62nd Brigade, Royal Field Artillery.
B Battery, 153rd Brigade, Royal Field Artillery.
83rd Battery, Royal Field Artillery (Lahore).
22nd Canadian (Howitzer) Brigade.
24th Heavy Battery, Royal Garrison Artillery.
115th Heavy Battery, Royal Garrison Artillery.
122nd Heavy Battery, Royal Garrison Artillery.
3rd Siege Battery, Royal Garrison Artillery.
12th Siege Battery, Royal Garrison Artillery.
9th Field Company, Royal Engineers.
56th Field Company, Royal Engineers.
70th Field Company, Royal Engineers.
77th Field Company, Royal Engineers.
1st (Cheshire) Field Company, Royal Engineers.
170th Tunnelling Company, Royal Engineers.
172nd Tunnelling Company, Royal Engineers.
173rd Tunnelling Company, Royal Engineers.
253rd Tunnelling Company, Royal Engineers.
12th Divisional Signal Company, Royal Engineers.
24th Trench Mortar Battery.
76/1st Trench Mortar Battery.
No. 2 Squadron, Royal Flying Corps.
No. 6 Squadron, Royal Flying Corps.
2nd Battalion, Grenadier Guards.
1st Battalion, Coldstream Guards.
2nd Battalion, Irish Guards.
1st Battalion, Welsh Guards.
11th (Service) Battalion, The Royal Scots (Lothian Regiment).
1st Battalion, The Queen's (Royal West Surrey Regiment).
7th (Service) Battalion, The King's Own (Royal Lancaster Regiment).
8th (Service) Battalion, The King's Own (Royal Lancaster Regiment).
1st Battalion, Northumberland Fusiliers.

12th (Service) Battalion, Northumberland Fusiliers.
1st Battalion, Royal Warwickshire Regiment.
8th Battalion, Royal Warwickshire Regiment (Territorial).
8th (Service) Battalion, Royal Fusiliers (City of London Regiment).
9th (Service) Battalion Royal Fusiliers (City of London Regiment).
4th (Extra Reserve) Battalion, The King's Liverpool Regiment.
l/8th (Irish) Battalion, The King's Liverpool Regiment (Territorial).
7th (Service) Battalion, Lincolnshire Regiment.
l/4th Battalion, Suffolk Regiment (Territorial).
7th (Service) Battalion, Suffolk Regiment.
8th (Service) Battalion, Somerset Light Infantry.
7th (Service) Battalion, Bedfordshire Regiment.
l/4th Battalion, The Prince of Wales's Own (West Yorkshire Regiment) (Territorial).
2nd Battalion, Lancashire Fusiliers.
11th (Service) Battalion, Lancashire Fusiliers.
15th (Service) Battalion, Lancashire Fusiliers.
17th (Service) Battalion, Lancashire Fusiliers.
2nd Battalion, Royal Welsh Fusiliers.
15th (Service) Battalion, Royal Welsh Fusiliers.
8th (Service) Battalion, King's Own Scottish Borderers.
7th (Service) Battalion, Royal Inniskilling Fusiliers.
9th (Service) Battalion, Royal Inniskilling Fusiliers.
10th (Service) Battalion, Royal Inniskilling Fusiliers.
1/6th Battalion, Gloucestershire Regiment (Territorial).
1st Battalion, East Lancashire Regiment.
7th (Service) Battalion, East Surrey Regiment.
8th (Service) Battalion, East Surrey Regiment.
9th (Service) Battalion, West Riding Regiment.
2nd Battalion, The Border Regiment.
7th (Service) Battalion, The Border Regiment.
11th (Service) Battalion, The Border Regiment.
7th (Service) Battalion, Royal Sussex Regiment.
8th (Service) Battalion, Royal Sussex Regiment.
8th (Service) Battalion, South Staffordshire Regiment.
1st Battalion, Dorsetshire Regiment.
1/4th Battalion, Oxfordshire and Buckinghamshire Light Infantry (Territorial).
1st Battalion Northamptonshire Regiment.
5th (Service) Battalion, Northamptonshire Regiment.
6th (Service) Battalion, NorthamptonshireRegiment.

1st Battalion, The King's (Shropshire Light Infantry).
1st Battalion, Duke of Cambridge's Own (Middlesex Regiment).
2nd Battalion, Duke of Cambridge's Own (Middlesex Regiment).
2nd Battalion, King's Royal Rifle Corps.
6th (Service) Battalion, The Duke of Edinburgh's (Wiltshire Regiment).
18th (Service) Battalion, Manchester Regiment.
1st Battalion, The Prince of Wales's (North Staffordshire Regiment).
8th (Service) Battalion, The Prince of Wales's (North Staffordshire Regiment).
17th (Service) Battalion, Highland Light Infantry.
8th (Service) Battalion, Seaforth Highlanders (Ross-shire Buffs, The Duke of Albany's).
1st Battalion, The Gordon Highlanders.
2nd Battalion, The Royal Irish Rifles.
9th (Service) Battalion, The Royal Irish Rifles.
1st Battalion, Princess Victoria's (Royal Irish Fusiliers).
2nd Battalion, Princess Louise's (Argyll & Sutherland Highlanders).
9th (Service) Battalion, Royal Munster Fusiliers.
3rd Battalion, The Rifle Brigade (The Prince Consort's Own).
5th Canadian Infantry Battalion.
7th Canadian Infantry Battalion.
29th Canadian Infantry Battalion.
49th Canadian Infantry Battalion.

9. The activity described above has its counterpart in rear of our lines in the training which is carried out continuously. During the periods of relief all formations, and especially the newly created ones, are instructed and practised in all classes of the present and other phases of warfare. A large number of schools also exist for the instruction of individuals especially in the use and theory of the less familiar weapons, such as bombs and grenades.

There are schools for young staff officers and regimental officers, for candidates for commissions, etc. In short, every effort is made to take advantage of the closer contact with actual warfare, and to put the finishing touches, often after actual experience in the trenches, to the training received at home.

10. During the period under review the forces under my command have been considerably augmented by the arrival of new formations from home, and the transfer of others released from service in the Near East. This increase has made possible the relief of a French Army, to which I have already referred, at the time of the Battle of Verdun. Among the newly arrived forces is the "Anzac" Corps. With them, the Canadians, and a portion of the South

African Overseas Force which has also arrived, the Dominions now furnish a valuable part of the Imperial Forces in France.

Since the date of the last Despatch, but before I assumed command, the Indian Army Corps left this country for service in the East. They had given a year's valuable and gallant service under conditions of warfare which they had not dreamt of, and in a climate peculiarly difficult for them to endure. I regret their departure, but I do not doubt that they will continue to render gallant and effective service elsewhere, as they have already done in this country.

11. I take this opportunity to bring to notice the admirable work which the Royal Flying Corps has continued to perform, in spite of much unfavourable weather, in carrying out reconnaissance duties, in taking photographs – an important aid to reconnaissance which has been brought to a high pitch of perfection – and in assisting the work of our Artillery by registering targets, and locating hostile batteries. In the performance of this work they have flown in weather when no hostile aeroplane ventured out, and they have not hesitated to fly low, under fire of the enemy's guns, when their duties made it necessary to do so. They have also carried out a series of bombing raids on hostile aerodromes and points of military importance. A feature of the period under review has been the increased activity of the enemy's aircraft, in suitable weather. But the enemy's activity has been mainly on his own side of the line, and has aimed chiefly at interrupting the work carried out by our machines. In order to carry on the work in spite of this opposition, which was for a time rendered more effective by the appearance in December of a new and more powerful type of enemy machine, it has been necessary to provide an escort to accompany our reconnaissance aeroplanes, and fighting in the air, which was formerly exceptional, has now become an everyday occurrence.

The observers, no less than the pilots, have done excellent service, and many fine feats have been performed by both. Developments on the technical side of the Air Service have been no less remarkable and satisfactory than the progress made on the purely military side. Much inventive genius has been displayed; and our equipment for photography, wireless telegraphy, bomb-dropping and offensive action generally has been immensely improved; while great skill has been shown in keeping the flying machines themselves in good flying condition.

12. The continuance of siege warfare has entailed for the Royal Engineers work of a particularly arduous and important kind extending from the front trenches to the Base Ports. In the performance of this work the Officers, Non-commissioned Officers and men of the Field Companies and other units of the Corps have continued to exhibit a very high standard of skill, courage, and devotion to duty.

13. The work of the Tunnelling Companies calls for special mention. Increased mining activity on the part of the enemy has invariably been answered with enterprise combined with untiring energy on the part of our miners, who in carrying out duties always full of danger have shown that they possess in the highest degree the qualities of courage, perseverance, and self-sacrifice. Their importance in the present phase of warfare is very great.

14. The excellent work done by the Corps of Military Police is worthy of mention. This Corps is inspired by a high sense of duty, and in the performance of its share in the maintenance of discipline it has shown both zeal and discretion.

15. All branches of the Medical Services deserve the highest commendation for the successful work done by them, both at the Front and on the Lines of Communication. The sick rate has been consistently low; there has been no serious epidemic, and enteric fever, the bane of armies in the past, has almost completely disappeared owing to preventive measures energetically carried out.

The results of exposure incidental to trench warfare during the winter months were to a very great extent kept in check by careful application of the precautions recommended and taught by regimental Medical Officers.

The wounded have been promptly and efficiently dealt with, and their evacuation to the Base has been rapidly accomplished.

The close co-operation which has existed between the officers of the Regular Medical Service of the Army and those members of the civil medical profession, who have patriotically given their valuable services to the Army, has largely contributed to the prevention of disease and to the successful treatment and comfort of the sick and wounded. As part of the Medical Services, the Canadian Army Medical Corps has displayed marked efficiency and devotion to duty.

16. The Commission of Graves Registration and Enquiries has, since it first undertook this work eighteen months ago, registered and marked over 50,000 graves. Without its labours many would have remained unidentified. It has answered several thousand enquiries from relatives and supplied them with photographs. Flowers and shrubs have been planted in most of the cemeteries which are sufficiently far removed from the firing line, and all cemeteries which it is possible to work in during the daytime are now being looked after by non-commissioned officers and men of this unit.

17. The valuable nature of the work performed by the officers of the Central Laboratory and the Chemical Advisers with the Armies in investigations into

the nature of the gasses and other new substances used in hostile attacks, and in devising and perfecting means of protecting our troops against them, is deserving of recognition. The efforts of these officers materially contributed to the failure of the Germans in their attack of 19th December 1915, as well as in the various gas attacks since made.

18. The stream of additional personnel and material arriving from England, and the move of complete formations to and from the East during the period under review, have thrown a great deal of work on our Base Ports and on the Advanced Base. The staff and personnel at these stations have coped most ably with the work of forwarding and equipping the various units passing through their hands, and I desire to bring their good work to notice.

19. The large increases made to our forces have necessitated a great expansion in the resources of our Lines of Communication, and I have been greatly struck by the forethought shown by the Administrative Services in anticipating the requirements of the Armies in the Field and in the provision made to satisfy these requirements.

The Base Ports have been developed to the utmost possible extent, advanced Depots have been provided, and communications have been improved to ensure punctual distribution to the troops.

Labour has been organised in order to develop local resources, especially in the matter of timber for defences and hutting, and stone for road maintenance, whereby considerable reductions have been made possible in the shipments from over sea.

Economy has attended the good methods adopted, and the greatest credit is due to all concerned for the results obtained.

20. I desire to acknowledge here the valuable assistance rendered by the naval transport officers on the Lines of Communication. They have worked with and for the Army most untiringly, efficiently, and with the utmost harmony.

I also desire to acknowledge the indebtedness of the Army to the Royal Navy for their unceasing and uniformly successful care in securing the safety of our transport service on the seas.

21. I wish to acknowledge the work done in the reproduction of maps by the Ordnance Survey Department. Over 90 per cent. of the maps used in this country are reproduced and printed in England by the Ordnance Survey, and the satisfactory supply is largely due to the foresight and initiative displayed by this Department. I can now count on obtaining an issue of as many as 10,000 copies of any map within one week of sending it home for reproduction.

22. I have forwarded under a separate letter the names of the Officers, Non-Commissioned Officers and Men whom I wish to bring to notice for gallant and distinguished service.

23. I cannot close this Despatch without some reference to the work of my predecessor in Command, Field-Marshal Viscount French. The Field-Marshal, starting the war with our small Expeditionary Force, faced an enemy far superior in numbers and fully prepared for this great campaign. During the long and anxious time needed for the improvisation of the comparatively large force now serving in this country, he overcame all difficulties, and before laying down his responsibilities he had the satisfaction of seeing the balance of advantage swing steadily in our favour. Those who have served under him appreciate the greatness of his achievement.

I have the honour to be,
Your Lordship's most obedient Servant,
D. HAIG, General,
Commander-in-Chief, The British Forces in France.

SIR DOUGLAS HAIG'S DESPATCH OF 23 DECEMBER 1916

The Battle of the Somme

War Office,
29th December, 1916.

The following Despatch has been received by the Secretary of State for War from General Sir Douglas Haig, G.C.B., Commanding-in-Chief, the British Forces in France:-

General Headquarters,
23rd December, 1916.

MY LORD,

I have the honour to submit the following report on the operations of the Forces under my Command since the 19th May, the date of my last Despatch.

1. The principle of an offensive campaign during the summer of 1916 had already been decided on by all the Allies. The various possible alternatives on the Western front had been studied and discussed by General Joffre and myself, and we were in complete agreement as to the front to be attacked by the combined French and British Armies. Preparations for our offensive had made considerable progress; but as the date on which the attack should begin was dependent on many doubtful factors, a final decision on that point was deferred until the general situation should become clearer.

Subject to the necessity of commencing operations before the summer was too far advanced, and with due regard to the general situation, I desired to postpone my attack as long as possible. The British Armies were growing in numbers and the supply of munitions was steadily increasing. Moreover a very large proportion of the officers and men under my command were still far from being fully trained, and the longer the attack could be deferred the more efficient they would become. On the other hand the Germans were continuing to press their attacks at Verdun, and both there and on the Italian front, where the Austrian offensive was gaining ground, it was evident that the strain might become too great to be borne unless timely action were taken to relieve it. Accordingly, while maintaining constant touch with General Joffre in regard to all these considerations, my preparations were pushed on, and I agreed, with the consent of H.M. Government, that my attack should be launched whenever the general situation required it with as great a force as I might then be able to make available.

2. By the end of May the pressure of the enemy on the Italian front had assumed such serious proportions that the Russian campaign was opened early in June, and the brilliant successes gained by our Allies against the Austrians at once caused a movement of German troops from the Western to the Eastern front. This, however, did not lessen the pressure on Verdun. The heroic defence of our French Allies had already gained many weeks of inestimable value and had caused the enemy very heavy losses; but the strain continued to increase. In view, therefore, of the situation in the various theatres of war, it was eventually agreed between General Joffre and myself that the combined French and British offensive should not be postponed beyond the end of June.

The object of that offensive was threefold:

   (i.) To relieve the pressure on Verdun.
   (ii.) To assist our Allies in the other theatres of war by stopping any further transfer of German troops from the Western front.
   (iii.) To wear down the strength of the forces opposed to us.

3. While my final preparations were in progress the enemy made two unsuccessful attempts to interfere with my arrangements. The first, directed on the 21st May against our positions on the Vimy Ridge, south and south-east of Souchez, resulted in a small enemy gain of no strategic or tactical importance; and rather than weaken my offensive by involving additional troops in the task of recovering the lost ground, I decided to consolidate a position in rear of our original line.

The second enemy attack was delivered on the 2nd June on a front of over one and a half miles from Mount Sorrell to Hooge, and succeeded in penetrating to a maximum depth of 700 yards. As the southern part of the lost position commanded our trenches I judged it necessary to recover it, and by an attack launched on the 13th June, carefully prepared and well executed, this was successfully accomplished by the troops on the spot.

Neither of these enemy attacks succeeded in delaying the preparations for the major operations which I had in view.

4. These preparations were necessarily very elaborate and took considerable time.

Vast stocks of ammunition and stores of all kinds had to be accumulated beforehand within a convenient distance of our front. To deal with these many miles of new railways – both standard and narrow gauge – and trench tramways were laid. All available roads were improved, many others were made, and long causeways were built over marshy valleys. Many additional dug-outs had to be provided as shelter for the troops, for use as dressing stations for the wounded, and as magazines for storing ammunition, food, water, and engineering material. Scores of miles of deep communication trenches had to be dug, as well as trenches for telephone wires, assembly and assault trenches, and numerous gun emplacements and observation posts.

Important mining operations were undertaken, and charges were laid at various points beneath the enemy's lines.

Except in the river valleys, the existing supplies of water were hopelessly insufficient to meet the requirements of the numbers of men and horses to be concentrated in this area as the preparations for our offensive proceeded. To meet this difficulty many wells and borings were sunk, and over one hundred pumping plants were installed. More than one hundred and twenty miles of water mains were laid, and everything was got ready to ensure an adequate water supply as our troops advanced.

Much of this preparatory work had to be done under very trying conditions, and was liable to constant interruption from the enemy's fire. The weather, on the whole, was bad, and the local accommodation totally insufficient for housing the troops employed, who consequently had to content themselves with such rough shelter as could be provided in the circumstances. All this labour, too, had to be carried out in addition to fighting and to the everyday work of maintaining existing defences. It threw a very heavy strain on the troops, which was borne by them with a cheerfulness beyond all praise.

5. The enemy's position to be attacked was of a very formidable character, situated on a high, undulating tract of ground, which rises to more than 500 feet above sea-level, and forms the watershed between the Somme on the one side and the rivers of south-western Belgium on the other. On the southern face of this watershed, the general trend of which is from east-south-east to west-north-west, the ground falls in a series of long irregular spurs and deep depressions to the valley of the Somme. Well down the forward slopes of this face the enemy's first system of defence, starting from the Somme near Curlu, ran at first northwards for 3,000 yards, then westwards for 7,000 yards to near Fricourt, where it turned nearly due north, forming a great salient angle in the enemy's line.

Some 10,000 yards north of Fricourt the trenches crossed the River Ancre, a tributary of the Somme, and still running northwards passed over the summit of the watershed, about Hebuterne and Gommecourt, and then down its northern spurs to Arras.

On the 20,000 yards front between the Somme and the Ancre the enemy had a strong second system of defence, sited generally on or near the southern crest of the highest part of the watershed, at an average distance of from 3,000 to 5,000 yards behind his first system of trenches.

During nearly two years' preparation he had spared no pains to render these defences impregnable. The first and second systems each consisted of several lines of deep trenches, well provided with bomb-proof shelters and with numerous communication trenches connecting them. The front of the trenches in each system was protected by wire entanglements, many of them in two belts forty yards broad, built of iron stakes interlaced with barbed wire, often almost as thick as a man's finger.

The numerous woods and villages in and between these systems of defence had been turned into veritable fortresses. The deep cellars, usually to be found in the villages, and the numerous pits and quarries common to a chalk country were used to provide cover for machine guns and trench mortars. The existing cellars were supplemented by elaborate dug-outs, sometimes in two storeys, and these were connected up by passages as much as thirty feet below the surface of the ground. The salients in the enemy's line, from which he could bring enfilade fire across his front, were made into self-contained forts, and often protected by mine fields; while strong redoubts and concrete machine gun emplacements had been constructed in positions from which he could sweep his own trenches should these be taken. The ground lent itself to good artillery observation on the enemy's part, and he had skilfully arranged for cross fire by his guns.

These various systems of defence, with the fortified localities and other supporting points between them, were cunningly sited to afford each other mutual assistance and to admit of the utmost possible development of enfilade and flanking fire by machine guns and artillery. They formed, in short, not merely a series of successive lines, but one composite system of enormous depth and strength.

Behind his second system of trenches, in addition to woods, villages and other strong points prepared for defence, the enemy had several other lines already completed; and we had learnt from aeroplane reconnaissance that he was hard at work improving and strengthening these and digging fresh ones between them and still further back.

In the area above described, between the Somme and the Ancre, our front line trenches ran parallel and close to those of the enemy, but below them. We had good direct observation on his front system of trenches and on the various defences sited on the slopes above us between his first and second systems; but the second system itself, in many places, could not be observed from the ground in our possession, while, except from the air, nothing could be seen of his more distant defences.

North of the Ancre, where the opposing trenches ran transversely across the main ridge, the enemy's defences were equally elaborate and formidable. So far as command of ground was concerned, we were here practically on level terms; but, partly as a result of this, our direct observation over the ground held by the enemy was not so good as it was further south. On portions of this front the opposing first line trenches were more widely separated from each other; while in the valleys to the north were many hidden gun positions from which the enemy could develop flanking fire on our troops as they advanced across the open.

6. The period of active operations dealt with in this despatch divides itself roughly into three phases. The first phase opened with the attack of the 1st July, the success of which evidently came as a surprise to the enemy and caused considerable confusion and disorganisation in his ranks. The advantages gained on that date and developed during the first half of July may be regarded as having been rounded off by the operations of the 14th July and three following days, which gave us possession of the southern crest of the main plateau between Delville Wood and Bazentin-le-Petit.

We then entered upon a contest lasting for many weeks, during which the enemy, having found his strongest defences unavailing, and now fully alive to his danger, put forth his utmost efforts to keep his hold on the main ridge. This stage of the battle constituted a prolonged and severe struggle for mastery between the contending armies, in which, although progress was slow and difficult, the confidence of our troops in their ability to win was never shaken. Their tenacity and determination proved more than equal to their task, and by the first week in September they had established a fighting superiority that has left its mark on the enemy, of which possession of the ridge was merely the visible proof.

The way was then opened for the third phase, in which our advance was pushed down the forward slopes of the ridge and further extended on both flanks until, from Morval to Thiepval, the whole plateau and a good deal of ground beyond were in our possession. Meanwhile our gallant Allies, in addition to great successes south of the Somme, had pushed their advance, against equally determined opposition and under most difficult tactical conditions, up the long slopes on our immediate right, and were now preparing to drive the enemy from the summit of the narrow and difficult portion of the main ridge which lies between the Combles Valley and the River Tortille, a stream flowing from the north into the Somme just below Peronne.

7. Defences of the nature described could only be attacked with any prospect of success after careful artillery preparation. It was accordingly decided that our bombardment should begin on the 24th June, and a large force of artillery was brought into action for the purpose. Artillery bombardments were also carried out daily at different points on the rest of our front, and during the period from the 24th June to 1st July gas was discharged with good effect at

more than forty places along our line upon a frontage which in total amounted to over 15 miles. Some 70 raids, too, were undertaken by our infantry between Gommecourt and our extreme left north of Ypres during the week preceding the attack, and these kept me well informed as to the enemy's dispositions, besides serving other useful purposes.

On the 25th June the Royal Flying Corps carried out a general attack on the enemy's observation balloons, destroying nine of them, and depriving the enemy for the time being of this form of observation.

8. On July 1st, at 7.30 a.m., after a final hour of exceptionally violent bombardment, our infantry assault was launched. Simultaneously the French attacked on both sides of the Somme, co-operating closely with us.

The British main front of attack extended from Maricourt on our right, round the salient at Fricourt, to the Ancre in front of St. Pierre Divion. To assist this main attack by holding the enemy's reserves and occupying his artillery, the enemy's trenches north of the Ancre, as far as Serre inclusive, were to be assaulted simultaneously; while further north a subsidiary attack was to be made on both sides of the salient at Gommecourt.

I had entrusted the attack on the front from Maricourt to Serre to the Fourth Army, under the command of General Sir Henry S. Rawlinson, Bart., K.C.B., K.C.V.O., with five Army Corps at his disposal. The subsidiary attack at Gommecourt was carried out by troops from the Army commanded by General Sir E.H.H. Allenby, K.C.B.

Just prior to the attack the mines which had been prepared under the enemy's lines were exploded, and smoke was discharged at many places along our front. Through this smoke our infantry advanced to the attack with the utmost steadiness, in spite of the very heavy barrage of the enemy's guns. On our right our troops met with immediate success, and rapid progress was made. Before midday Montauban had been carried, and shortly afterwards the Briqueterie, to the east, and the whole of the ridge to the west of the village were in our hands. Opposite Mametz part of our assembly trenches had been practically levelled by the enemy artillery, making it necessary for our infantry to advance to the attack across 400 yards of open ground. Nonetheless they forced their way into Mametz, and reached their objective in the valley beyond, first throwing out a defensive flank towards Fricourt on their left. At the same time the enemy's trenches were entered north of Fricourt, so that the enemy's garrison in that village was pressed on three sides. Further north, though the villages of La Boisselle and Ovillers for the time being resisted our attack, our troops drove deeply into the German lines on the flanks of these strongholds, and so paved the way for their capture later. On the spur running south from Thiepval the work known as the Leipzig Salient was stormed, and severe fighting took place for the possession of the village and its defences. Here and north of the valley of the Ancre as far as Serre, on the left flank of our attack, our initial successes were not sustained. Striking progress was made at many points and parties of troops penetrated the enemy's positions to the outer defences of Grandcourt, and also to Pendant Copse and Serre; but the enemy's continued resistance at Thiepval and Beaumont Hamel made it impossible to forward reinforcements and ammunition, and, in spite of their gallant efforts, our troops were forced to withdraw during the night to their own lines.

The subsidiary attack at Gommecourt also forced its way into the enemy's positions; but there met with such vigorous opposition, that as soon as it was considered that the attack had fulfilled its object our troops were withdrawn.

9. In view of the general situation at the end of the first day's operations, I decided that the best course was to press forward on a front extending from our junction with the French to a point halfway between La Boisselle and Contalmaison, and to limit the offensive on our left for the present to a slow and methodical advance. North of the Ancre such preparations were to be made as would hold the enemy to his positions, and enable the attack to be resumed there later if desirable. In order that General Sir Henry Rawlinson might be left free to concentrate his attention on the portion of the front where the attack was to be pushed home, I also decided to place the operations against the front, La Boisselle to Serre, under the command of General Sir Hubert de la P. Gough, K.C.B., to whom I accordingly allotted the two northern corps of Sir Henry Rawlinson's army. My instructions to Sir Hubert Gough were that his Army was to maintain a steady pressure on the front from La Boisselle to the Serre Road, and to act as a pivot, on which our line could swing as our attacks on his right made progress towards the north.

10. During the succeeding days the attack was continued on these lines. In spite of strong counter-attacks on the Briqueterie and Montauban, by midday on the 2nd July our troops had captured Fricourt, and in the afternoon and evening stormed Fricourt Wood and the farm to the north. During the 3rd and 4th July Bernafay and Caterpillar Woods were also captured, and our troops pushed forward to the railway north of Mametz. On these days the reduction of La Boisselle was completed after hard fighting, while the outskirts of Contalmaison were reached on the 5th July. North of La Boisselle also the enemy's forces opposite us were kept constantly engaged, and our holding in the Leipzig Salient was gradually increased.

To sum up the results of the fighting of these five days, on a front of over six miles, from the Briqueterie to La Boisselle, our troops had swept over the whole of the enemy's first and strongest system of defence, which he had done his utmost to render impregnable. They had driven him back over a distance of more than a mile, and had carried four elaborately fortified villages.

The number of prisoners passed back at the close of the 5th July had already reached the total of ninety-four officers and 5,724 other ranks.

11. After the five days' heavy and continuous fighting just described it was essential to carry out certain readjustments and reliefs of the forces engaged. In normal conditions of enemy resistance the amount of progress that can be made at any time without a pause in the general advance is necessarily limited. Apart from the physical exhaustion of the attacking troops and the considerable distances separating the enemy's successive main systems of defence, special artillery preparation was required before a successful assault could be delivered. Meanwhile, however, local operations were continued in spite of much unfavourable weather. The attack on Contalmaison and Mametz Wood was undertaken on the 7th July, and after three days' obstinate fighting, in the course of which the enemy delivered several powerful counter-attacks, the village and the whole of the wood, except its northern border, were finally secured. On the 7th July also a footing was gained in the outer defences of Ovillers, while on the 9th July on our extreme right Maltz Horn Farm – an important point on the spur north of Hardecourt – was secured.

A thousand yards north of this farm our troops had succeeded at the second attempt in establishing themselves on the 8th July in the southern end of Trones Wood. The enemy's positions in the northern and eastern parts of this wood were very strong, and no less than eight powerful German counter-attacks were made here during the next five days. In the course of this struggle portions of the wood changed hands several times; but we were left eventually, on the 13th July, in possession of the southern part of it.

12. Meanwhile Mametz Wood had been entirely cleared of the enemy, and with Trones Wood also practically in our possession we were in a position to undertake an assault upon the enemy's second system of defences. Arrangements were accordingly made for an attack to be delivered at daybreak on the morning of the 14th July against a front extending from Longueval to Bazentin-le-Petit Wood, both inclusive. Contalmaison Villa, on a spur 1,000 yards west of Bazentin-le-Petit Wood, had already been captured to secure the left flank of the attack, and advantage had been taken of the progress made by our infantry to move our artillery forward into new positions. The preliminary bombardment had opened on the 11th July. The opportunities offered by the ground for enfilading the enemy's lines were fully utilised and did much to secure the success of our attack.

13. In the early hours of the 14th July the attacking troops moved out over the open for a distance of from about 1,000 to 1,400 yards, and lined up in the darkness just below the crest and some 300 to 500 yards from the enemy's trenches. Their advance was covered by strong patrols, and their correct deployment had been ensured by careful previous preparations. The whole movement was carried out unobserved and without touch being lost in any case. The decision to attempt a night operation of this magnitude with an Army, the bulk of which has been raised since the beginning of the war, was perhaps the highest tribute that could be paid to the quality of our troops. It would not have been possible but for the most careful preparation and forethought, as well as thorough reconnaissance of the ground which was in many cases made personally by Divisional, Brigade and Battalion Commanders and their staffs before framing their detailed orders for the advance.

The actual assault was delivered at 3.25 a.m. on the 14th July, when there was just sufficient light to be able to distinguish friend from foe at short ranges, and along the whole front attacked our troops, preceded by a very effective artillery barrage, swept over the enemy's first trenches and on into the defences beyond.

On our right the enemy was driven from his last foothold in Trones Wood, and by 8.0 a.m. we had cleared the whole of it, relieving a body of 170 men who had maintained themselves all night in the northern corner of the wood, although completely surrounded by the enemy. Our position in the wood was finally consolidated, and strong patrols were sent out from it in the direction of Guillemont and Longueval. The southern half of this latter village was already in the hands of the troops who had advanced west of Trones Wood. The northern half, with the exception of two strong points, was captured by 4.0 p.m. after a severe struggle.

In the centre of our attack Bazentin-le-Grand village and wood were also gained, and our troops pushing northwards captured Bazentin-le-Petit village, and the cemetery to the east. Here the enemy counter-attacked twice about midday without success, and again in the afternoon, on the latter occasion momentarily reoccupying the northern half of the village as far as the church. Our troops immediately returned to the attack, and drove him out again with heavy losses. To the left of the village Bazentin-le-Petit Wood was cleared, in spite of the considerable resistance of the enemy along its western edge, where we successfully repulsed a counter-attack. In the afternoon further ground was gained to the west of the Wood, and posts were established immediately south of Pozieres.

The enemy's troops, who had been severely handled in these attacks and counter-attacks, began to show signs of disorganisation, and it was reported early in the afternoon that it was possible to advance to High Wood. General

Rawlinson, who had held a force of cavalry in readiness for such an eventuality, decided to employ a part of it. As the fight progressed small bodies of this force had pushed forward gradually, keeping in close touch with the development of the action and prepared to seize quickly any opportunity that might occur. A squadron now came up on the flanks of our infantry, who entered High Wood at about 8.0 p.m., and, after some hand-to-hand fighting, cleared the whole of the Wood with the exception of the northern apex. Acting mounted in co-operation with the infantry the cavalry came into action with good effect, killing several of the enemy and capturing some prisoners.

14. On the 15th July the battle still continued, though on a reduced scale. Arrow Head Copse, between the southern edge of Trones Wood and Guillemont, and Waterlot Farm on the Longueval – Guillemont Road, were seized, and Delville Wood was captured and held against several hostile counterattacks. In Longueval fierce fighting continued until dusk for the possession of the two strong points and the orchards to the north of the village. The situation in this area made the position of our troops in High Wood somewhat precarious, and they now began to suffer numerous casualties from the enemy's heavy shelling. Accordingly orders were given for their withdrawal, and this was effected during the night of the 15/16th July without interference by the enemy. All the wounded were brought in.

In spite of repeated enemy counter-attacks further progress was made on the night of the 16th July along the enemy's main second line trenches north-west of Bazentin-le-Petit Wood to within 500 yards of the north-east corner of the village of Pozieres, which our troops were already approaching from the South.

Meanwhile the operations further north had also made progress. Since the attack of the 7th July the enemy in and about Ovillers had been pressed relentlessly, and gradually driven back by incessant bombing attacks and local assaults, in accordance with the general instructions I had given to General Sir Hubert Gough. On the 16th July a large body of the garrison of Ovillers surrendered, and that night and during the following day, by a direct advance from the west across No Man's Land, our troops carried the remainder of the village and pushed out along the spur to the north and eastwards towards Pozieres.

15. The results of the operations of the 14th July and subsequent days were of considerable importance. The enemy's second main system of defence had been captured on a front of over three miles. We had again forced him back more than a mile, and had gained possession of the southern crest of the main ridge on a front of 6,000 yards. Four more of his fortified villages and three

woods had been wrested from him by determined fighting, and our advanced troops had penetrated as far as his third line of defence. In spite of a resolute resistance and many counter-attacks, in which the enemy had suffered severely, our line was definitely established from Maltz Horn Farm, where we met the French left, northwards along the eastern edge of Trones Wood to Longueval, then westwards past Bazentin-le-Grand to the northern corner of Bazentin-le-Petit and Bazentin-le-Petit Wood, and then westwards again past the southern face of Pozieres to the north of Ovillers. Posts were established at Arrow Head Copse and Waterlot Farm, while we had troops thrown forward in Delville Wood and towards High Wood, though their position was not yet secure.

I cannot speak too highly of the skill, daring, endurance and determination by which these results had been achieved. Great credit is due to Sir Henry Rawlinson for the thoroughness and care with which this difficult undertaking was planned; while the advance and deployment made by night without confusion, and the complete success of the subsequent attack, constitute a striking tribute to the discipline and spirit of the troops engaged, as well as to the powers of leadership and organisation of their commanders and staffs.

During these operations and their development on the 15th a number of enemy guns were taken, making our total captures since the 1st July 8 heavy howitzers, 4 heavy guns, 42 field and light guns and field howitzers, 30 trench mortars and 52 machine guns. Very considerable losses had been inflicted on the enemy, and the prisoners captured amounted to over 2,000, bringing the total since the 1st July to over 10,000.

16. There was strong evidence that the enemy forces engaged on the battle front had been severely shaken by the repeated successes gained by ourselves and our Allies; but the great strength and depth of his defences had secured for him sufficient time to bring up fresh troops, and he had still many powerful fortifications, both trenches, villages and woods, to which he could cling in our front and on our flanks.

We had, indeed, secured a footing on the main ridge, but only on a front of 6,000 yards; and desirous though I was to follow up quickly the successes we had won, it was necessary first to widen this front.

West of Bazentin-le-Petit the villages of Pozieres and Thiepval, together with the whole elaborate system of trenches round, between and on the main ridge behind them, had still to be carried. An advance further east would, however, eventually turn these defences, and all that was for the present required on the left flank of our attack was a steady, methodical, step by step advance as already ordered.

On our right flank the situation called for stronger measures. At Delville Wood and Longueval our lines formed a sharp salient, from which our front ran on the one side westwards to Pozieres, and on the other southwards to Maltz Horn Farm. At Maltz Horn Farm our lines joined the French, and the Allied front continued still southwards to the village of Hem on the Somme.

This pronounced salient invited counterattacks by the enemy. He possessed direct observation on it all round from Guillemont on the south-east to High Wood on the northwest. He could bring a concentric fire of artillery to bear not only on the wood and village, but also on the confined space behind, through which ran the French communications as well as ours, where great numbers of guns, besides ammunition and impedimenta of all sorts, had necessarily to be crowded together. Having been in occupation of this ground for nearly two years he knew every foot of it, and could not fail to appreciate the possibilities of causing us heavy loss there by indirect artillery fire; while it was evident that, if he could drive in the salient in our line and so gain direct observation on to the ground behind, our position in that area would become very uncomfortable.

If there had not been good grounds for confidence that the enemy was not capable of driving from this position troops who had shown themselves able to wrest it from him, the situation would have been an anxious one. In any case it was clear that the first requirement at the moment was that our right flank, and the French troops in extension of it, should swing up into line with our centre. To effect this, however, strong enemy positions had to be captured both by ourselves and by our Allies.

From Delville Wood the main plateau extends for 4,000 yards east-north-east to Les Boeufs and Morval, and for about the same distance south-eastwards to Leuze and Bouleau Woods, which stand above and about 1,000 yards to the west of Combles. To bring my right up into line with the rest of my front it was necessary to capture Guillemont, Falfemont Farm and Leuze Wood, and then Ginchy and Bouleaux Wood. These localities were naturally very strong, and they had been elaborately fortified. The enemy's main second line system of defence ran in front of them from Waterlot Farm, which was already in our hands, south-eastwards to Falfemont Farm, and thence southwards to the Somme. The importance of holding us back in this area could not escape the enemy's notice, and he had dug and wired many new trenches, both in front of and behind his original lines. He had also brought up fresh troops, and there was no possibility of taking him by surprise.

The task before us was therefore a very difficult one and entailed a real trial of strength between the opposing forces. At this juncture its difficulties were increased by unfavourable weather. The nature of the ground limited the possibility of direct observation by our artillery fire, and we were consequently much dependent on observation from the air. As in that element we had attained almost complete superiority, all that we required was a clear atmosphere; but with this we were not favoured for several weeks. We had rather more rain than is usual in July and August, and even when no rain fell there was an almost constant haze and frequent low clouds.

In swinging up my own right it was very important that the French line north of the Somme should be advanced at the same time in close combination with the movement of the British troops. The line of demarcation agreed on between the French commander and myself ran from Maltz Horn Farm due eastwards to the Combles Valley and then north-eastwards up that valley to a point midway between Sailly-Saillisel and Morval. These two villages had been fixed upon as the objectives, respectively, of the French left and of my right. In order to advance in co-operation with my right, and eventually to reach Sailly-Saillisel, our Allies had still to fight their way up that portion of the main ridge which lies between the Combles Valley on the west and the River Tortille on the east. To do so they had to capture, in the first place, the strongly fortified villages of Maurepas, Le Forest, Rancourt and Fregicourt, besides many woods and strong systems of trenches. As the high ground on each side of the Combles Valley commands the slopes of the ridge on the opposite side, it was essential that the advance of the two armies should be simultaneous and made in the closest co-operation. This was fully recognised by both armies and our plans were made accordingly.

To carry out the necessary preparations to deal with the difficult situation outlined above a short pause was necessary to enable tired troops to be relieved and guns to be moved forward; while at the same time old communications had to be improved and new ones made. Entrenchments against probable counterattacks could not be neglected, and fresh dispositions of troops were required for the new attacks to be directed eastwards.

It was also necessary to continue such pressure on the rest of our front, not only on the Ancre but further south, as would make it impossible for the enemy to devote himself entirely to resisting the advance between Delville Wood and the Somme. In addition it was desirable further to secure our hold on the main ridge west of Delville Wood by gaining more ground to our front in that direction. Orders were therefore issued in accordance with the general considerations explained above, and, without relaxing pressure along the enemy's front from Delville Wood to the West, preparations for an attack on Guillemont were pushed on.

17. During the afternoon of the 18th July the enemy developed his expected counterattack against Delville Wood, after heavy preliminary shelling. By sheer weight of numbers and at very heavy cost he forced his way through the

northern and north-eastern portions of the wood and into the northern half of Longueval, which our troops had cleared only that morning. In the south-east corner of the wood he was held up by a gallant defence, and further south three attacks on our positions in Waterlot Farm failed.

This enemy attack on Delville Wood marked the commencement of the long closely contested struggle which was not finally decided in our favour till the fall of Guillemont on the 3rd September, a decision which was confirmed by the capture of Ginchy six days later. Considerable gains were indeed made during this period; but progress was slow and bought only by hard fighting. A footing was established in High Wood on the 20th July and our line linked up thence with Longueval. A subsequent advance by the Fourth Army on the 23rd July on a wide front from Guillemont to near Pozieres found the enemy in great strength all along the line, with machine guns and forward troops in shell holes and newly constructed trenches well in front of his main defences. Although ground was won the strength of the resistance experienced showed that the hostile troops had recovered from their previous confusion suf-ficiently to necessitate long and careful preparation before further successes on any great scale could be secured.

An assault delivered simultaneously on this date by General Gough's Army against Pozieres gained considerable results, and by the morning of the 25th July the whole of that village was carried, including the cemetery, and important progress was made along the enemy's trenches to the north-east. That evening, after heavy artillery preparation, the enemy launched two more powerful counterattacks, the one directed against our new position in and around High Wood and the other delivered from the north-west of Delville Wood. Both attacks were completely broken up with very heavy losses to the enemy.

On the 27th July the remainder of Delville Wood was recovered, and two days later the northern portion of Longueval and the orchards were cleared of the enemy, after severe fighting, in which our own and the enemy's artillery were very active.

18. On the 30th July the village of Guillemont and Falfemont Farm to the south-east were attacked, in conjunction with a French attack north of the Somme. A battalion entered Guillemont, and part of it passed through to the far side; but as the battalions on either flank did not reach their objectives, it was obliged to fall back, after holding out for some hours on the western edge of the village. In a subsequent local attack on the 7th August our troops again entered Guillemont, but were again compelled to fall back owing to the failure of a simultaneous effort against the enemy's trenches on the flanks of the village.

The ground to the south of Guillemont was dominated by the enemy's positions in and about that village. It was therefore hoped that these positions might be captured first, before an advance to the south of them in the direction of Falfemont Farm was pushed further forward. It had now become evident, however, that Guillemont could not be captured as an isolated enterprise without very heavy loss, and, accordingly, arrangements were made with the French Army on our immediate right for a series of combined attacks, to be delivered in progressive stages, which should embrace Maurepas, Falfemont Farm, Guillemont, Leuze Wood and Ginchy.

An attempt on the 16th August to carry out the first stage of the pre-arranged scheme met with only partial success, and two days later, after a preliminary bombardment, lasting thirty-six hours, a larger combined attack was undertaken. In spite of a number of enemy counter-attacks – the most violent of which, levelled at the point of junction of the British with the French, succeeded in forcing our Allies and ourselves back from a part of the ground won – very valuable progress was made, and our troops established themselves in the outskirts of Guillemont village and occupied Guillemont Station. A violent counterattack on Guillemont Station was repulsed on the 23rd August, and next day further important progress was made on a wide front north and east of Delville Wood.

19. Apart from the operations already described, others of a minor character, yet involving much fierce and obstinate fighting, continued during this period on the fronts of both the British Armies. Our lines were pushed forward wherever possible by means of local attacks and by bombing and sapping, and the enemy was driven out of various forward positions from which he might hamper our progress. By these means many gains were made which, though small in themselves, in the aggregate represented very considerable advances. In this way our line was brought to the crest of the ridge above Martinpuich, and Pozieres Windmill and the high ground north of the village were secured, and with them observation over Martinpuich and Courcelette and the enemy's gun positions in their neighbourhood and around Le Sars. At a later date our troops reached the defences of Mouquet Farm, north-west of Pozieres, and made progress in the enemy's trenches south of Thiepval. The enemy's counter-attacks were incessant and frequently of great violence, but they were made in vain and at heavy cost to him. The fierceness of the fighting can be gathered from the fact that one regiment of the German Guards Reserve Corps which had been in the Thiepval salient opposite Mouquet Farm is known to have lost 1,400 men in fifteen days.

20. The first two days of September on both Army fronts were spent in preparation for a more general attack, which the gradual progress made

during the preceding month had placed us in a position to undertake. Our assault was delivered at 12 noon on the 3rd September on a front extending from our extreme right to the enemy trenches on the right bank of the Ancre, north of Hamel. Our Allies attacked simultaneously on our right.

Guillemont was stormed and at once consolidated, and our troops pushed on unchecked to Ginchy and the line of the road running south to Wedge Wood. Ginchy was also seized, but here in the afternoon we were very strongly counter-attacked. For three days the tide of attack and counter-attack swayed backwards and forwards amongst the ruined houses of the village, till, in the end, for three days more the greater part of it remained in the enemy's possession. Three counter-attacks made on the evening of the 3rd September against our troops in Guillemont all failed with considerable loss to the enemy. We also gained ground north of Delville Wood and in High Wood, though here an enemy counter-attack recovered part of the ground won.

On the front of General Gough's Army, though the enemy suffered heavy losses in personnel, our gain in ground was slight.

21. In order to keep touch with the French who were attacking on our right, the assault on Falfemont Farm on the 3rd September was delivered three hours before the opening of the main assault. In the impetus of their first rush our troops reached the farm, but could not hold it. Nevertheless, they pushed on to the north of it, and on the 4th September delivered a series of fresh assaults upon it from the west and north.

Ultimately this strongly fortified position was occupied piece by piece, and by the morning of the 5th September the whole of it was in our possession. Meanwhile further progress had been made to the north-east of the farm, where considerable initiative was shown by the local commanders. By the evening of the same day our troops were established strongly in Leuze Wood, which on the following day was finally cleared of the enemy.

22. In spite of the fact that most of Ginchy and of High Wood remained in the enemy's hands, very noteworthy progress had been made in the course of these four days' operations, exceeding anything that had been achieved since the 14th July. Our right was advanced on a front of nearly two miles to an average depth of nearly one mile, penetrating the enemy's original second line of defence on this front, and capturing strongly fortified positions at Falfemont Farm, Leuze Wood, Guillemont, and south-east of Delville Wood, where we reached the western outskirts of Ginchy. More important than this gain in territory was the fact that the barrier which for seven weeks the enemy had maintained against our further advance had at last been

broken. Over 1,000 prisoners were made and many machine guns taken or destroyed in the course of the fighting.

23. Preparations for a further attack upon Ginchy continued without intermission, and at 4.45 p.m. on the 9th September the attack was reopened on the whole of the Fourth Army front. At Ginchy and to the north of Leuze Wood it met with almost immediate success. On the right the enemy's line was seized over a front of more than 1,000 yards from the southwest corner of Bouleaux Wood in a north-westerly direction to a point just south of the Guillemont-Morval tramway. Our troops again forced their way into Ginchy, and passing beyond it carried the line of enemy trenches to the east. Further progress was made east of Delville Wood and south and east of High Wood.

Over 500 prisoners were taken in the operations of the 9th September and following days, making the total since the 1st July over 17,000.

24. Meanwhile the French had made great progress on our right, bringing their line forward to Louage Wood (just south of Combles) – Le Forest – Clery-sur-Somme, all three inclusive. The weak salient in the Allied line had therefore disappeared and we had gained the front required for further operations.

Still more importance, however, lay in the proof afforded by the results described of the ability of our new Armies not only to rush the enemy's strongest defences, as had been accomplished on the 1st and 14th July, but also to wear down and break his power of resistance by a steady, relentless pressure, as they had done during the weeks of this fierce and protracted struggle. As has already been recounted, the preparations made for our assault on the 1st July had been long and elaborate; but though the enemy knew that an attack was coming, it would seem that he considered the troops already on the spot, secure in their apparently impregnable defences, would suffice to deal with it. The success of that assault, combined with the vigour and determination with which our troops pressed their advantage, and followed by the successful night attack of the 14th July, all served to awaken him to a fuller realisation of his danger. The great depth of his system of fortification, to which reference has been made, gave him time to reorganise his defeated troops, and to hurry up numerous fresh divisions and more guns. Yet in spite of this, he was still pushed back, steadily and continuously. Trench after trench, and strong point after strong point were wrested from him. The great majority of his frequent counter-attacks failed completely, with heavy loss; while the few that achieved temporary local success purchased it dearly, and were soon thrown back from the ground they had for the moment regained.

The enemy had, it is true, delayed our advance considerably, but the effort had cost him dear; and the comparative collapse of his resistance during the last few days of the struggle justified the belief that in the long run decisive victory would lie with our troops, who had displayed such fine fighting qualities and such indomitable endurance and resolution.

25. Practically the whole of the forward crest of the main ridge, on a front of some 9,000 yards from Delville Wood to the road above Mouquet Farm, was now in our hands, and with it the advantage of observation over the slopes beyond. East of Delville Wood, for a further 3,000 yards to Leuze Wood, we were firmly established on the main ridge; while further east, across the Combles Valley, the French were advancing victoriously on our right. But though the centre of our line was well placed, on our flanks there was still difficult ground to be won. From Ginchy the crest of the high ground runs northwards for 2,000 yards, and then eastward, in a long spur, for nearly 4,000 yards. Near the eastern extremity of this spur stands the village of Morval, commanding a wide field of view and fire in every direction. At Leuze Wood my right was still 2,000 yards from its objective at this village, and between lay a broad and deep branch of the main Combles Valley, completely commanded by the Morval spur, and flanked, not only from its head north-east of Ginchy, but also from the high ground east of the Combles Valley, which looks directly into it.

Up this high ground beyond the Combles Valley the French were work-ing their way towards their objective at Sailly-Saillisel, situated due east of Morval, and standing at the same level. Between these two villages the ground falls away to the head of the Combles Valley, which runs thence in a south-westerly direction. In the bottom of this valley lies the small town of Combles, then well fortified and strongly held, though dominated by my right at Leuze Wood, and by the French left on the opposite heights. It had been agreed between the French and myself that an assault on Combles would not be necessary, as the place could be rendered untenable by pressing forward along the ridges above it in on either side.

The capture of Morval from the south presented a very difficult problem, while the capture of Sailly-Saillisel, at that time some 3,000 yards to the north of the French left, was in some respects even more difficult. The line of the French advance was narrowed almost to a defile by the extensive and strongly fortified wood of St. Pierre Vaast on the one side, and on the other by the Combles Valley, which, with the branches running out from it, and the slopes on each side, is completely commanded, as has been pointed out, by the heights bounding the valley on the east and west.

On my right flank, therefore, the progress of the French and British forces was still interdependent, and the closest co-operation continued to be neces-sary in order to gain the further ground required to enable my centre to advance on a sufficiently wide front. To cope with such a situation unity of command is usually essential, but in this case the cordial good feeling between the Allied Armies, and the earnest desire of each to assist the other, proved equally effective, and removed all difficulties.

On my left flank the front of General Gough's Army bent back from the main ridge near Mouquet Farm down a spur descending south-westwards, and then crossed a broad valley to the Wonderwork, a strong point situated in the enemy's front-line system near the southern end of the spur on the higher slopes of which Thiepval stands. Opposite this part of our line we had still to carry the enemy's original defences on the main ridge above Thiepval, and in the village itself, defences which may fairly be described as being as nearly impregnable as nature, art, and the unstinted labour of nearly two years could make them.

Our advance on Thiepval, and on the defences above it, had been carried out up to this date, in accordance with my instructions given on the 3rd July, by a slow and methodical progression, in which great skill and much patience and endurance had been displayed with entirely satisfactory results. General Gough's Army had, in fact, acted most successfully in the required manner as a pivot to the remainder of the attack. The Thiepval defences were known to be exceptionally strong, and as immediate possession of them was not necessary to the development of my plans after the 1st July, there had been no need to incur the heavy casualties to be expected in an attempt to rush them. The time was now approaching, although it had not yet arrived, when their capture would become necessary; but from the positions we had now reached and those which we expected shortly to obtain, I had no doubt that they could be rushed when required without undue loss. An important part of the remaining positions required for my assault on them was now won by a highly successful enterprise carried out on the evening of the 14th September, by which the Wonderwork was stormed.

26. The general plan of the combined Allied attack which was opened on the 15th September was to pivot on the high ground south of the Ancre and north of the Albert – Bapaume road, while the Fourth Army devoted its whole effort to the rearmost of the enemy's original systems of defence between Morval and Le Sars. Should our success in this direction warrant it I made arrangements to enable me to extend the left of the attack to embrace the villages of Martinpuich and Courcelette. As soon as our advance on this front had reached the Morval line, the time would have arrived to bring forward my left across the Thiepval Ridge. Meanwhile on my right our Allies arranged to continue the line of advance in close co-operation with me from the Somme to the slopes above Combles; but directing their main effort northwards

against the villages of Rancourt and Fregicourt, so as to complete the isolation of Combles and open the way for their attack upon Sailly-Saillisel.

27. A methodical bombardment was commenced at 6.0 a.m. on the 12th September and was continued steadily and uninterruptedly till the moment of attack.

At 6.20 a.m. on the 15th September the infantry assault commenced, and at the same moment the bombardment became intense. Our new heavily armoured cars, known as "Tanks," now brought into action for the first time, successfully co-operated with the infantry, and coming as a surprise to the enemy rank and file gave valuable help in breaking down their resistance. The advance met with immediate success on almost the whole of the front attacked. At 8.40 a.m. tanks were seen to be entering Flers, followed by large numbers of troops. Fighting continued in Flers for some time, but by 10.0 a.m. our troops had reached the north side of the village, and by midday had occupied the enemy's trenches for some distance beyond. On our right our line was advanced to within assaulting distance of the strong line of defence running before Morval, Les Boeufs and Gueudecourt, and on our left High Wood was at last carried after many hours of very severe fighting, reflecting great credit on the attacking battalions. Our success made it possible to carry out during the afternoon that part of the plan which provided for the capture of Martinpuich and Courcelette, and by the end of the day both these villages were in our hands. On the 18th September the work of this day was completed by the capture of the Quadrilateral, an enemy stronghold which had hitherto blocked the progress of our right towards Morval. Further progress was also made between Flers and Martinpuich.

28. The result of the fighting of the 15th September and following days was a gain more considerable than any which had attended our arms in the course of a single operation since the commencement of the offensive. In the course of one day's fighting we had broken through two of the enemy's main defensive systems and had advanced on a front of over six miles to an average depth of a mile. In the course of this advance we had taken three large villages, each powerfully organised for prolonged resistance. Two of these villages had been carried by assault with short preparation in the course of a few hours' fighting. All this had been accomplished with a small number of casualties in comparison with the troops employed, and in spite of the fact that, as was afterwards discovered, the attack did not come as a complete surprise to the enemy.

The total number of prisoners taken by us in these operations since their commencement on the evening of the 14th September amounted at this date to over 4,000, including 127 officers.

29. Preparations for our further advance were again hindered by bad weather, but at 12.35 p.m. on the 25th September, after a bombardment commenced early in the morning of the 24th, a general attack by the Allies was launched on the whole front between the Somme and Martinpuich. The objectives on the British front included the villages of Morval, Les Boeufs and Gueudecourt, and a belt of country about 1,000 yards deep curving round the north of Flers to a point midway between that village and Martinpuich. By nightfall the whole of these objectives were in our hands, with the exception of the village of Gueudecourt, before which our troops met with very serious resistance from a party of the enemy in a section of his fourth main system of defence.

On our right our Allies carried the village of Rancourt, and advanced their line to the outskirts of Fregicourt, capturing that village also during the night and early morning. Combles was therefore nearly surrounded by the Allied forces, and in the early morning of the 26th September the village was occupied simultaneously by the Allied forces, the British to the north and the French to the south of the railway. The capture of Combles in this inexpensive fashion represented a not inconsiderable tactical success. Though lying in a hollow, the village was very strongly fortified, and possessed, in addition to the works which the enemy had constructed, exceptionally large cellars and galleries, at a great depth underground, sufficient to give effectual shelter to troops and material under the heaviest bombardment. Great quantities of stores and ammunition of all sorts were found in these cellars when the village was taken.

On the same day Gueudecourt was carried, after the protecting trench to the west had been captured in a somewhat interesting fashion. In the early morning a Tank started down the portion of the trench held by the enemy from the north-west, firing its machine guns and followed by bombers. The enemy could not escape, as we held the trench at the southern end. At the same time an aeroplane flew down the length of the trench, also firing a machine gun at the enemy holding it. These then waved white handkerchiefs in token of surrender, and when this was reported by the aeroplane the infantry accepted the surrender of the garrison. By 8.30 a.m. the whole trench had been cleared, great numbers of the enemy had been killed, and 8 officers and 362 other ranks made prisoners. Our total casualties amounted to five.

30. The success of the Fourth Army had now brought our advance to the stage at which I judged it advisable that Thiepval should be taken, in order to bring our left flank into line and establish it on the main ridge above that village, the possession of which would be of considerable tactical value in future operations.

Accordingly at 12.25 p.m on the 26th September, before the enemy had been given time to recover from the blow struck by the Fourth Army, a general attack was launched against Thiepval and the Thiepval Ridge. The objective consisted of the whole of the high ground still remaining in enemy hands extending over a front of some 3,000 yards north and east of Thiepval, and including, in addition to that fortress, the Zollern Redoubt, the Stuff Redoubt, and the Schwaben Redoubt, with the connecting lines of trenches.

The attack was a brilliant success. On the right our troops reached the system of enemy trenches which formed their objectives without great difficulty. In Thiepval and the strong works to the north of it the enemy's resistance was more desperate. Three waves of our attacking troops carried the outer defences of Mouquet Farm, and, pushing on, entered Zollern Redoubt, which they stormed and consolidated. In the strong point formed by the buildings of the Farm itself, the enemy garrison, securely posted in deep cellars, held out until 6.0 p.m., when their last defences were forced by a working party of a Pioneer Battalion acting on its own initiative.

On the left of the attack fierce fighting, in which Tanks again gave valuable assistance to our troops, continued in Thiepval during that day and the following night, but by 8.30 a.m. on the 27th September the whole of the village of Thiepval was in our hands.

Some 2,300 prisoners were taken in the course of the fighting on the Thiepval Ridge on these and the subsequent days, bringing the total number of prisoners taken in the battle area in the operations of the 14th-30th September to nearly 10,000. In the same period we had captured 27 guns, over 200 machine guns, and some 40 trench mortars.

31. On the same date the south and west sides of Stuff Redoubt were carried by our troops, together with the length of trench connecting that strong point with Schwaben Redoubt to the west and also the greater part of the enemy's defensive line eastwards along the northern slopes of the ridge. Schwaben Redoubt was assaulted during the afternoon, and in spite of counter attacks, delivered by strong enemy reinforcements, we captured the whole of the southern face of the Redoubt and pushed out patrols to the northern face and towards St. Pierre Divion.

Our line was also advanced north of Courcelette, while on the Fourth Army front a further portion of the enemy's fourth system, of defence north-west of Gueudecourt was carried on a front of a mile. Between these two points the enemy fell back upon his defences running in front of Eaucourt l'Abbaye and Le Sars and on the afternoon and evening of the 27th September our troops were able to make a very considerable advance in this area without encountering serious opposition until within a few hundred yards of this line. The ground thus occupied extended to a depth of from 500 to 600 yards on a front of nearly two miles between the Bazentin-le-Petit, Ligny, Thilloy and Albert – Bapaume roads.

Destremont Farm, south-west of Le Sars, was carried by a single company on the 29th September, and on the afternoon of the 1st October a successful attack was launched against Eaucourt l'Abbaye and the enemy defences to the east and west of it, comprising a total front of about 3,000 yards. Our artillery barrage was extremely accurate, and contributed greatly to the success of the attack. Bomb fighting continued among the buildings during the next two days, but by the evening of the 3rd October the whole of Eaucourt l'Abbaye was in our hands.

32. At the end of September I had handed over Morval to the French, in order to facilitate their attacks on Sailly-Saillisel, and on the 7th October, after a postponement rendered necessary by three days' continuous rain, our Allies made a considerable advance in the direction of the latter village. On the same day the Fourth Army attacked along the whole front from Les Boeufs to Destremont Farm in support of the operations of our Allies.

The village of Le Sars was captured, together with the Quarry to the north-west, while considerable progress was made at other points along the front attacked. In particular, to the east of Gueudecourt, the enemy's trenches were carried on a breadth of some 2,000 yards, and a footing gained on the crest of the long spur which screens the defences of Le Transloy from the south-west. Nearly 1,000 prisoners were secured by the Fourth Army in the course of these operations.

33. With the exception of his positions in the neighbourhood of Sailly-Saillisel, and his scanty foothold on the northern crest of the high ground above Thiepval, the enemy had now been driven from the whole of the ridge lying between the Tortille and the Ancre.

Possession of the north-western portion of the ridge north of the latter village carried with it observation over the valley of the Ancre between Miraumont and Hamel and the spurs and valleys held by the enemy on the right bank of the river. The Germans, therefore, made desperate efforts to cling to their last remaining trenches in this area, and in the course of the three weeks following our advance made repeated counter-attacks at heavy cost in the vain hope of recovering the ground they had lost. During this period our gains in the neighbourhood of Stuff and Schwaben Redoubts were gradually increased and secured in readiness for future operations; and I was quite confident of the ability of our troops, not only to repulse the enemy's attacks, but to clear him entirely from his last positions on the ridge whenever it should suit my plans to do so. I was, therefore, well content with the situation on this flank.

Along the centre of our line from Gueudecourt to the west of Le Sars similar considerations applied. As we were already well down the forward slopes of the ridge on this front, it was for the time being inadvisable to make any serious advance. Pending developments elsewhere all that was necessary or indeed desirable was to carry on local operations to improve our positions and to keep the enemy fully employed.

On our eastern flank, on the other hand, it was important to gain ground. Here the enemy still possessed a strong system of trenches covering the villages of Le Transloy and Beaulencourt and the town of Bapaume; but, although he was digging with feverish haste, he had not yet been able to create any very formidable defences behind this line. In this direction, in fact, we had at last reached a stage at which a successful attack might reasonably be expected to yield much greater results than anything we had yet attained. The resistance of the troops opposed to us had seriously weakened in the course of our recent operations, and there was no reason to suppose that the effort required would not be within our powers.

This last completed system of defence, before Le Transloy, was flanked to the south by the enemy's positions at Sailly-Saillisel and screened to the west by the spur lying between Le Transloy and Les Boeufs. A necessary preliminary, therefore, to an assault upon it was to secure the spur and the Sailly-Saillisel heights. Possession of the high ground at this latter village would at once give a far better command over the ground to the north and north-west, secure the flank of our operations towards Le Transloy, and deprive the enemy of observation over the Allied communications in the Combles Valley. In view of the enemy's efforts to construct new systems of defence behind the Le Transloy line, it was desirable to lose no time in dealing with the situation.

Unfortunately, at this juncture, very unfavourable weather set in and continued with scarcely a break during the remainder of October and the early part of November. Poor visibility seriously interfered with the work of our artillery, and constant rain turned the mass of hastily dug trenches for which we were fighting into channels of deep mud. The country roads, broken by countless shell craters, that cross the deep stretch of ground we had lately won, rapidly became almost impassable, making the supply of food, stores and ammunition a serious problem. These conditions multiplied the difficulties of attack to such an extent that it was found impossible to exploit the situation with the rapidity necessary to enable us to reap the full benefits of the advantages we had gained.

None the less my right flank continued to assist the operations of our Allies against Saillisel, and attacks were made to this end, whenever a slight improvement in the weather made the co-operation of artillery and infantry at all possible. The delay in our advance, however, though unavoidable, had given the enemy time to reorganise and rally his troops. His resistance again became stubborn and he seized every favourable opportunity for counter-attacks. Trenches changed hands with great frequency, the conditions of ground making it difficult to renew exhausted supplies of bombs and ammunition, or to consolidate the ground won, and so rendering it an easier matter to take a battered trench than to hold it.

34. On the 12th and 18th September further gains were made to the east of the Les Boeufs – Gueudecourt line and east of Le Sars, and some hundreds of prisoners were taken. On these dates, despite all the difficulties of ground, the French first reached and then captured the villages of Sailly-Saillisel, but the moment for decisive action was rapidly passing away, while the weather showed no signs of improvement. By this time, too, the ground had already become so bad that nothing less than a prolonged period of drying weather, which at that season of the year was most unlikely to occur, would suit our purpose.

In these circumstances, while continuing to do all that was possible to improve my position on my right flank, I determined to press on with preparations for the exploitation of the favourable local situation on my left flank. At midday on the 21st October, during a short spell of fine, cold weather, the line of Regina Trench and Stuff Trench, from the west Courcelette – Pys road westward to Schwaben Redoubt, was attacked with complete success. Assisted by an excellent artillery preparation and barrage, our infantry carried the whole of their objectives very quickly and with remarkably little loss, and our new line was firmly established in spite of the enemy's shell fire. Over 1,000 prisoners were taken in the course of the day's fighting, a figure only slightly exceeded by our casualties.

On the 23rd October, and again on the 5th November, while awaiting better weather for further operations on the Ancre, our attacks on the enemy's positions to the east of Les Boeufs and Gueudecourt were renewed, in conjunction with French operations against the Sailly-Saillisel heights and St. Pierre Vaast Wood. Considerable further progress was achieved. Our footing on the crest of the Le Transloy Spur was extended and secured, and the much contested tangle of trenches at our junction with the French left at last passed definitely into our possession. Many smaller gains were made in this neighbourhood by local assaults during these days, in spite of the difficult conditions of the ground. In particular, on the 10th November, after a day of improved weather, the portion of Regina Trench lying to the east of the Courcelette – Pys Road was carried on a front of about 1,000 yards.

Throughout these operations the enemy's counter-attacks were very numerous and determined, succeeding indeed in the evening of the 23rd October in regaining a portion of the ground east of Le Sars taken from him by our attack on that day. On all other occasions his attacks were broken by our artillery or infantry and the losses incurred by him in these attempts, made frequently with considerable effectives, were undoubtedly very severe.

35. On the 9th November the long continued bad weather took a turn for the better, and thereafter remained dry and cold, with frosty nights and misty mornings, for some days. Final preparations were therefore pushed on for the attack on the Ancre, though, as the ground was still very bad in places, it was necessary to limit the operations to what it would be reasonably possible to consolidate and hold under the existing conditions.

The enemy's defences in this area were already extremely formidable when they resisted our assault on the 1st July, and the succeeding period of four months had been spent in improving and adding to them in the light of the experience he had gained in the course of our attacks further south. The hamlet of St. Pierre Divion and the villages of Beaucourt-sur-Ancre and Beaumont Hamel, like the rest of the villages forming part of the enemy's original front in this district, were evidently intended by him to form a permanent line of fortifications, while he developed his offensive elsewhere. Realising that his position in them had become a dangerous one, the enemy had multiplied the number of his guns covering this part of his line, and at the end of October introduced an additional Division on his front between Grandcourt and Hebuterne.

36. At 5 a.m. on the morning of the 11th November the special bombardment preliminary to the attack was commenced. It continued with bursts of great intensity until 5.45 a.m. on the morning of the 13th November, when it developed into a very effective barrage covering the assaulting infantry.

At that hour our troops advanced on the enemy's position through dense fog, and rapidly entered his first line trenches on almost the whole of the front attacked, from east of Schwaben Redoubt to the north of Serre. South of the Ancre, where our assault was directed northwards against the enemy's trenches on the northern slopes of the Thiepval ridge, it met with a success altogether remarkable for rapidity of execution and lightness of cost. By 7.20 a.m. our objectives east of St. Pierre Divion had been captured, and the Germans in and about that hamlet were hemmed in between our troops and the river. Many of the enemy were driven into their dugouts and surrendered, and at 9.0 a.m. the number of prisoners was actually greater than the attacking force. St. Pierre Divion soon fell, and in this area nearly 1,400 prisoners were taken by a single division at the expense of less than 600 casualties. The rest of our forces operating south of the Ancre attained their objectives with equal completeness and success.

North of the river the struggle was more severe, but very satisfactory results were achieved. Though parties of the enemy held out for some hours during the day in strong points at various places along his first line and in Beaumont Hamel, the main attack pushed on. The troops attacking close to the right bank of the Ancre reached their second objectives to the west and north-west of Beaucourt during the morning, and held on there for the remainder of the day and night, though practically isolated from the rest of our attacking troops. Their tenacity was of the utmost value, and contributed very largely to the success of the operations.

At nightfall our troops were established on the western outskirts of Beaucourt, in touch with our forces south of the river, and held a line along the station road from the Ancre towards Beaumont Hamel, where we occupied the village. Further north the enemy's first line system for a distance of about half-a-mile beyond Beaumont Hamel was also in our hands. Still further north – opposite Serre – the ground was so heavy that it became necessary to abandon the attack at an early stage; although, despite all difficulties, our troops had in places reached the enemy's trenches in the course of their assault.

Next morning, at an early hour, the attack was renewed between Beaucourt and the top of the spur just north of Beaumont Hamel. The whole of Beaucourt was carried, and our line extended to the north-west along the Beaucourt road across the southern end of the Beaumont Hamel spur. The number of our prisoners steadily rose, and during this and the succeeding days our front was carried forward eastwards and northwards up the slopes of the Beaumont Hamel spur.

The results of this attack were very satisfactory, especially as before its completion bad weather had set in again. We had secured the command of the Ancre valley on both banks of the river at the point where it entered the enemy's lines, and, without great cost to ourselves, losses had been inflicted on the enemy which he himself admitted to be considerable. Our final total of prisoners taken in these operations, and their development during the subsequent days, exceeded 7,200, including 149 officers.

37. Throughout the period dealt with in this despatch the rôle of the other armies holding our defensive line from the northern limits of the battle front to beyond Ypres was necessarily a secondary one, but their task was neither light nor unimportant. While required to give precedence in all respects to the needs of the Somme battle, they were responsible for the security of the

line held by them and for keeping the enemy on their front constantly on the alert. Their rôle was a very trying one, entailing heavy work on the troops and constant vigilance on the part of Commanders and Staffs. It was carried out to my entire satisfaction, and in an unfailing spirit of unselfish and broad-minded devotion to the general good, which is deserving of the highest commendation.

Some idea of the thoroughness with which their duties were performed can be gathered from the fact that in the period of four and a half months from the 1st July some 360 raids were carried out, in the course of which the enemy suffered many casualties and some hundreds of prisoners were taken by us. The largest of these operations was undertaken on the 19th July in the neighbourhood of Armentieres. Our troops penetrated deeply into the enemy's defences, doing much damage to his works and inflicting severe losses upon him.

38. The three main objects with which we had commenced our offensive in July had already been achieved at the date when this account closes; in spite of the fact that the heavy autumn rains had prevented full advantage being taken of the favourable situation created by our advance, at a time when we had good grounds for hoping to achieve yet more important successes.

Verdun had been relieved; the main German forces had been held on the western front; and the enemy's strength had been very considerably worn down.

Any one of these three results is in itself sufficient to justify the Somme battle. The attainment of all three of them affords ample compensation for the splendid efforts of our troops and for the sacrifices made by ourselves and our Allies. They have brought us a long step forward towards the final victory of the Allied cause.

The desperate struggle for the possession of Verdun had invested that place with a moral and political importance out of all proportion to its military value. Its fall would undoubtedly have been proclaimed as a great victory for our enemies, and would have shaken the faith of many in our ultimate success. The failure of the enemy to capture it, despite great efforts and very heavy losses, was a severe blow to his prestige, especially in view of the confidence he had openly expressed as to the results of the struggle.

Information obtained both during the progress of the Somme battle and since the suspension of active operations has fully established the effect of our offensive in keeping the enemy's main forces tied to the western front. A movement of German troops eastward, which had commenced in June as a result of the Russian successes, continued for a short time only after the opening of the Allied attack. Thereafter the enemy forces that moved east consisted, with one exception, of divisions that had been exhausted in the Somme battle, and these troops were always replaced on the western front by fresh divisions. In November the strength of the enemy in the western theatre of war was greater than in July, notwithstanding the abandonment of his offensive at Verdun. It is possible that if Verdun had fallen large forces might still have been employed in an endeavour further to exploit that success. It is, however, far more probable, in view of developments in the eastern theatre, that a considerable transfer of troops in that direction would have followed. It is therefore justifiable to conclude that the Somme offensive, not only relieved Verdun, but held large forces which would otherwise have been employed against our Allies in the east.

The third great object of the Allied operations on the Somme was the wearing down of the enemy's powers of resistance. Any statement of the extent to which this has been attained must depend in some degree on estimates. There is, nevertheless, sufficient evidence to place it beyond doubt that the enemy's losses in men and material have been very considerably higher than those of the Allies, while morally the balance of advantage on our side is still greater.

During the period under review a steady deterioration took place in the moral of large numbers of the enemy's troops. Many of them, it is true, fought with the greatest determination, even in the latest encounters, but the resistance of still larger numbers became latterly decidedly feebler than it had been in the earlier stages of the battle. Aided by the great depth of his defences, and by the frequent reliefs which his resources in men enabled him to effect, discipline and training held the machine together sufficiently to enable the enemy to rally and reorganise his troops after each fresh defeat. As our advance progressed, four-fifths of the total number of divisions engaged on the Western front were thrown one after another into the Somme battle, some of them twice, and some three times; and towards the end of the operations, when the weather unfortunately broke, there can be no doubt that his power of resistance had been very seriously diminished.

The total number of prisoners taken by us in the Somme battle between the 1st July and the 18th November is just over 38,000, including over 800 officers. During the same period we captured 29 heavy guns, 96 field guns and field howitzers, 136 trench mortars, and 514 machine guns.

So far as these results are due to the action of the British forces, they have been attained by troops the vast majority of whom had been raised and trained during the war. Many of them, especially amongst the drafts sent to replace wastage, counted their service by months, and gained in the Somme battle their first experience of war. The conditions under which we entered the war had made this unavoidable. We were compelled either to use hastily trained and inexperienced officers and men, or else to defer the offensive until we had trained them. In this latter case we should have failed our Allies. That these troops should have accomplished so much under such conditions, and against an Army and a nation whose chief concern for so many years has been preparation for war, constitutes a feat of which the history of our nation records no equal. The difficulties and hardships cheerfully overcome, and the endurance, determination, and invincible courage shown in meeting them, can hardly be imagined by those who have not had personal experience of the battle, even though they have themselves seen something of war.

The events which I have described in this Despatch forms but a bare outline of the more important occurrences. To deal in any detail even with these without touching on the smaller fights and the ceaseless work in the trenches continuing day and night for five months, is not possible here. Nor have I deemed it permissible in this Despatch, much as I desired to do so, to particularise the units, brigades, or divisions especially connected with the different events described. It would not be possible to do so without giving useful information to the enemy. Recommendations for individual rewards have been forwarded separately, and in due course full details will be made known. Meanwhile, it must suffice to say that troops from every part of the British Isles, and from every Dominion and quarter of the Empire, whether Regulars, Territorials, or men of the New Armies, have borne a share in the Battle of the Somme. While some have been more fortunate than others in opportunities for distinction, all have done their duty nobly.

Among all the long roll of victories borne on the colours of our regiments, there has never been a higher test of the endurance and resolution of our infantry. They have shown themselves worthy of the highest traditions of our race, and of the proud records of former wars.

Against such defences as we had to assault – far more formidable in many respects than those of the most famous fortresses in history – infantry would have been powerless without thoroughly efficient artillery preparation and support. The work of our artillery was wholly admirable, though the strain on the personnel was enormous. The excellence of the results attained was the more remarkable, in view of the shortness of the training of most of the junior officers, and of the N.C.Os. and men. Despite this, they rose to a very high level of technical and tactical skill, and the combination between artillery and infantry, on which, above everything, victory depends, was an outstanding feature of the battle. Good even in July, it improved with experience, until in the latter assaults it approached perfection.

In this combination between infantry and artillery the Royal Flying Corps played a highly important part. The admirable work of this Corps has been a very satisfactory feature of the battle. Under the conditions of modern war the duties of the Air Service are many and varied. They include the regulation and control of artillery fire by indicating targets and observing and reporting the results of rounds; the taking of photographs of enemy trenches, strong points, battery positions, and of the effect of bombardments; and the observation of the movements of the enemy behind his lines.

The greatest skill and daring has been shown in the performance of all these duties, as well as in bombing expeditions. Our Air Service has also co-operated with our infantry in their assaults, signalling the position of our attacking troops and turning machine guns on to the enemy infantry and even on to his batteries in action.

Not only has the work of the Royal Flying Corps to be carried out in all weathers and under constant fire from the ground, but fighting in the air has now become a normal procedure, in order to maintain the mastery over the enemy's Air Service. In these fights the greatest skill and determination have been shown, and great success has attended the efforts of the Royal Flying Corps. I desire to point out, however, that the maintenance of mastery in the air, which is essential, entails a constant and liberal supply of the most up-to-date machines, without which even the most skilful pilots cannot succeed.

The style of warfare in which we have been engaged offered no scope for cavalry action, with the exception of the one instance already mentioned, in which a small body of cavalry gave useful assistance in the advance on High Wood.

Intimately associated with the artillery and infantry in attack and defence the work of various special services contributed much towards the successes gained.

Trench mortars, both heavy and light, have become an important adjunct to artillery in trench warfare, and valuable work has been done by the personnel in charge of these weapons. Considerable experience has been gained in their use, and they are likely to be employed even more frequently in the struggle in future.

Machine guns play a great part – almost a decisive part under some conditions – in modern war, and our Machine Gun Corps has attained to considerable proficiency in their use, handling them with great boldness and skill. The highest value of these weapons is displayed on the defensive rather than in the offensive, and we were attacking. Nevertheless, in attack also machine guns can exercise very great influence in the hands of men with a quick eye for opportunity and capable of a bold initiative. The Machine Gun Corps, though comparatively recently formed, has done very valuable work and will increase in importance.

The part played by the new armoured cars – known as "tanks" – in some of the later fights has been brought to notice by me already in my daily reports.

These cars proved of great value on various occasions, and the personnel in charge of them performed many deeds of remarkable valour.

The employment by the enemy of gas and of liquid flame as weapons of offence compelled us not only to discover ways to protect our troops from their effects but also to devise means to make use of the same instruments of destruction. Great fertility of invention has been shown, and very great credit is due to the special personnel employed for the rapidity and success with which these new arms have been developed and perfected, and for the very great devotion to duty they have displayed in a difficult and dangerous service. The Army owes its thanks to the chemists, physiologists and physicists of the highest rank who devoted their energies to enabling us to surpass the enemy in the use of a means of warfare which took the civilised world by surprise. Our own experience of the numerous experiments and trials necessary before gas and flame could be used, of the great preparations which had to be made for their manufacture, and of the special training required for the personnel employed, shows that the employment of such methods by the Germans was not the result of a desperate decision, but had been prepared for deliberately.

Since we have been compelled, in self defence, to use similar methods, it is satisfactory to be able to record, on the evidence of prisoners, of documents captured, and of our own observation, that the enemy has suffered heavy casualties from our gas attacks, while the means of protection adopted by us have proved thoroughly effective.

Throughout the operations Engineer troops, both from home and over-seas, have played an important rôle, and in every engagement the Field Companies, assisted by Pioneers, have co-operated with the other arms with the greatest gallantry and devotion to duty.

In addition to the demands made on the services of the Royal Engineers in the firing line, the duties of the Corps during the preparation and development of the offensive embraced the execution of a vast variety of important works, to which attention has already been drawn in this despatch. Whether in or behind the firing line, or on the lines of communication, these skilled troops have continued to show the power of resource and the devotion to duty by which they have ever been characterised.

The Tunnelling Companies still maintain their superiority over the enemy underground, thus safeguarding their comrades in the trenches. Their skill, enterprise and courage have been remarkable, and, thanks to their efforts, the enemy has nowhere been able to achieve a success of any importance by mining.

During the Battle of the Somme the work of the Tunnelling Companies contributed in no small degree to the successful issue of several operations.

The Field Survey Companies have worked throughout with ability and devotion, and have not only maintained a constant supply of the various maps required as the battle progressed, but have in various other ways been of great assistance to the artillery.

The Signal Service, created a short time before the war began on a very small scale, has expanded in proportion with the rest of the Army, and is now a very large organisation.

It provides the means of inter-communication between all the Armies and all parts of them, and in modern war requirements in this respect are on an immense and elaborate scale. The calls on this service have been very heavy, entailing a most severe strain, often under most trying and dangerous conditions. Those calls have invariably been met with conspicuous success, and no service has shown a more whole-hearted and untiring energy in the fulfilment of its duty.

The great strain of the five months' battle was met with equal success by the Army Service Corps and the Ordnance Corps, as well as by all the other Administrative Services and Departments, both on the Lines of Communication and in front of them. The maintenance of large armies in a great battle under modern conditions is a colossal task. Though bad weather often added very considerably to the difficulties of transport, the troops never wanted for food, ammunition, or any of the other many and varied requirements for the supply of which these Services and Departments are responsible. This fact in itself is the highest testimony that can be given to the energy and efficiency with which the work was conducted.

In connection with the maintenance and supply of our troops, I desire to express the obligation of the Army to the Navy for the unfailing success with which, in the face of every difficulty, the large numbers of men and the vast quantities of material required by us have been transported across the seas.

I also desire to record the obligation of the Army in the Field to the various authorities at home, and to the workers under them – women as well as men – by whose efforts and self-sacrifice all our requirements were met. Without the vast quantities of munitions and stores of all sorts provided, and without the drafts of men sent to replace wastage, the efforts of our troops could not have been maintained.

The losses entailed by the constant fighting threw a specially heavy strain on the Medical Services. This has been met with the greatest zeal and efficiency. The gallantry and devotion with which officers and men of the regimental medical service and Field Ambulances have discharged their duties is shown by the large number of the R.A.M.C. and Medical Corps of the Dominions who have fallen in the Field. The work of the Medical Services behind the front has been no less arduous. The untiring professional zeal and marked ability of the surgical specialists and consulting surgeons, combined with the skill and devotion of the medical and nursing staffs, both at the Casualty Clearing Stations in the Field and the Stationary and General Hospitals at the Base, have been beyond praise. In this respect also the Director General has on many occasions expressed to me the immense help the British Red Cross Society have been to him in assisting the R.A.M.C. in their work.

The health of the troops has been most satisfactory, and, during the period to which this despatch refers, there has been an almost complete absence of wastage due to disease of a preventable nature.

With such large forces as we now have in the Field, the control exercised by a Commander-in-Chief is necessarily restricted to a general guidance, and great responsibilities devolve on the Army Commanders.

In the Somme Battle these responsibilities were entrusted to Generals Sir Henry Rawlinson and Sir Hubert Gough, commanding respectively the Fourth and Fifth Armies, who for five months controlled the operations of very large forces in one of the greatest, if not absolutely the greatest struggle that has ever taken place.

It is impossible to speak too highly of the great qualities displayed by these commanders throughout the battle. Their thorough knowledge of the profession, and their cool and sound judgment, tact and determination proved fully equal to every call on them. They entirely justified their selection for such responsible commands.

The preparations for the battle, with the exception of those at Gomme-court, were carried out under Sir Henry Rawlinson's orders. It was not until after the assault of the 1st July that Sir Hubert Gough was placed in charge of a portion of the front of attack, in order to enable Sir Henry Rawlinson to devote his whole attention to the area in which I then decided to concentrate the main effort.

The Army Commanders have brought to my notice the excellent work done by their Staff Officers and Technical Advisers, as well as by the various commanders and staffs serving under them, and I have already submitted the names of the various officers and others recommended by them.

I desire also to record my obligation to my own Staff at General Head Quarters and on the Lines of Communication, and to the various Technical Advisers attached thereto for their loyal and untiring assistance.

Throughout the operations the whole Army has worked with a remarkable absence of friction and with a self-sacrifice and whole-hearted devotion to the common cause which is beyond praise. This has ensured and will continue to ensure the utmost concentration of effort. It is indeed a privilege to work with such officers and with such men.

I cannot close this Despatch without alluding to the happy relations which continue to exist between the Allied Armies and between our troops and the civil population in France and Belgium. The unfailing co-operation of our Allies, their splendid fighting qualities, and the kindness and goodwill universally displayed towards us have won the gratitude, as well as the respect and admiration, of all ranks of the British Armies.

In conclusion, I desire to add a few words as to future prospects.

The enemy's power has not yet been broken, nor is it yet possible to form an estimate of the time the war may last before the objects for which the Allies are fighting have been attained. But the Somme battle has placed beyond doubt the ability of the Allies to gain those objects. The German Army is the mainstay of the Central Powers, and a full half of that Army, despite all the advantages of the defensive, supported by the strongest fortifications, suffered defeat on the Somme this year. Neither victors nor the vanquished will forget this; and, though bad weather has given the enemy a respite, there will un-doubtedly be many thousands in his ranks who will begin the new campaign with little confidence in their ability to resist our assaults or to overcome our defence.

Our new Armies entered the battle with the determination to win and with confidence in their power to do so. They have proved to themselves, to the enemy, and to the world that this confidence was justified, and in the fierce struggle they have been through they have learned many valuable lessons which will help them in the future.

I have the honour to be,
Your Lordship's obedient Servant,
D. HAIG,
General, Commanding-in-Chief,
British Armies in France.

SIR DOUGLAS HAIG'S DESPATCH OF 31 MAY 1917

Battle of the Ancre and the German withdrawal to the Hindenburg Line

War Office,
19th June, 1917.

The following Despatch has been received by the Secretary of State for War from Field-Marshal Sir Douglas Haig, G.C.B., Commanding-in-Chief, British Armies in France.

GENERAL HEAD QUARTERS,
BRITISH ARMIES IN FRANCE.
31*st May*, 1917.

MY LORD,

I have the honour to submit the following Report on the operations of the British Armies in France from the 18th November, 1916, to the commencement of our present offensive.

Nature of Operations.

(1) My plans for the winter, already decided on at the opening of the period under review, were based on several considerations:-

The enemy's strength had been considerably reduced by the severe and protracted struggle on the Somme battlefields, and so far as circumstances and the weather would permit it was most desirable to allow him no respite during the winter.

With this object, although possibilities were limited by the state of the ground under winter conditions, I considered it feasible to turn to good account the very favourable situation then existing in the region of the River Ancre as a result of the Somme battle.

Our operations prior to the 18th November, 1916, had forced the enemy into a very pronounced salient in the area between the Ancre and the Scarpe Valleys, and had obtained for us greatly improved opportunities for observation over this salient. A comparatively short further advance would give us complete possession of the few points south of the Ancre to which the enemy still clung, and would enable us to gain entire command of the spur above Beaumont Hamel. Thereafter, the configuration of the ground in the neighbourhood of the Ancre Valley was such that every fresh advance would enfilade the enemy's positions and automatically open up to the observation of our troops some new part of his defences. Arrangements could therefore be made for systematic and deliberate attacks to be delivered on selected positions, to gain further observation for ourselves and deprive the enemy of that advantage. By these means the enemy's defences would be continually outflanked, and we should be enabled to direct our massed artillery fire with such accuracy against his trenches and communications as to make his positions in the Ancre Valley exceedingly costly to maintain.

With the same object in view a number of minor enterprises and raids were planned to be carried out along the whole front of the British Armies.

In addition to the operations outlined above, preparations for the resumption of a general offensive in the spring had to be proceeded with in due course. In this connection, steps had to be taken to overcome the difficulties which a temporary lack of railway facilities would place in the way of completing our task within the allotted time. Provision had also to be made to cope with the effect of winter conditions upon work and roads, a factor to which the prolonged frost at the commencement of the present year subsequently gave especial prominence. Another very important consideration was the training of the forces under my command. It was highly desirable that during the winter the troops engaged in the recent prolonged fighting should be given an adequate period out of the line for training, rest and refitting.

Certain modifications of my programme in this respect eventually became necessary. To meet the wishes of our Allies in connection with the plan of operations for the spring of 1917, a gradual extension of the British front southwards as far as a point opposite the town of Roye was decided on in January, and was completed without incident of importance by the 26th February, 1917. This alteration entailed the maintenance by British forces of an exceptionally active front of 110 miles, including the whole of the Somme battle front, and combined with the continued activity maintained throughout the winter interfered to no small extent with my arrangements for reliefs. The training of the troops had consequently to be restricted to such limited opportunities as circumstances from time to time permitted.

The operations on the Ancre, however, as well as the minor enterprises and raids to which reference has been made, were carried out as intended. Besides gaining valuable position and observation by local attacks in the neighbourhood of Bouchavesnes, Sailly-Saillisel and Grandcourt, these raids and minor enterprises were the means of inflicting heavy casualties on the enemy, and contributed very appreciably to the total of 5,284 prisoners taken from him in the period under review.

OPERATIONS ON THE ANCRE.

The Enemy's Position.

(2) At the conclusion of the operations of the 13th November and following days the enemy still held the whole of the Ancre Valley from Le Transloy to Grandcourt, and his first line of defence lay along the lower northern slopes of the Thiepval Ridge.

North of the Ancre, he still held the greater part of the spur above Beaumont Hamel. Beyond that point the original German front line, in which the enemy had established himself two years previously, ran past Serre, Gommecourt and Monchy-au-Bois to the northern slopes of the main watershed, and then north-east down to the valley of the River Scarpe east of Arras.

Besides the positions held by him on our immediate front, and in addition to the fortified villages of the Ancre Valley with their connecting trenches, the enemy had prepared along the forward crest of the ridge north of the Ancre Valley a strong second system of defence. This consisted of a double line of trenches, heavily wired, and ran north-west from Saillisel past Le Transloy to the Albert – Bapaume Road, where it turned west past Grevillers and Loupart Wood and then northwest again past Achiet-le-Petit to Bucquoy. This system, which was known as the Le Transloy-Loupart line, both by reason of its situation and as a result of the skill and industry expended on its preparation, constituted an exceedingly strong natural defensive position; second only to that from which the enemy had recently been driven on the Morval – Thiepval Ridge. Parallel to this line, but on the far side of the crest, he had constructed towards the close of the past year a third defensive system on the line Rocquigny, Bapaume, Ablainzevelle.

Operations Commenced.

(3) The first object of our operations in the Ancre Valley was to advance our trenches to within assaulting distance of the Le Transloy – Loupart line.

Accordingly, on the 18th November, 1916, before the rapidly deteriorating condition of the ground had yet made an undertaking on so considerable a scale impossible, an attack was delivered against the next German line of defence, overlooking the villages of Pys and Grandcourt. Valuable positions were gained on a front of about 5,000 yards, while a simultaneous attack north of the Ancre considerably improved the situation of our troops in the Beaucourt Valley.

By this time winter conditions had set in, and along a great part of our new front movement across the open had become practically impossible. During the remainder of the month, therefore, and throughout December, our energies were principally directed to the improvement of our own trenches and of roads and communications behind them. At the same time the necessary rearrangement of our artillery was completed, so as to take full advantage of the opportunities afforded by our new positions for concentration of fire.

The Beaumont Hamel Spur.

(4) As soon as active operations again became possible, proceedings were commenced to drive the enemy from the remainder of the Beaumont Hamel Spur. In January a number of small operations were carried out with this object, resulting in a progressive improvement of our position. Before the end of the month the whole of the high ground north and east of Beaumont Hamel was in our possession, we had pushed across the Beaucourt Valley 1,000 yards north of Beaucourt Village, and had gained a footing on the southern slopes of the spur to the east.

The most important of these attacks was undertaken at dawn on the morning of the 11th January against a system of hostile trenches extending for some 1,500 yards along the crest of the spur east and north-east of Beaumont Hamel. By 8.30 a.m. all our objectives had been captured, together with over 200 prisoners. That afternoon an enemy counterattack was broken up by our artillery.

Throughout the whole of the month's fighting in this area, in which over 500 German prisoners were taken by us, our casualties were exceedingly light. This satisfactory circumstance can be attributed mainly to the close and skilful co-operation between our infantry and artillery, and to the excellence of our artillery preparation and barrages. These in turn were made possible by the opportunities for accurate observation afforded by the high ground north of Thiepval and by the fine work done by our aircraft.

Grandcourt.

(5) Possession of the Beaumont Hamel Spur opened up a new and extensive field of action for our artillery. The whole of the Beaucourt Valley and the western slopes of the spur beyond from opposite Grandcourt to Serre now lay exposed to our fire. Operations were, therefore, at once commenced under the cover of our guns to clear the remainder of the valley south of the Serre Hill, and to push our line forward to the crest of the spur.

On the night of the 3rd/4th February an important German line of defence on the southern slopes of this spur, forming part of the enemy's original second line system north of the Ancre, was captured by our troops on a front of about three-quarters of a mile. The enemy's resistance was stubborn, and hard fighting took place, which lasted throughout the whole of the following day and night. During this period a number of determined counter-attacks were beaten off by our infantry or dispersed by our artillery, and by the

5th February we had gained the whole of our objectives. In this operation, in which the excellence of our artillery co-operation was very marked, we took 176 prisoners and four machine guns.

This success brought our front forward north of the Ancre to a point level with the centre of Grandcourt, and made the enemy's hold on his position in that village and in his more western defences south of the river very precarious. It was not unexpected, therefore, when on the morning of the 6th February our patrols reported that the last remaining portion of the old German second line system south of the river, lying between Grandcourt and Stuff Redoubt, had been evacuated. The abandoned trenches were occupied by our troops the same morning. Constant reconnaissances were sent out by us to keep touch with the enemy and to ascertain his movements and intentions. Grandcourt itself was next found to be clear of the enemy, and by 10 a.m. on the morning of the 7th February was also in our possession. That night we carried Baillescourt Farm, about half way between Beaucourt and Miraumont, capturing 87 prisoners.

The Advance against Serre.

(6) The task of driving the enemy from his position in the Beaucourt Valley was resumed on the night of the 10th/11th February. Our principal attack was directed against some 1,500 yards of a strong line of trenches, the western end of which was already in our possession, lying at the southern foot of the Serre Hill. Our infantry were formed up after dark, and at 8.30 p.m. advanced under our covering artillery barrage. After considerable fighting in the centre and towards the left of our attack, the whole of the trench line which formed our objective was gained, with the exception of two strong points which held out for a few days longer. At 5 a.m. a determined counter-attack from the direction of Puisieux-au-Mont was beaten off by our artillery and machine gun fire. Two other counterattacks on the 11th February and a third on the 12th February were equally unsuccessful.

The Advance towards Miraumont.

(7) The village of Serre now formed the point of a very pronounced salient, which our further progress along the Ancre Valley would render increasingly difficult, if not impossible, for the enemy to hold. Accordingly, an operation on a somewhat larger scale than anything hitherto attempted since the new year, was now undertaken. Its object was to carry our line forward along the spur which runs northwards from the main Morval – Thiepval Ridge about Courcelette, and so gain possession of the high ground at its northern extremity. The possession of this high ground, besides commanding the approaches to Pys and Miraumont from the south, would give observation over the upper valley of the Ancre, in which many hostile batteries were

situated in positions enabling their fire to be directed for the defence of the Serre sector. At the same time arrangements were made for a smaller attack on the opposite bank of the river, designed to seize a portion of the Sunken Road lying along the eastern crest of the second spur north of the Ancre and so obtain control of the approaches to Miraumont from the west.

Our assault was delivered simultaneously on both banks of the Ancre at 5.45 a.m. on the 17th February. The night was particularly dark, and thick mist and heavy conditions of ground produced by the thaw that had just set in added to the difficulties with which our troops had to contend. The enemy was, moreover, on the alert, and commenced a heavy barrage some time before the hour of our assault, while our attacking battalions were still forming up. None the less, our troops advanced to the assault with great gallantry. On the left of our attack our artillery preparation had been assisted by observation from the positions already won on the right bank of the Ancre. In consequence, our infantry were able to make a very considerable advance, and established themselves within a few hundred yards of Petit Miraumont. The right of our attack encountered more serious resistance, but here also valuable progress was made.

North of the Ancre our troops met with complete success. The whole of the position attacked, on a front of about half-a-mile, was secured without great difficulty, and an enemy counter-attack during the morning was easily driven off.

Next day, at 11.30 a.m., the enemy delivered a second counter-attack from the north with considerable forces, estimated at two battalions, upon our new positions north of the river. His advancing waves came under the concentrated fire of our artillery and machine guns while still some distance in front of our lines, and were driven back in disorder with exceedingly heavy losses.

Eleven officers and 588 other ranks were taken prisoners by us in these operations.

Miraumont and Serre Evacuated.

(8) The ground gained by these two attacks, and by minor operations carried out during the succeeding days, gave us the observation we desired, as well as complete command over the German artillery positions in the upper Ancre Valley and over his defences in and around Pys and Miraumont. The constant bombardment by our artillery, combined with the threat of an attack in which his troops would have been at great disadvantage, accordingly decided the enemy to abandon both villages. Our possession of Miraumont, however, gravely endangered the enemy's positions at Serre by opening up for us possibilities of a further advance northwards, while the loss of Serre would speedily render Puisieux-au-Mont and Gommecourt equally difficult of

defence. There was, therefore, good ground to expect that the evacuation of Pys and Miraumont would shortly be followed by a withdrawal on a more considerable scale. This, in fact, occurred.

On the 24th February the enemy's positions before Pys, Miraumont and Serre were found by our patrols to have been evacuated, and were occupied by our troops. Our patrols were then at once pushed forward, supported by strong infantry detachments, and by the evening of the 25th February the enemy's first system of defence from north of Gueudecourt to west of Serre, and including Luisenhof Farm, Warlencourt-Eaucourt, Pys, Miraumont, Beauregard Dovecot and Serre, had fallen into our hands. The enemy offered some opposition with machine guns at selected strong points in his line, and his artillery actively shelled the areas from which he had withdrawn; but the measures taken to deal with such tactics proved adequate, and the casualties inflicted on our troops were light.

The enemy's retirement at this juncture was greatly favoured by the weather. The prolonged period of exceptional frost, following on a wet autumn, had frozen the ground to a great depth. When the thaw commenced in the third week of February the roads, disintegrated by the frost, broke up, the sides of trenches fell in, and the area across which our troops had fought their way forward returned to a condition of slough and quagmire even worse than that of the previous autumn. On the other hand, the condition of the roads and the surface of the ground behind the enemy steadily improved the further he withdrew from the scene of the fighting. He was also materially assisted by a succession of misty days, which greatly interfered with the work of our aeroplanes. Over such ground and in such conditions rapid pursuit was impossible. It is greatly to the credit of all ranks concerned that, in spite of all difficulties, constant touch was maintained with the enemy and that timely information was obtained of his movements.

Le Barque and Gommecourt.

(9) Resistance of a more serious character was encountered in a strong secondary line of defence which, from a point in the Le Transloy – Loupart line due west of the village of Beaulencourt, crossed in front of Ligny-Thilloy and Le Barque to the southern defences of Loupart Wood. Between the 25th February and the 2nd March a series of attacks were carried out against this line, and the enemy was gradually driven out of his positions. By the evening of the latter day the whole line of trenches and the villages of Le Barque, Ligny-Thilloy and Thilloy had in turn been captured. One hundred and twenty-eight prisoners and a number of trench-mortars and machine guns were taken in this fighting, in the course of which the enemy made several vigorous but unsuccessful counter-attacks.

Meanwhile rapid progress had been made on the remainder of the front of our advance. On the 27th February the enemy's rearguards in Puisieux-au-Mont were driven to their last positions of defence in the neighbourhood of the church, and to the north-west of the village our front was extended to within a few hundred yards of Gommecourt. That evening our patrols entered Gommecourt Village and Park, following closely upon the retreating enemy, and by 10 p.m. Gommecourt and its defences had been occupied. Next morning the capture of Puisieux-au-Mont was completed.

Irles.

(10) The enemy had, therefore, been driven back to the Le Transloy – Loupart line, except that he still held the village of Irles, which formed a salient to his position, and was linked up to it at Loupart Wood and Achiet-le-Petit by well-constructed and well-wired trenches.

Accordingly, our next step was to take Irles, as a preliminary to a larger undertaking against the Le Transloy – Loupart line itself; but before either operation could be attempted exceedingly heavy work had to be done in the improvement of roads and communications, and in bringing forward guns and ammunition. The following week was devoted to these very necessary tasks. Meanwhile, operations were limited to small enterprises, designed to keep in touch with the enemy and to establish forward posts which might assist in the forthcoming attack. The assault on Irles and its defences was delivered at 5.25 a.m. on the morning of the 10th March, and was completely successful. The whole of our objectives were captured, and in the village and the surrounding works 289 prisoners were taken, together with sixteen machine guns and four trench mortars. Our casualties were very light, being considerably less than the number of our prisoners.

The Loupart Line.

(11) The way was now open for the main operation against the centre of the Le Transloy – Loupart line, which throughout the 11th March was heavily shelled by all natures of our artillery. So effective was this bombardment that during the night of the 12th-13th March the enemy once more abandoned his positions, and fell back on the parallel system of defences already referred to on the reverse side of the ridge. Grevillers and Loupart Wood were thereupon occupied by our troops, and methodical preparations were at once begun for an attack on the enemy's next line of defence.

THE ENEMY'S RETREAT.
The General Withdrawal.

(12) For some time prior to this date a number of indications had been observed which made it probable that the area of the German withdrawal would be yet further extended.

It had been ascertained that the enemy was preparing a new defensive system, known as the Hindenburg Line, which, branching off from his original defences near Arras, ran south-eastwards for twelve miles to Queant, and thence passed west of Cambrai towards St. Quentin. Various "switches" branching off from this line were also under construction. The enemy's immediate concern appeared to be to escape from the salient between Arras and Le Transloy, which would become increasingly difficult and dangerous to hold as our advance on the Ancre drove ever more deeply into his defences. It was also evident, however, from the preparations he was making that he contemplated an eventual evacuation of the greater salient between Arras and the Aisne Valley, north-west of Rheims.

Constant watch had accordingly been kept along the whole front south of Arras, in order that instant information might be obtained of any such development. On the 14th March patrols found portions of the German front line empty in the neighbourhood of St. Pierre Vaast Wood. Acting on the reports of these patrols, during that night and the following day our troops occupied the whole of the enemy's trenches on the western edge of the wood. Little opposition was met, and by the 16th March we held the western half of Moislains Wood, the whole of St. Pierre Vaast Wood with the exception of its north-eastern corner, and the enemy's front trenches as far as the northern outskirts of Sailly-Saillisel.

Meanwhile, on the evening of the 15th March, further information had been obtained which led me to believe that the enemy's forces on our front south of the Somme had been reduced, and that his line was being held by rearguard detachments supported by machine guns, whose withdrawal might also be expected at any moment. The Corps Commanders concerned were immediately directed to confirm the situation by patrols. Orders were thereafter given for a general advance, to be commenced on the morning of the 17th March along our whole front from the Roye Road to south of Arras.

Bapaume and Peronne.

(13) Except at certain selected localities, where he had left detachments of infantry and machine guns to cover his retreat, such as Chaulnes, Vaux Wood, Bapaume and Achiet-le-Grand, the enemy offered little serious opposition to our advance on this front, and where he did so his resistance was rapidly overcome. Before nightfall on the 17th March Chaulnes and Bapaume had been captured, and advanced bodies of our troops had pushed deeply into the enemy's positions at all points from Damery to Monchy-au-Bois. On our right our Allies made rapid progress also and entered Roye.

On the 18th March and subsequent days our advance continued, in co-operation with the French. In the course of this advance the whole intricate system of German defences in this area, consisting of many miles of powerful, well-wired trenches which had been constructed with immense labour and worked on till the last moment, were abandoned by the enemy and passed into the possession of our troops.

At 7 a.m. on the 18th March our troops entered Peronne and occupied Mont St. Quentin, north of the town. To the south our advanced troops established themselves during the day along the western bank of the Somme from Peronne to just north of Epenancourt. By 10 p.m. on the same day Brie Bridge had been repaired by our engineers sufficiently for the passage of infantry in single file, and our troops crossed to the east bank of the river, in spite of some opposition. Further south French and British cavalry entered Nesle.

North of Peronne equal progress was made, and by the evening of the 18th March our troops had entered the German trench system known as the Beugny – Ypres Line, beyond which lay open country as far as the Hindenburg Line. On the same day the left of our advance was extended to Beaurains, which was captured after slight hostile resistance.

By the evening of the 19th March our infantry held the line of the Somme from Canizy to Peronne, and infantry outposts and cavalry patrols had crossed the river at a number of points. North of Peronne our infantry had reached the line Bussu, Barastre, Velu, St. Leger, Beaurains, with cavalry in touch with the enemy at Nurlu, Bertincourt, Noreuil, and Henin-sur-Cojeul. Next day considerable bodies of infantry and cavalry crossed to the east of the Somme, and a line of cavalry outposts with infantry in support was established from south of Germaine, where we were in touch with the French, through Hancourt and Nurlu to Bus. Further north we occupied Morchies.

Difficulty of Communications.

(14) By this time our advance had reached a stage at which the increasing difficulty of maintaining our communications made it imperative to slacken the pace of our pursuit. South of Peronne, the River Somme, the bridges over which had been destroyed by the retreating enemy, presented a formidable obstacle. North of Peronne the wide belt of devastated ground over which the Somme battle had been fought offered even greater difficulties to the passage of guns and transport.

We were advancing, therefore, over country in which all means of communication had been destroyed, against an enemy whose armies were still intact and capable of launching a vigorous offensive should a favourable opening present itself. Strong detachments of his infantry and cavalry occupied points of advantage along our line of advance, serving to keep the enemy informed of our progress and to screen his own movements. His guns, which had already been withdrawn to previously prepared positions, were available at any moment to cover and support a sudden counter-stroke, while the conditions of the country across which we were moving made the progress of our own artillery unavoidably slow. The bulk of the enemy's forces were known to be holding a very formidable defensive system, upon which he could fall back should his counter-stroke miss its aim. On the other hand, our troops as they moved forward left all prepared defences further and further behind them. In such circumstances the necessity for caution was obvious. At different stages of the advance successive lines of resistance were selected and put in a state of defence by the main bodies of our infantry, while cavalry and infantry outposts maintained touch with the enemy and covered the work of consolidation. Meanwhile, in spite of the enormous difficulties which the condition of ground and the ingenuity of the enemy had placed in our way, the work of repairing and constructing bridges, roads and railways was carried forward with most commendable rapidity.

Enemy Resistance Increasing.

(15) North of the Bapaume – Cambrai Road between Noreuil and Neuville-Vitasse our advance had already brought us to within two or three miles of the Hindenburg Line, which entered the old German front line system at Tilloy-lez-Mofflaines. The enemy's resistance now began to increase along our whole front, extending gradually southwards from the left flank of our advance where our troops had approached most nearly to his new main defensive position.

A number of local counter-attacks were delivered by the enemy at different points along our line. In particular five separate attempts were made to recover Beaumetz-lez-Cambrai, which we had captured on the 21st March, and the farm to the north of the village. All failed with considerable loss to the enemy.

Meanwhile our progress continued steadily, and minor engagements multiplied from day to day all along our front. In these we were constantly successful, and at small cost to ourselves took many prisoners and numerous machine guns and trench mortars. In every fresh position captured large numbers of German dead testified to the obstinacy of the enemy's defence and the severity of his losses.

Our cavalry took an active part in this fighting, and on the 27th March in particular carried out an exceedingly successful operation, in the course of which a squadron drove the enemy from Villers Faucon and a group of neighbouring villages, capturing 23 prisoners and four machine guns. In another series of engagements on the 1st and 2nd April, in which Savy and Selency were taken and our line advanced to within two miles of St. Quentin, we captured 91 prisoners and six German field guns. The enemy's casualties were particularly heavy.

On the 2nd April, also, an operation on a more important scale was undertaken against the enemy's positions north of the Bapaume – Cambrai Road. The enemy here occupied in considerable strength a series of villages and well-wired trenches, forming an advanced line of resistance to the Hindenburg Line. A general attack on these positions was launched in the early morning of the 2nd April on a front of over ten miles, from Doignies to Henin-sur-Cojeul, both inclusive. After fighting which lasted throughout the day the entire series of villages was captured by us, with 270 prisoners, four trench mortars and 25 machine guns.

The Hindenburg Line.

(16) By this date our troops were established on the general line Selency, Jeancourt, Epehy, Ruyaulcourt, Doignies, Mercatel, Beaurains. East of Selency, and between Doignies and our old front line east of Arras, our troops were already close up to the main Hindenburg defences. Between Selency and Doignies the enemy still held positions some distance in advance of his new system. During the succeeding days our efforts were directed to driving him from these advanced positions, and to pushing our posts forward until contact had been established all along our front south of Arras with the main defences of the Hindenburg Line. Fighting of some importance again took place on the 4th and 5th April in the neighbourhood of Epehy and Havrincourt Wood, in which Ronssoy, Lempire and Metz-en-Couture were captured by us, together with 100 prisoners, two trench mortars and eleven machine guns.

General Review.

(17) Certain outstanding features of the past five months' fighting call for brief comment before I close this report.

In spite of a season of unusual severity, a winter campaign has been conducted to a successful issue under most trying and arduous conditions. Activity on our battle-front has been maintained almost without a break from the conclusion of last year's offensive to the commencement of the present operations. The successful accomplishment of this part of our general plan has already enabled us to realise no inconsiderable instalment of the fruits of the Somme Battle, and has gone far to open the road to their full achievement. The courage and endurance of our troops has carried them triumphantly through a period of fighting of a particularly trying nature, in which they have been subjected to the maximum of personal hardship and physical strain. I cannot speak too highly of the qualities displayed by all ranks of the Army.

I desire also to place on record here my appreciation of the great skill and energy displayed by the Army Commanders under whose immediate orders the operations described above were carried out. The ability with which the troops in the Ancre area were handled by General Sir Hubert Gough, and those further south, on our front from Le Transloy to Roye, by General Sir Henry Rawlinson, was in all respects admirable.

The retreat to which the enemy was driven by our continued success re-introduced on the Western front conditions of warfare which had been absent from that theatre since the opening months of the war. After more than two years of trench warfare considerable bodies of our troops have been engaged under conditions approximating to open fighting, and cavalry has been given an opportunity to perform its special duties. Our operations south of Arras during the latter half of March are, therefore, of peculiar interest, and the results achieved by all arms have been most satisfactory. Although the delib-erate nature of the enemy's withdrawal enabled him to choose his own ground for resistance, and to employ every device to inflict losses on our troops, our casualties, which had been exceedingly moderate throughout the operations on the Ancre during the period of the retreat became exceptionally light. The prospect of a more general resumption of open fighting can be regarded with great confidence.

The systematic destruction of roads, railways and bridges in the evacuated area made unprecedented demands upon the Royal Engineers, already heavily burdened by the work entailed by the preparations for our spring offensive. Our steady progress, in the face of the great difficulties confronting us, is the best testimony to the energy and thoroughness with which those demands were met.

The bridging of the Somme at Brie, to which reference has already been made, is an example of the nature of the obstacles with which our troops were met and of the rapidity with which those obstacles were overcome. In this instance six gaps had to be bridged across the canal and river, some of them of considerable width and over a swift flowing stream. The work was com-menced on the morning of the 18th March, and was carried out night and day in three stages. By 10 p.m. on the same day footbridges for infantry had been completed, as already stated. Medium type bridges for horse transport and cavalry were completed by 5 a.m. on the 20th March, and by 2 p.m. on the 28th March, or four and a-half days after they had been begun, heavy bridges capable of taking all forms of traffic had taken the place of the lighter type. Medium type deviation bridges were constructed as the heavy bridges were begun, so that from the time the first bridges were thrown across the river traffic was practically continuous.

Throughout the past winter the question of transport, in all its forms, has presented problems of a most serious nature, both in the battle area and behind the lines. On the rapid solution of these problems the success or failure of our operations necessarily largely depended.

At the close of the campaign of 1916 the steady growth of our Armies and the rapid expansion of our material resources had already taxed to the utmost the capacity of the roads and railways then at our disposal. Existing broad and narrow gauge railways were insufficient to deal with the increasing volume of traffic, an undue proportion of which was thrown upon the roads. As winter conditions set in these rapidly deteriorated, and the difficulties of maintenance and repair became almost overwhelming. An increase of railway facilities of every type and on a large scale was therefore imperatively and urgently necessary to relieve the roads. For this purpose rails, material and rolling stock were required immediately in great quantities, while at a later date our wants in these respects were considerably augmented by a large programme of new construction in the area of the enemy's withdrawal.

The task of obtaining the amount of railway material required to meet the demands of our Armies, and of carrying out the work of construction at the rate rendered necessary by our plans, in addition to providing labour and material for the necessary repair of roads, was one of the very greatest difficulty. Its successful accomplishment reflects the highest credit on the Transportation Service, of whose efficiency and energy I cannot speak too highly. I desire to acknowledge in the fullest manner the debt that is owed to all who assisted in meeting a most difficult situation, and especially to Major-General Sir Eric Geddes, Director-General of Transportation, to whose great ability, organising power and energy the results achieved are primarily due. I am glad to take this opportunity also to acknowledge the valuable assistance given to us by the Chemin de Fer du Nord, by which the work of the Transportation Service was greatly facilitated.

I wish also to place on record here the fact that the successful solution of the problem of railway transport would have been impossible had it not been for the patriotism of the railway companies at home and in Canada. They did not hesitate to give up the locomotives and rolling stock required to meet our needs, and even to tear up track in order to provide us with the necessary rails. The thanks of the Army are due also to those who have accepted so cheerfully the inconvenience caused by the consequent diminution of the railway facilities available for civil traffic.

The various other special services, to the excellence of whose work I was glad to call attention in my last Despatch, have continued to discharge their duties with the same energy and efficiency displayed by them during the

Somme Battle, and have rendered most valuable assistance to our artillery and infantry.

I desire also to repeat the well-merited tribute paid in my last Despatch to the different Administrative Services and Departments. The work entailed by the double task of meeting the requirements of our winter operations and preparing for our next offensive was very heavy, demanding unremitting labour and the closest attention to detail.

The fighting on the Ancre and subsequent advance made large demands upon the devotion of our Medical Services. The health of the troops during the period covered by this Despatch has been satisfactory, notwithstanding the discomfort and exposure to which they were subjected during the extreme cold of the winter, especially in the areas taken over from the enemy.

The loyal co-operation and complete mutual understanding that prevailed between our Allies and ourselves throughout the Somme Battle have been continued and strengthened by the events of the past winter, and in particular by the circumstances attending the enemy's withdrawal. During the latter part of the period under review, a very considerable tract of country has been won back to France by the combined efforts of the Allied troops. This result is regarded with lively satisfaction by all ranks of the British Armies in France. At the same time I wish to give expression to the feelings of deep sympathy and profound regret provoked among us by the sight of the destruction that war has wrought in a once fair and prosperous countryside.

I have the honour to be,
My Lord,
Your Lordship's obedient Servant,
D. HAIG,
Field-Marshal,
Commanding-in-Chief,
British Armies in France.

Index

ALSO AVAILABLE FROM
PEN & SWORD BOOKS...

AVAILABLE FROM ALL GOOD BOOKSHOPS
OR TO ORDER DIRECT
PLEASE CALL **01226 734222**

OR PRE-ORDER ONLINE VIA OUR WEBSITE:
WWW.PEN-AND-SWORD.CO.UK

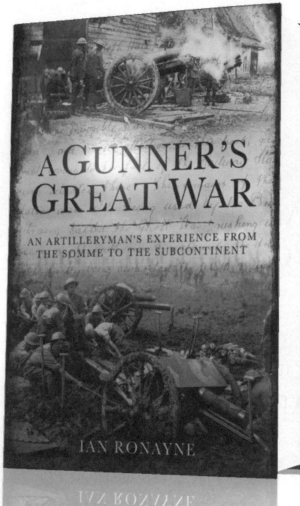

9781848846081 •
HB • 16 B&W plates •
192 pages • £19.99

If the First World War had not happened when it did, Channel Islander Clarence Ahier would almost certainly have led a mostly unremarkable life. But it did, and in October 1915, aged just 23-years-old, Clarence left his home and volunteered to join the British Army. He would spend the next two and half years serving as an artilleryman on the Western Front.

From the very beginning of his time at the front, he wrote a graphic and moving account of his experiences of war. The complete journal consists of around 25,000 words, with a focus on Clarence's experience during the Battle of the Somme, in the fighting around Ypres, and, after he was wounded for the second time, the journey to India and his time there as a member of the garrison. This will be supported by additional explanatory text.

WHAT THE CRITICS SAID:

'A Gunner's Great War is a graphic and moving account of an artilleryman's experience on the Western Front. An Interesting book for those who like artillery and WWI.'
ENGLISH HERITAGE

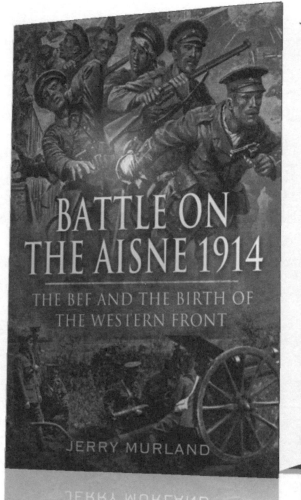

9781848847699 •
HB • 16 B&W plates •
256 pages • £19.99

The River Aisne featured prominently in August 1914 during the Retreat from Mons. A month later it was the scene of further desperate action when the BEF re-crossed it in their unsuccessful attempt to dislodge the German Army entrenched along the crest of the slopes on its northern bank.

Having already fought three major engagements and marched over 200 miles in a month, the battle proved hugely costly to the BEF. Indeed the three British Corps suffered losses of over 650 officers and some 12,000 men killed.

The author places the Aisne battles in their rightful context, both from the BEF and German viewpoints. In this detailed analysis he identifies the early deficiencies and lack of preparedness of the British Army staff and logistics organisation as well as friction among those within the command structure, all of which hampered effective operations.

WHAT THE CRITICS SAID:

'The author's narrative is clear, easy to read and engaging...the stories, quotes and anecdotes bring life to the proceedings and reveal weaknesses in British structure, tactics and command. Well worth a read.'
THE LONG, LONG TRAIL

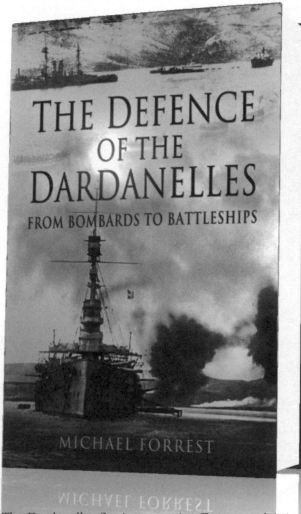

THE DEFENCE
OF THE
DARDANELLES
FROM BOMBARDS TO BATTLESHIPS

MICHAEL FORREST

9781781590522 •
HB • 120 integrated images •
272 pages • £25.00

The Dardanelles Strait, separating Europe and Asia Anatolia, was fortified in the fifteenth century with massive bronze bombards causing any unwelcome ships to run a truly formidable gauntlet. So it proved on 18 March 1915 when a powerful fleet of British and French warships attempted to force a passage to allow minesweepers to clear the Strait. The attack failed at the cost of three ships sunk and three more seriously damaged. The Allied inability to control the Strait necessitated and, crucially, delayed the disastrous Allied invasion of Gallipoli that cost the lives of some 250,000 men.

The author makes an in-depth study of the Turkish defences that caused such loss to the Royal Navy and French allies and reveals that the Ottoman army and Turkey's coastal defences relied almost entirely on the German firm of Krupp for guns. This choice was a crucial element to the successful defence of the Dardanelles. Using excellent illustrations he also examines the relative strengths of the Royal and French Navies and Turkish coastal defences.

This definitive work examines the flaws of Winston Churchill's strategy and identifies the inadequacies of pitting warships against shore fortifications. Damningly, the author's research proves that British intelligence sources had previously assessed that a naval attack alone would not succeed.

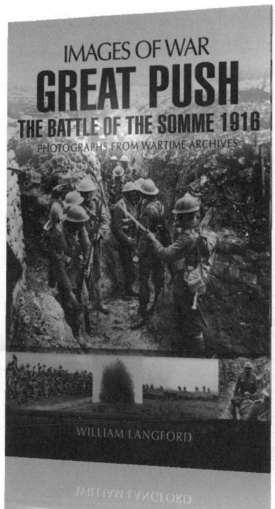

9781781590416 •
PB • 250 integrated images •
240 pages • £16.99

In 1916, Sir Douglas Haig, commanding the BEF, began his great offensive to drive the invaders off the ground they had been occupying for over a year and a half. The 'Great Push', as the offensive was advertised to the nation, began 1 July 1916. A glossy picture magazine was produced to inform the British public of the progress of the offensive. Over a four month period until the Battle of the Somme faded away in November the magazine appeared with the following advertising blurb:

'Sir Douglas Haig's Great Push; The Battle of the Somme; A popular, pictorial and authoritative work on one of the Greatest Battles in History, illustrated by about 700 wonderful Official Photographs and Cinematograph Films; By Arrangement With the War Office; beautifully printed on the Best English Art Paper.'

As is well known, the Great Push turned out to be little more than a nudge, but, for the sake of national morale, the British public had to be encouraged to believe that all was going well; especially in view of the horrific casualties wrecking the lives of families throughout the land.

WHAT THE CRITICS SAID:

'Another good photo reference in the Images of War series, and fascinating if you are interested in WW1.'
Military Modelling

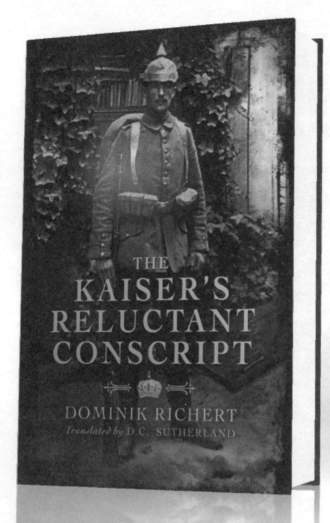

9781781590331 •
HB • 8 B&W plates •
288 pages • £19.99

In 1914 Dominik Richert was involved in fighting on the French border and was then moved to northern France where he was in combat with Indian troops. In 1915 he was sent to the East and took part in the Battle for Mount Zwinin in the Carpathians and the subsequent invasion of the western parts of the Ukraine and of eastern Poland. In 1917 he took part in the capture of Riga before returning to the Western Front in 1918, where he saw German tanks in action at the battle of Villers-Brettoneux.

No longer believing in the war, he subsequently crossed no-man's land and surrendered to the French, becoming a 'deserteur Alsacienne'. The book ends with his return home early in 1919.

This superb memoir gives a fascinating insight into the War as experienced by the Germans, and into the development of the author's attitude to it. Yes, Richert fights to survive, but he feels little respect for, or allegiance, to his own army or the society which sent him to war.

WHAT THE CRITICS SAID:

'This is an unusual, educational and absorbing memoir of an infantryman's Great War and I recommend it.'
THE LONG, LONG TRAIL

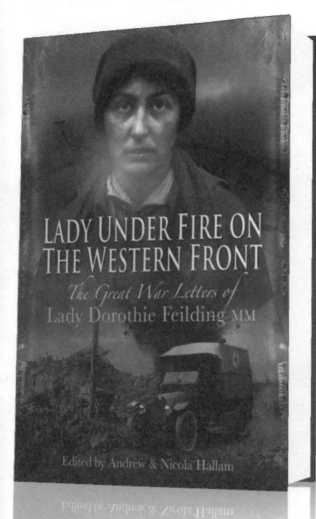

9781848843226 •
HB • 16 B&W plates •
240 pages • £19.99

Also Available as an eBook –
Epub: 9781844682140
Kindle: 9781844682157

When Britain went to war in 1914 Lady Dorothie Feilding, the twenty-five-year-old daughter of the Earl of Denbigh, wasted no time in volunteering for the Munro Motor Ambulance Corps. Spending nearly four years on the Western Front in Belgium driving ambulances, she had the distinction of being the first woman to be awarded the Military Medal for her bravery as well as the *Croix de Guerre* and the Belgian Order of Leopold.

Fortunately the hundreds of letters that she wrote to her family at Newnham Paddox, near Rugby, have been discovered and carefully edited by Andy and Nicola Hallam. These reflect the tragedy and horror of war and also the tensions of being a woman at the front contending with shells, traumatic wounds, gossip, lice, vehicle maintenance and inconvenient marriage proposals.

WHAT THE CRITICS SAID:

'Extraordinary letters written by an aristocratic heroine of the First World War...'
THE EXPRESS

'A useful addition to the relatively small collection of Great War works about those dedicated to easing the lot of the soldier on the Western Front.'
THE WESTERN FRONT ASSOCIATION STAND TO! MAGAZINE

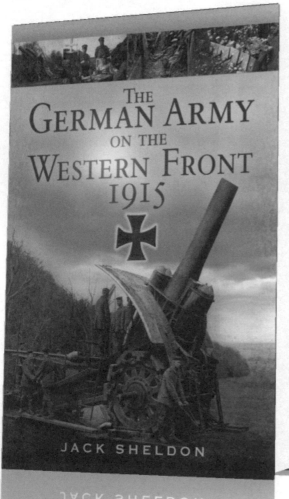

THE
GERMAN ARMY
ON THE
WESTERN FRONT
1915

JACK SHELDON

9781848844667 •
HB • 16 B&W plates •
336 pages • £25.00

Also Available as an eBook –
Epub: 9781783032266
Kindle: 9781783032259

With the Central Powers holding the initiative throughout, 1915 was the year that largely determined the way the remainder of the war would be fought. Constantly on the offensive in the vast open spaces of the Eastern Front, the German Army stood on the strategic defensive in the West. There, with minimal ground-holding forces and thanks to skillful deployment of limited reserves of men and guns, it repulsed with bloody losses every attempt by the Western Allies to drive it from occupied France and Belgium.

Shortages of weapons, equipment and ammunition forced both sides to tool up for what was clearly becoming a long war of attrition. Although the Western Front had stabilized by the end of 1914, this did not mean that tactical thinking and developments also stood still. Every Allied attempt to break the deadlock elicited a response from the German defenders, who brought the tactics of positional warfare to a high state of refinement. Trench systems increased in depth and complexity. The machine gun proved its lethality and the result for the Western Allies was one costly setback after another, with French losses reaching a staggering 1,000,000 fatalities by the end of the year.

This superbly researched book provides the clearest and most comprehensive German perspective yet on this period of the War. It covers such well-known actions as Neuve Chapelle, Ypres, where gas was used on a large scale for the first time, Aubers Ridge and Loos as well as the appalling clashes in Champagne and the Argonne Forest.

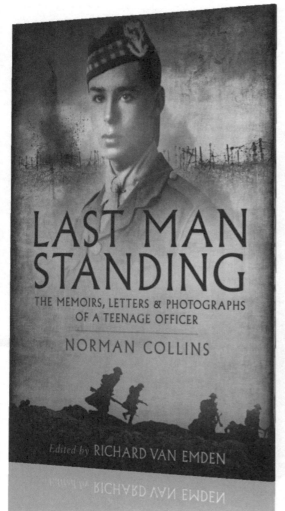

9781848848658 •
PB • Illustrated throughout
• 208 pages • £12.99

Also Available as an eBook –
Epub: 9781781597750
Kindle: 9781781597767

It hardly seems credible today that a 19-year-old boy, just commissioned into the Seaforth Highlanders, could lead a platoon of men into the carnage of the Battle of the Somme. Norman Collins, the author of this superb memoir, was this remarkable man.

Using Norman's own words, *Last Man Standing* follows him from his childhood in Hartlepool to his subsequent service in France. The book also covers such shattering events as the German naval assault on Hartlepool in December 1914 when Norman was subjected to as big a bombardment as any occurring on the Western Front at that time. Norman's love for the men under his command shine out in this book and his stories are gripping and deeply moving. They are illustrated by a rare collection of private photographs taken at or near the front by Norman himself.

WHAT THE CRITICS SAID:

'Enthralling memoir. These letters form the freshest part of this book, full of detail about kit and food that obsessed soldiers but which do not find a place in the history books.'
WHO DO YOU THINK YOU ARE?

'This is a harrowing tale of battle, loss and the horrors of war.'
SCOTLAND MAGAZINE

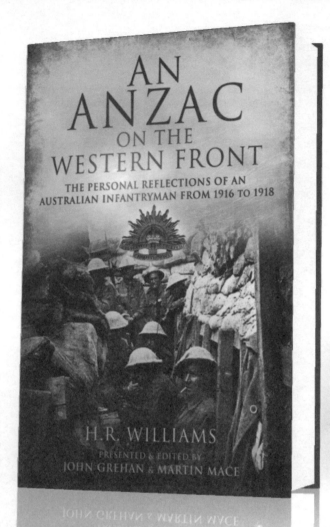

9781848847675 •
HB • 16 B&W plates •
208 pages • £19.99

Having enlisted in 1915 and serving in the 56th Battalion Australian Imperial Force, Harold Roy Williams had only arrived in France, from Egypt, on 30 June 1916. He describes the horrors of the Fromelles battlefield in shocking clarity and the conditions the troops had to endure are revealed in disturbing detail.

Surviving a later gas attack, Williams' subsequent postings read like a tour of the Western Front. Following the Somme there was the mud and squalor of the line south of Ypres, the German Spring Offensive of 1918, the Battle of Amiens – frequently described as the most decisive battle against the Germans in France and Flanders – the capture of Villers-Bretonneux and, finally, the assault on Péronne. This is his graphic description of his service in the First World War.

WHAT THE CRITICS SAID:

'A remarkably candid and graphic account of his wartime service, this book details Williams' journey from the Somme through to the German offensive in 1918, his wounding at the Battle of Péronne, and his eventful turn home.'
BRITAIN AT WAR MAGAZINE

Tracing Your Family History?

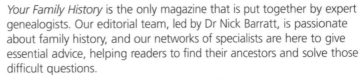

Read Your Family HISTORY

ESSENTIAL ADVICE FROM THE EXPERTS

FREE COPY!

Your Family History is the only magazine that is put together by expert genealogists. Our editorial team, led by Dr Nick Barratt, is passionate about family history, and our networks of specialists are here to give essential advice, helping readers to find their ancestors and solve those difficult questions.

In each issue we feature a **Beginner's Guide** covering the basics for those just getting started, a **How To** … section to help you to dig deeper into your family tree and the opportunity to **Ask The Experts** about your tricky research problems. We also include a **Spotlight** on a different county each month and a **What's On** guide to the best family history courses and events, plus much more.

Receive a free copy of *Your Family History* magazine and gain essential advice and all the latest news. To request a free copy of a recent back issue, simply e-mail your name and address to marketing@your-familyhistory.com or call 01226 734302*.

Your Family History is in all good newsagents and also available on subscription for six or twelve issues. For more details on how to take out a subscription, call 01778 392013 or visit **www.your-familyhistory.co.uk**.

Alternatively read issue 31 online completely free using this QR code

*Free copy is restricted to one per household and available while stocks last.

www.your-familyhistory.com